My Wanderlust Diaries

A Compilation of Travel Stories, Misadventures, and
Life Lessons from a Solo Female Backpacker

Melissa Kittrell

Fulton Books, Inc.
Meadville, PA

Published by Fulton Books 2021

ISBN 978-1-64952-649-6 (paperback)
ISBN 978-1-64952-650-2 (digital)

Printed in the United States of America

PREFACE

As she rolled up the gravel driveway in her beat-up Chevy, I could tell she had been drinking again. Our giant rottweilers in the front yard, which she collected like souvenirs, began their normal barking and pulling at their chains like wild jackals to welcome her arrival. I couldn't even keep track of her schedule anymore or even know for sure if she was indeed working or just pulling an all-nighter at the neighborhood pub. I didn't even care anymore. I had only a few short weeks left in my high school year in Podunk, Oklahoma, and I was free.

I was always a smart girl, usually the first in my class and unbelievably independent. I was an overachiever; despite having an alcoholic mother, I had something inside me that drove me to strive for excellence. Maybe it was the fear of not wanting to start a squabble with my warden or maybe it was something deeper that I would unbury at a later date, but my upbringing should have left me in the welfare line with the rest of the white trash I was brought up with. I never cared for anyone setting my agenda or telling me what to do; how I ended up in the military was a surprise to those that knew me well. I had a couple of scholarships all lined up, but on a not-so-special Tuesday, for no particular reason, I found myself opening the old yellow phone book and thumbing through the tattered pages to find the military recruitment section. I did not even like organized sports, but for some reason, that was beyond me, I became hell-bent to do something different and to escape the shackles of small-town life. I wanted to escape the heartache and frustration of living with a bipolar single mom and forge a path of my own not bound by any obligations.

I tried the phone number for the Coast Guard—busy signal. I eyeballed the Marines, thinking how badass that would be, but I knew my limitations. Never doing a pull-up and my heaviest lifting was a sousaphone I played in the marching band, I knew that might be reason enough to think twice about the Marines. In landlocked Oklahoma, the time I did on the water was bass fishing with my buddies, but my real excitement was noodling season. This was the one thing that Pauls Valley was known for besides idle town gossip and a church on every corner—the catfish noodling. I was quite proficient at this sport and would even pride myself for going out at night while my mom was at work and wandering along the Washita River checking my trot lines and venturing out to prey upon my baited barrels that hosted the giant river kings. I would scoop the mammoths out of the river with my bare hands. As I looked at my noodling scars on my young tanned skin, I decided that the Navy was my ticket out of this one horse town. The recruiter couldn't have arranged a meeting quick enough after he checked my 4.0 grade point average. Within one week, I was pledged into the United States Navy as a Nuclear Machinist's Mate under the Delayed Entry Program.

When my mother heard of what I had done, she began to cry, but I was fueled by a fire inside that even a mother's tears couldn't extinguish. I was ready for an adventure that was more than the Friday night-lights of the varsity football game or the sound of the aftermarket exhaust on my high school crush's Camaro, making his rounds as I worked the neighborhood Sonic as a carhop. The first plane ride in my adult life was to Great Lakes, Illinois, via Chicago O'Hare. My extra-long pale blond hair that extended past my butt was hacked off to my ears—a small price to pay for what I was longing for. There was a somber disposition that reflected in the mirror; proudly standing was a once band geek wearing a pressed military Navy white uniform. Nothing could hide the glimmer in my bright green eyes as I set my sights on the next chapter. This begins the story of my untamable wanderlust.

Welcome to the Burmese Thunderdome

The cloud of the COVID-19 crisis had finally cast its dark shadow over my beloved Myanmar. The Burmese had tricked themselves into believing their country had zero cases of the virus. I knew that was nonsense, but over the weeks, I heard many locals proudly proclaim how their country was disease-free because of the hot climate and how safe it was. In reality, this third-world country had no way to test for the virus. No test = No results = No virus. Surrounding countries knew Myanmar was at risk and started to increase restrictions on travelers from this La La Land, boasting they were the last holdout of no corona. Finally, reality sank in with the citizens getting sick with flu-like symptoms and they changed their tune. Not only was there a lack of medical infrastructure, but there was a lack of education as well; so when the naive locals now heard that their country was contaminated, the icy finger pointed to the foreigners.

Overnight, things changed for me. Most hotels and hostels were ordered to refuse accommodation to foreigners. Flight restrictions and land border closures on the entire perimeter of the country left many travelers completely stuck with no other options. The hostel owners showed compassion, but they couldn't make an exception—lights out at midnight and everyone was on the streets. I frantically tried to book flights out of country, but the light at the end of the tunnel was growing dimmer by the second. My only hope at this point was Bangkok, but they had some crazy restrictions I would have to overcome, but it was my only hope.

My hostel was the last holdout with a few travelers frantically absorbing all the internet bandwidth, trying to book flights out of country. I had found one and felt a hint of relief when an e-mail confirmation came through with a flight from Mandalay to Bangkok. I grew nervous as the anxiety from a sobbing German girl filled the air of the common room. She was overly dramatic on a FaceTime call with her friends back home going over every detail in the most cinematic fashion—you would have thought she was in the infantry of WWI by the way she spoke and the lack of self-awareness to the atmosphere she was creating, it disgusted me. Almost everyone was headed to Yangon via a night bus that was a bumpy twelve-hour ride away. I felt a little uneasy, knowing that almost every flight I had tried to book had been canceled last minute, but I tried to remain hopeful. It was a new awful phenomenon happening during this mass exodus of travelers called "Ghost Flights," where you could book it, but the flight would never leave the ground and you would get a cancellation notice once the airline computer systems caught up to reality. Booking flights during this crazy time reminded me of an Italian household cooking spaghetti. I filled my head with visions of a rotund Italian mother boiling her noodles and periodically throwing one on the wall to see if it stuck; if the noodle sticks, dinner was ready. Unfortunately for me, my flight booking experience was the metaphor of a slimy limp noodle that fell to the floor. I had over seven noodles that lay at my feet from failed flight attempts, but I had hoped this next one would stick.

As the Germans all piled their bags at the entry in preparation to catch the bus, I checked my e-mail one last time before heading to my bunk to grab a couple of hours sleep before my flight the next morning. There was a new e-mail—flight canceled; I had just been ghosted—AGAIN! I tried not to let the anxiety of now eight sloppy noodles of failed flights in the books for me but instead dashed to my dorm and threw all contents of my pack on the floor. I was like an F-18 Hornet that was too fat to fly—if it was not necessary and imperative to get me home, it was trashed. I needed to dump weight to make my travels as simple as possible and allow me flexibility to move to whatever mechanism of travel would take me and not be burdened with baggage: My little sun hat gifted to me from Cho in Yangon—trash. My eco water bottle from the elephant camp—trash. I even went through every piece of paper in my travel notebook. If the paper served no purpose, in the waste bin it went; every ounce counted at this point. Despite the hot temperatures of Myanmar, I layered my clothes like a Sherpa to minimize my pack size. With my bags packed, I dashed to the bus station, where I met the Germans and other travelers bound for Yangon. I had no ticket, but I forcefully pleaded with the sales clerk to let me board the bus. As she made me wait, I watched the Germans load their multiple packs into the cargo hold alongside the local farmer's giant bags of potatoes and dried fish. The clerk told me all seats were full, but just as all hope was almost lost, the driver pulled out a tiny little plastic stool and placed it in the aisle beside his driver's seat. The little pink chair looked like something a toddler would use and was dirty and cracked, but I did not care. I threw my pack in the aisle and sat on my little stool, thankful.

It was going to be a long ride to Yangon from Nyaungshwe and made even longer when my tiny plastic stool broke, leaving me with a wobbly three-legged contraption. I tried to fix it by leveling my pack underneath but eventually just gave up and lay in the middle of the aisle, snuggling my backpack like a body pillow. I couldn't sleep, but I tried to just close my eyes and focus on my breathing. My anxiety was through the roof as I was forced to hear the German girl continue her saga to a family member on her phone and the smell of the dried fish made its way to my nose from the corroded holes in the deck structure of the lower cargo hold. I knew I needed to stay strong, both physically and mentally at this point. A sick mind will undoubtedly create a sick body, and I needed to appear as healthy as possible if I was going to stand any chance in getting into Thailand. I remembered my travel friends of the past that tried to teach me meditation on the floating reeds of Lake Titicaca. I did not buy into the meditation thing then, but I needed this skill now to slow my heart rate. I slowly breathed in the rancid fish air and exhaled slowly, paying attention to the fullness of my lungs and the feeling of my hot breath over my chapped lips. I continued the exercise, trying to drown out the chaos around me. Just then, something hit the windshield of the bus, sending the driver into a complete outrage. As I held onto my pack like riding an inflatable pool toy, I popped up from my nook I made on the dirty bus floor. I listened to the driver explain that an overloaded farm truck had dumped some potatoes, and one bounced up and smashed his window, making a giant crack across the glass. I examined the damage as I took note of the absent rearview mirror, missing control knobs and electrical tape holding something seemingly important together…a little crack in the windshield only added character to this chariot from hell at this point. Finally, the roads settled out and the little dancing Buddha trinket hanging from the remnants of the rearview mirror support slowed and the calmness of the night set in for the long overnight journey.

I couldn't sleep—no chance. I took advantage of the time by keeping the driver company and chatting with him. He told me to call him Sam, and I admired that he spoke almost perfect English. As the kilometers rolled on the bus's odometer, Sam entertained me by teaching me some Burmese language. I had a deep interest in understanding some of heated words he yelled after the rogue potato incident, and he taught me how to say "Fuck off, you piece of shit" in Burmese. You never know when that might come in handy, but he also taught me the pleasantries I had struggled with—*who knew how long I might be stuck in Myanmar, and it could be useful.* As I finally was starting to feel a bit of levity in the dark cloud of Burma, the damn German girl came trotting up the aisle, obviously pissed about something. As she tried to make her way to the driver, she stepped on my bag and straddled me in the process with her crotch in my face as she complained that her seat wouldn't recline like the others. I never wanted to punch someone in the twat so badly as I sat in the disgusting floor, listening to this bawl-bag complain about the fucking recline of her chair! Sam vigilantly kept his eyes on the road as he seemed to ignore her woes. She just kept standing there—in my little piece of the world—contaminating it with her dark aura. I pushed her off my bag as I backed her up the aisle. I told her Sam did not speak English and ended my sentence with "——." As you might have guessed, it was Burmese for "Fuck off, you piece of shit" as she cowardly skulked back to her seat. Sam just started laughing as we continued our ride to Yangon.

After what felt like an eternity of bumps and lumps of banging my knees on the hard floor, we finally arrived in Yangon. After twelve hours with no internet, I had no idea what status the world was in as I heard others discussing how India was now in complete and total lockdown—no outside activities in a land of billions seemed like madness, but that wasn't my problem... I needed to be first to that ticket counter for a ride into Bangkok. Being in the aisle proved a huge bonus as I was first off the bus with no wait for multiple baggage from the cargo hold. I found the only airline that still flew to Thailand, and with any luck, there might just be a spot for me.

The sales clerk told me I would likely not be allowed on the flight because the rules had tightened for Thailand overnight. I would need travel insurance of $100,000, a health certificate issued within the past forty-eight hours stating I was COVID-19 virus-free from a certified physician, and then the new rule: an onward flight out of Bangkok within twenty-four hours of landing. I had briefly checked my e-mail before boarding the bus, and the US Embassy had replied to my e-mail and warned me this restriction might go into effect and that flights to Thailand would likely end the following day. The only international flights would be through Doha in the Persian Gulf region—the complete opposite end of the world and direct competition for flights with fleeing Europeans. I had to catch this flight, so I told her to book it and let me worry about immigration and the rules. She made a couple of hesitant phone calls but told me I could not be officially ticketed until check in, which was in thirty minutes.

With nothing to do but fret, I thought about connecting to the free thirty-minute Wi-Fi to distract my mind with Facebook, but I refrained and organized my paperwork. Thank God, I had bought travel insurance, and I just figured I would bullshit my way through the ticket counter with saying my onward flight would be changed as soon as I got to Bangkok or that I would just show a screenshot of one of my ghost flights that had been canceled would suffice. Now the tricky one—a health certificate. I had heard that Thailand was going to force this requirement and planned ahead, knowing that there was not a single facility in Myanmar that offered these tests. The government only had seventy tests total in custody, and they all went to the military. The embassy had warned me of this in their e-mail and offered me advice on some key words that had to be present in the health certificate. With Google Translate as my friend, I translated the verbiage to Burmese and a friend / savior / wonderful human (that shall remain nameless) created a document for me with an obscure clinic and physician in Nyaungshwe that I had found on the internet. With half the document looking like foreign Spaghettios of loops and hoops that symbolized the Burmese alphabet, I had in my hands something I prayed would suffice. Now I had nothing to do but wait.

The line had already started to form with frantic travelers, unclear of the new restrictions and poorly prepared for the circus. I tried to keep my cool as I listened to the travelers in front of me try to baffle the check-in counter attendants, but I was astounded at the level of detail these airline ladies belabored with. As the travelers began to lose their tempers, backup employees were brought in, almost acting as bouncers to the chaotic scene. As I eavesdropped, I realized my plan to bullshit about my onward flight stood no chance of success as each traveler was thoroughly checked with personal phone calls to the onward airline, verifying the twenty-four-hour requirement. To ensure travelers did not try anything shady, bags had to be checked to your home destination with zero exceptions. The check-in line was moving at a snail pace with the attendants and bouncers verifying every little detail. I quickly connected to the free airport thirty-minute Wi-Fi for a last ditch effort to find a plane leaving Bangkok within twenty-four hours. I had found one. It was expensive, but I knew anything going to the Middle East would have much graver consequences than a hefty ticket price, so I quickly put in all my information and waited for the payment to process. Just as I was up next, the confirmation code appeared.

As I showed all my information and laid out all my paperwork, a bouncer that looked like a Burmese edition of *Mad Max* came up to the counter and showed specific interest in my papers. Southeast Asia doesn't grow men like him as he seemed to be a freak of nature with his height and broad shoulders. His jet-black hair was styled in a wild fauxhawk, and it seemed he had charcoal eyeliner on that intensified his black eyes; all he needed was some leather and chain mail to complete his ominous presence. He was my villain in my plight to get home… I could feel it. As I showed all my documents, he wanted to double-check them all. I was legit in almost everything, except my fraudulent health certificate. The lady had seemed to pass it off, but as he examined it, my heart sank to the bottom of my chest as I hid my complete panic under my face mask. He picked up the phone and dialed the number on the certificate as I waited. As someone on the other end picked up the phone, all the Burmese chatter bounced off my eardrums like grenades as I wondered my fate from the phone call. The scenarios played out in my head from just missing this flight to possibly ending up in a Burmese jail for trying to pull a fast one, but at least I would have my lodging covered on a positive note. Finally, he handed the clerk my paperwork, and with a nod, she issued me my boarding pass. With one last obstacle, the clerk said that I couldn't have my onward flight with my current booking that had a transition of two different airports in the same city. My bags had to be checked the entire way to Seattle, and it wasn't possible with my layover. With only my pack I had whittled down to bare essentials, I told her it wasn't a problem since I wasn't checking bags, and I grabbed my boarding pass and headed to immigration.

A moment of relief set in as I scurried to the next stop, searching overhead for signs to lead me to the next checkpoint. As I locked in on the sign directing me, I shrieked as I felt a tap on my right shoulder. As I turned around, it was him—the villain, Mad Max. As I figured my goose was cooked and I couldn't even find words to utter, he handed over a small pocket-size book that must have fallen out of my paperwork in the hustle at the counter. He gave me a half smile as I grabbed my book, and he disappeared into the crowd. As I opened up my little novelty from Nepal, a page had been accidentally dog-eared, and I opened it up to see writing I think I divinely needed to read at that moment: *The stinking pigpen and the fragrant rose are two aspects of the same existence.* When I had bought the book, it was merely for some material on leadership quotes I use with my team at work with life lessons from Buddha, and I had no idea the role it would play in my travels when I needed those words the most. Looking back now, I know that book was always a part of this crazy jigsaw puzzle that would play into my path home. This simple little quote was more than the ink on paper for me—it was a message. Pain is a part of the process. Everything that had happened to me had happened for a reason. If I had not listened to the woes of the German girl explaining her itinerary over and over again, I wouldn't have known where and when to catch the bus to Yangon, where I was seated in the dirty floor clutching my minimal possessions, allowing me first access to a ticket out, narrowly escaping the closing wormhole of Myanmar.

All the challenges I encountered armored me with the weapons I needed to beat the Thunderdome. What could have been a stinking pen of literal rotting fish and perceived misfortune were actually blessings in disguise—a rose that was hiding in the stinking Burma bus all along. I realized that I could not celebrate too much. I might have passed this checkpoint, but this was only victory for Level 1, and I wasn't "out" but merely still in the game. I might have conquered the Burmese Thunderdome, but what was Bangkok going to bring me...maybe a swarm of locusts to spice things up?

Level 2, Thailand: Ready, Player One?

FROM THE AUTHOR

*A*s I sat in the airport stuck in Thailand, I had nothing to do but wait. The constant fretting and worry would do nothing but create bloody little nubs from chewing my fingernails while I watched the flight cancellation board. As I sat in the airport lounge, I had a moment of clarity as I finished writing a diary entry about the ordeal of getting out of Myanmar. I had always wanted to compile my entire collection of diary entries into a book, but life has a way of filling up your time, and as the years kept passing and the trips I took came and went, my diary entries just sat on the notepad of my phone. For nostalgia, I read a few and remembered some of the best times in my life. I noticed how in the beginning stages of my travels, I was so scared, but excited about the smallest things…and now I was stuck in an airport after making fraudulent health certificates to get me home after some of the wildest adventures from traveling during a pandemic. I realized that I wanted to tell my story. I used my time in the airport and the next two weeks in a mandatory quarantine to buckle down and make it happen. If you are reading this, I was successful.

As I traveled the world, many of the people I met had no idea that one day, our exploits together would end up in a book. To protect the innocent (and not so innocent), I have changed most of the names in the book. For storytelling purposes, sometimes I combined characters to make the story flow better. Sometimes events were not chronological and I switched up a few details to help the reader understand the general story line. All my stories are based on experiences I had around the globe with the amazing travel buddies I made along the way.

I hope you enjoy my book; it was a labor of love that took over eight years to create. My earlier diary entries have a different style than my later writing. Just like the evolution of growing up, my first diaries I was experiencing everything for the first time like a baby learning to crawl. As I became more experienced with navigating travel and learning from the seasoned backpackers, I was able to capture not only the events in a day, but I was able to start relating them to the common things that everyone thinks about and make my writing more of a "think piece" at times. My misadventures became life lessons I was able to share with my readers, and now I pass them onto you. I endeavored to share not only the beauty in the travel destinations but also give the reader something to think about that could relate to anyone and everyone about the things that affect us all. I hope this book inspires you to create your own adventure novel, whether from a safari Jeep in Africa or your backyard. I hope you are taking advantage of the beauty we are surrounded with each and every day and living your best life. We only have one life to live... make your adventure story a best seller!

PROLOGUE

My First
India And Thailand

Many young kids start their adult lives with a "gap year" of travel—sometimes sandwiched after high school and college or maybe even a few years after…but not me. I had already had many life experiences and even a career in the Navy that left me as a "senior" backpacker to the usual twenty-year-old, but my age or experiences did not matter. I needed a change.

My time in the US Navy had granted me a wonderful education as a Nuclear Machinist's Mate and some of the best friends a person could ask for, but my transition to civilian life was difficult as I struggled to make ends meet working as a waitress at a local burger joint. I had the normal twenty-year-old problems with loving the wrong man and trying to figure out what I stood for. I was thankful to get a job with the local Naval Shipyard in Washington State, where I had an upward trajectory if I only would have kept my head on straight. Unfortunately, I liked to learn the hard way as I let my emotions guide my path and cloud my judgment. After a tough year of losing love and then losing my father, I needed a reset. I couldn't pretend I was okay any longer; the consequences of doing so seemed more dire than losing my job. Just as I had done that day I raised my hand and swore into the active service of the military, I just as quickly looked at a map and tried to find somewhere that would not make me think of home—a place that I would not think of all I had lost at every corner. I did not know exactly what my soul needed at that time, but I knew I would not find it in Washington. So with very little thought, I booked my first solo backpacking trip. I had never done this before, but looking back now, it was that moment when I thought I was the most broken that I had made a choice that would forever change my life. The moment I bought that ticket was the initial spark that fueled the fire of my wanderlust, an attribute that would later become my identity and the adventure that would make me whole.

Wanderlust Diaries: My First...India

I had no idea what I was doing. I could barely figure out how to get to my hostel, so how was I ever going to navigate a two-month solo trip was still under review in my head. India was an assault to the senses. From the smells, the sounds, and the chaos I witnessed, my brain could barely process it all. I didn't know how to do the backpacker thing. I had only really done minimal explorations in the Navy, and when I did, it usually involved finding the closest pub with a strict buddy rule in place. I had unwittingly booked a tour before I had left the States with a hope that I would meet some other travelers to begin my adventure. I felt lost but alive as I stayed close to my hostel that was in the middle of feral New Delhi in the Paharganj, a backpacker central enclave, bustling with tiny shops and markets next to the Main Bazaar. I was uncomfortable...like a new baby experiencing everything for the first time. As scared as I was, I had never felt as alive as I watched the locals burn trash on the streets while a man in a turban ground spices to make chai masala tea in his dirty scorched pot. I watched the little old ladies in colorful saris chase a cow through the alleyways to bless the sacred bovine. This was unlike anything I had ever seen before, and my mind was a million miles away from any of the strife of back home.

The next morning, I waited on the street corner for my guide to arrive as I watched the city spring to life. I must have looked so out of place waiting. My hostel had a unique sort of security, where the owner slept on the floor in front of the entryway. I did not want my early morning departure to bother him, so I carefully opened the door and stepped over his body and the threshold to the streets littered with rubbish. I'll never forget the smile on my guide's face as he saw me standing there waiting. His name was Surrendir, and at that time, I had no way of knowing what an impact he would have on my life. All I saw was a smile that comforted my anxiety in that chaotic place filled with the sounds of beeping horns and the buzz of rickshaw drivers barreling down the narrow streets. He helped me load my backpack into his little white sedan, and we were off. My normal American brain that warned me of the perils of trusting strangers had to be rewired, and there was a kindness in Surrendir's face that put me at ease.

We made our way out of the city, driving past numerous shantytowns, where the people basically lived in thatch huts or boxes. I had known poverty in my lifetime, but I had never seen anything like this before. I resisted the urge to take photographs, but the vision of children running barefoot in the garbage of the streets of India would always live with me from that day forward. Surrendir's name was shortened to "Surri" for me as we progressed from an awkward hello to tongue-tied language translations to eventually friends. He spoke very little English, so we spent most of the four-hour drive learning each other's language. My Lonely Planet phrase book totally failed me. Surri barely understood anything I said, but a friendly smile and giggle would always mend any frustration from the language barrier. I did manage to talk to him about his life. He was thirty years old, married, and his wife and children lived 250 kilometers away, and he only got to see them once a year. He worked in Delhi to make money to support his family and was astounded with my stories of coming home every day to see my friends and loved ones.

Surri's driving scared me, and I wished he would pay more attention to the road instead of looking at me when I rambled on about my thoughts and ideas; they weren't nearly as important as the treacherous highway. After watching me cringe at the close calls, he had the idea to insist I get behind the wheel; I don't know why I ever said yes, but I did. I had never even driven in England at this point, so driving on the other side of the road on the outskirts of Delhi was utter pandemonium. Surri just laughed and sang to the Hindi tunes on the radio while I dodged camels, bikes, and tanker trucks while maneuvering down the highway in my manual right-hand drive car. I kept thinking he was a lunatic, but he just smiled and laughed as his Hindi deity Shiva danced in the rearview mirror while I honked and swerved through the labyrinth of obstacles. If Surri was a lunatic, he was in good company as I secretly enjoyed every second of the madness. I was alarmed when he started yelling, "Monkey! Monkeys!" I thought I misunderstood him, but he forced me to the side of the highway to discover a troop of monkeys where he bought a small bag of roasted peanuts from a street vendor. We took a quick break from the road while I fed the little beggar monkeys who seemed to have a routine of funny antics to earn their peanuts from the tourists.

We finally made it to Jaipur, the Pink City. The city was rich with history and culture, but you had to dig it out from under the trash and rubble. I had to teach my American mind to ignore the litter and look beyond it. It was hard to grasp how locals could throw their garbage on the streets as they did, but I started to gain insight that littering was not at the top of their priorities as most of them only had a cardboard box to call home. My blond hair drew attention as the locals would stare and the curious children would run up to stand beside me, requesting I break out my camera to take a photo with them. Surri handed me a scarf to place over my head as I made preps to enter my first Hindu temple. I had been to Japan with the Navy, but Westerners were common from the abundant military personnel; this felt different and authentic. I felt like a misstep here was more of a folly as I followed Surri's lead into the temple. As I entered, I took off my shoes, covered my head, and knelt on the floor beside Surri. I was reminded of my days growing up in Oklahoma, where I assisted my youth pastor conducting praise and worship in the church. I remembered the dancing and lifting of hands to honor the Lord, and a feeling of peace came over me, knowing that the people of the temple around me were doing their version of the same. The feeling of peace was short-lived when I felt a small splat on my head. A roost of pigeons overhead began to coo and fly around the upper chambers of the temple. I had just been shit on, and I wasn't sure what was more offensive—to uncover my head or just casually keep kneeling with excrement on my scarf. When I explained my dilemma to Surri once we exited, he just laughed as he gave my blond hair a tug with a cavalier grin on his face. We had our tour agenda, which was incredible, but some of the most memorable parts of my first few days came from simple moments like this with Surri.

Once in Jaipur, I rode a decorated elephant up to the Amber Fort. The palace was beyond words with olden day grandeur constructed from sandstone and marble. The marble pillars, gold, and many chambers for the royal wives, concubines, and servants were a sight to behold. Initially, I would have thought that only Surri and I with no other travelers would be a negative aspect of the trip, but that thought was quickly dispelled as we became so close. On the way back to Delhi, we got a flat tire, and despite the bedlam outside the car, I knew whatever plan Surri would concoct would be fine because I trusted him. When Surri told me to grab my bag and hop in the back of a truck that had pulled over, I didn't even question him. I was starting to become one with the chaos and learn that Dorothy just wasn't in Kansas anymore. The ride we hitched was in a chicken truck, but it did not only host chickens. There was a very curious goat that decided it wanted to nibble on my hair as we made our way back to the city. There were a lot of things I said I was sure Surri did not understand, but my one key phrase that always got him laughing was when I would exclaim, "This is craaaaazy," which it was, but I was indulging in it and soaking it up like a sponge.

One thing Surri made very clear was that he was no longer my "company driver" but my friend. With Surri, I was no longer in the tourist travel network, but I had found the key to the real India with him. He would take me places that pale faces would never go. Before Surri, I didn't know any better but to visit the establishments recommended by my Lonely Planet travel guide that were usually expensive and full of Westerners sitting at nice tables with their guidebook staged nearby. The places I went with Surri had delicious food served with inquisitive smiles instead of waiters expecting tips. I felt like Scarlett O'Hara with my local beau showing me off, and it was nice to be the Belle of the Indian ball!

Wanderlust Diaries: New Year, New Me at the Taj Mahal

I started the morning early. I couldn't sleep because of the street noise. It sounded like drums and music mixed with auto rickshaws honking all night—a frenzied symphony of sound that I was starting to grow accustomed to. Even with earplugs, the noise was relentless. I wandered the tiny streets filled with the rubbish of the prior night's tomfoolery to take a spot between the shoulders of two locals at the nearby chai stand. It was fascinating to watch the process as I warmed up while a neighborhood man started a fire with the street trash. The vendor would grind up the ginger and spices with a mortar and pestle and slowly stir and seep the tea. The process wasn't a short one, so during the wait, I would engage in conversation with the locals until Surri arrived to pick me up. I was wrong the first day when I thought I saw a bum with a fire in the street. This was what they did here. With India's population of over 1.3 billion people, the wealth was only in the top 1 percent. The common man in India would be a bum to American standards. I found it interesting how the locals wanted to talk to me about President Obama. They said he was a "good man." I just smiled and spoke graciously about him. It would not be appropriate, and they wouldn't understand why I would speak otherwise. I took notice on how this foreign land seemed to pay more attention to American politics than most Americans did. It was apparent the influence the United States had over the world. When Surri arrived, we left for Agra, and we even splurged a whopping three dollars to take the toll road instead of competing with camels and rickshaws on the local thoroughfare.

When we arrived, the first stop was a bucket-list destination I had only been to in my dreams—the Taj Mahal. It was everything I thought it would be of complete opulence, and it was absolutely stunning. Surri said he would wait for me in the car, but shocked by his comment, I insisted he join me and reminded him of his statements that he was not my "company driver" but my friend…and friends do not wait in the car. Surri said he could not afford the entry ticket even though his local fare was mere pennies on the dollar to my tourist fee. I told him not to worry about it and bought his ticket. I could not imagine a world where a local never laid eyes on this beautiful place in their backyard because of the expense of a two-dollar entrance. Surri was a mixed bag of emotions from what I could gather with his nonverbal communication. I could tell having me in tow while I casually held his arm made him excited but anxious at the same time. The prying eyes of the other drivers waiting at the entry gates and the looks from the guide I hired to explain the architecture made Surri question if he should indeed be my friend or step back and wait with the other drivers. Even though the caste system was supposedly abolished, it was still alive and well in India—anyone could see its presence in society. Surri was a driver, which was considered one step up from the untouchables. A guide was considered more prestigious than the drivers, so Surri walking as an equal with a tourist was considered to be living outside his class. I could tell it was weighing on his mind.

But aside from the lesson in societal norms, I was now free to indulge in this beautiful place. It was unimaginable the artwork and perfect symmetry of a structure that was built in the 1600s. The emperor, Shah Jahan, built this for his third wife that died in childbirth with his fourteenth child. Precious stones and gems were embedded in the marble, and the architects did remarkable things with optical illusions and using black onyx to inscribe chapters of the Koran throughout the palace chambers. Surri tried to emulate some of the silly things the guides were doing by insisting I try some of the cheeky photo shoots in front of the palace. Poses that involved jumping never appealed to me, but I went ahead a tried them for Surri's sake. I had been preaching to him to work on his English and maybe he could pursue becoming a guide. This seemed like a great practice session for him despite the dreadful photos he captured. After the Taj Mahal, we went to the Agra Fort, which was striking as well, considering it was the residence of the great emperors of the Mughal Dynasty before the capital shifted to Delhi.

Being far from the hostel, we decided to book a hotel nearby and enjoy the rest of the evening. It was New Year's Eve, and the festivities of the night were starting to ramp up with locals becoming more and more boisterous as the darkness grew closer. It was quite awkward, to say the least, with how to book a room for a tourist and a local—like oil and water, the two should never mix in the eyes of the innkeepers. Many of them refused lodging unless Surri took a lower-class room with the rest of the drivers in a different lodge. I did not want to spend the holiday alone in a tourist hotel, and I insisted that we could find a place for both of us. The only inn that agreed enforced a standard that I write a letter stating that I was fine with sharing a room with a local and signed my name. I had been sharing dormitory rooms with people from around the globe, so sharing a room with someone who had become my friend did not seem like such a big deal, but it was not normal for India.

Surri and I grabbed some dinner as we watched the city start to gurgle with the waywardness of the youth running through the streets. I desperately wanted to take part in the celebration, but I could tell this made Surri nervous as he continued to warn me that it wasn't safe and we needed to go to the hotel. As we walked back, I was startled by a loud BOOM in the distance. As I turned around, a twinkling of fireworks filled the sky and glowed above the monumental Taj Mahal in the background. *What a perfect day*, I thought to myself as my eyes matched the twinkling of the firecrackers. I looked to Surri, who must have misread my bliss for something more, and with a quick maneuver, he grabbed me by my waist and held me in a close embrace. He held my head close, and his dark brown eyes searched deep into my gaze, hoping for a sign of approval to his action. I could tell his next move involved a kiss, and as the pyrotechnics blazed over our heads, I could see what a magical moment it *could* be if I would let it. But there was a nagging sensation deep in my gut that could not be turned off. I wasn't in India to start a relationship; in fact, I wanted to get my head on straight from a failed one. Surri had become an important person to me. Our friendship that had no borders, societal norms, or bigotry with class lines made it even more special. I did not want to ruin that. As my Indian Rhett Butler waited patiently for his Scarlett to give in to the moment, I knew this would be a step that would taint a beautiful memory as I wiggled out of his embrace. "Only friends," I reminded him as I felt his anticipation dwindle like I had let the air out of a balloon.

We made our way back to the hotel, where the innkeeper gave his nonapproving smile as we entered. The space between us felt like we weren't even in the same room as Surri sheepishly retired to his bed and I stayed up to watch the fireworks cascade over the beautiful city from my window. It was a new year, and I refused to start it making old mistakes. As I watched the vibrant colors decorate the sky, I took in a deep breath and thought about how far I had come and how much more work I needed to do on myself. Changing my physical location was only temporary, and I had my work cut out for me to change the demons in my head, but I knew I was on the right path. I was not twenty years old anymore, and I had a failed marriage and a struggling career in my rearview mirror…but the chance to make it right. I knew my character was stronger than the résumé I had been building of lies and shortcomings, and I desperately wanted to figure out how to do that. I had flown over seven thousand miles to be in that spot at that moment, but I knew the path to bring me home as a new Melissa would not be as easy as just a plane ticket—it would be a journey that I needed to focus on every step of the way, but I was willing to put in the effort. Cheers to a New Year…and a new me.

Wanderlust Diaries: From the New to the Old

As we left Agra, Surri requested a pit stop at a small Hindi temple with a golden deity paramount in the structure. After seeing the beauties of the Taj Mahal and the other lavish structures on my trip thus far, I found it interesting that Surri wanted to stop at this small temple, which was no bigger than a Ford Pinto. It was like stopping at McDonald's after we had been eating at the Met, but I just watched him as he exited the car. He washed his hands in a pot of water and removed his shoes as he walked into the temple and rang the bells. He lit incense and waved it around the statues. The big finale was when he was rinsed with sacred water and given an orange dot on his forehead from a temple lady. He rang the bells as he turned and headed back to the car where his eyes met mine, observing the ritual through the ghostly fog on the windshield. I found the whole practice intriguing; temple meant something very special to the Hindis, and this short two minutes gave Surri the feeling of protection for our drive back to Delhi. I appreciated how it wasn't a long drawn out ordeal like the Sunday morning services I was accustomed to, but something personal that he attributed such significance and power. On the drive back, I introduced Surri to America's greatest: Jimmy Buffett, Johnny Cash, and the Rolling Stones from my iPod. "So many mobile phones," Surri exclaimed, as he noticed that I had my iPod, iPhone, international phone, and camera staged in my lap. I had feelings of guilt as I thought to myself that Surri had none of these—no common man of the service caste ever would. I used the drive past mustard plantations and spice gardens as time to help Surri with his English; if he ever was to become more than a driver, his English had to be better. We spoke back and forth, and he laughed at my horrible attempts at speaking Hindi as we took turns playing teacher.

We made a pit stop at a cultural site that was unbelievably ornate and appealed to me. The objective of this establishment was to educate about the Hindi culture, including their gods and prophets. My mini lessons with Surri were nice, but I needed more to truly understand the culture. I did not understand the religion, which was the backbone of the entire society. Whether it was the class system or the small deity Surri paid homage to before the car ride, I was ignorant of it all, and this was a chance for me to educate myself. I rented an audio guidebook to walk me through the lessons as I strolled from gallery to gallery, admiring the artwork, but mostly trying to absorb the information like a sponge. The Hindi religion was so different, with the gods looking different from any manlike creature or like the God worshipped in human form in the Bible. However, looking beyond the blue skin or multiple arms, I tried to listen to the message, which was simple. With almost textbook similar teachings to Buddha and Jesus, the resounding message of the Hindis was the same. Above all else, be a good person—love God and love each other; when faced with a choice of good or evil, choose to do good. All the wars fought over religion seemed like such waste when the underlying backbone of them all was so obvious. I felt connected to Surri. He thought the orange dot on his forehead was his protection just as I felt like my morning prayer and previous baptism in the Washita River of Oklahoma was my salvation; we were connected by our faith, and it did not matter anything beyond that.

Once in Delhi, I told Surri that I had planned to take a casual walking tour through Old Delhi. Surri laughed until he realized I was serious and insisted on joining me. I had started to feel bad that he was spending so much time with me instead of finding fares and making money, but Surri was insistent that he would not let me do this alone. Upon arriving in Old Delhi, I realized Surri was right… I was in no way prepared for the hysteria of Old Delhi. My Lonely Planet guidebook failed to tell me this relaxing walking tour would be more like a game of *Frogger* with dodging rickshaws, motorcycles, cars, and then my all-time favorite, the infamous groper. Being stuck in a mob of people, shoulder to shoulder, there was not much control over the flow of traffic. I was lucky just to stay close to Surri, but I saw something coming at me that raised an eyebrow. Coming in the mass of people was a man that had his arm raised above the crowd with his fingers extended like he was stretching them in preps of an exercise. As I passed by, I was completely appalled as the man dove his hand down in the crowd like an Olympic diver and tweaked my boob. Before I could even turn around, the man was gone, disappearing into the horde of people.

Old Delhi was different from the bazaars of New Delhi and the areas up north we had visited. The Muslim population was huge, and this was the first time I experienced this religion up close and personal. I had never seen a person wearing a full abaya or hijab, and these coverings seemed so odd to me. The full outer garments that only allowed a small slit for the eyes made me somewhat anxious considering I did not understand the religion. The eyes peering at me from the inside of the black dresses made me wonder what they saw when they looked at me. I was so obviously American with my blond hair in a messy ponytail and my blue jeans and blouse. I was the epitome of an open book. I felt there was secrecy hiding inside the robes and masks, and it made me apprehensive and uneasy. The call to prayer and wet markets were a lot to take in as I watched the live butchering of chickens on the streets while the blood pooled onto the sidewalks. The smells of death and incense permeated my nose while the loud speakers of the mosques chanted in foreign tongues prayers over the people of the city. I was on sensory overload and ready to head back to the familiar alleyways of New Delhi.

Wanderlust Diaries: Friends, Foes, and Final Days of Delhi

Surri and I checked out some final sights on my must-see bucket list of Delhi, such as the Lotus Temple and the Quintab Minar, which was the tallest stone tower/minar in India and was built in 1199 during Islamic rule. I had been so lucky to have Surri as my navigator through my first couple of weeks as a backpacker, but I knew I needed to learn how to travel on my own and Surri needed to take on a couple driving jobs to earn some money. I felt confident from some of my lessons with Surri on the proper street food and handy lessons in speaking the language, so I set off on my own to explore. I was starting to feel comfortable and noticed more of the good in people as I indulged in the little children that would run up to me and say hi. I felt somewhat like an exotic animal as locals requested photos with me now I didn't have Surri seeming to be my bodyguard and I was vulnerable and approachable.

After a day of just living in Delhi, exploring the bazaars and markets, I decided to take a local boy up on an offer for tea. His name was Kazaam, and he worked in a small shop across from my hostel. Every day, I was greeted with a friendly hello from him as I started my day, and he seemed genuinely friendly. As we walked along the labyrinth of alleyways in the Paharganj area, I started to become a little befuddled on why we hadn't stopped at one of the multiple chai stands I had grown to love. Kazaam told me that he knew of a better place, and it was then that my hackles started to go up as I took notice to my surroundings. He had led me to Connaught Place, which surrounded the train station and was dubbed as the hotbed for thieves and con artists in my guidebook. He wanted to go to this coffee shop that I had seen in passing that looked similar to a Starbucks. I didn't want to go to a commercial place like that when there were wonderful cups of chai in the streets for a nickel. My instincts told me something was wrong with this guy, but I figured one cup of coffee wouldn't hurt and then I would ditch him. Kazaam was much too friendly, and the words he spoke sent alarms off in my head as I saw through a routine I figured was used on tourists a time or two. He started to touch my hair and invade my personal space. I wanted to leave. He was so pushy and tried to make me think that I was being overly cautious. After all, what was just a drink? But I listened to my instincts as I jumped in a rickshaw and used some of my minimal language skills to direct the driver to my hostel. But Kazaam just wouldn't give up as he boarded the rickshaw and snuggled in next to me after giving the driver Hindi instructions to an alternate destination. I listened closely to the fast words coming from his mouth… Though I did not understand it all, I could make out the words "India Gate," which ironically was the location of a murder and rape of a tourist a couple of weeks prior. I had followed the story in the news before my trip, and with that final straw, I dispelled any bit of courtesy or etiquette protocol and forcefully kicked Kazaam out of the rickshaw. I'll never know if this was an overreaction, but I can never fault listening to my intuition, which was my eye into the soul. Intuition does not seek to appease others but was my only friend that I knew had my best interest at heart. I listened to it and returned home to my familiar chaos of the Paharganj.

The next morning, Surri was waiting for me in the hostel lobby to help me carry my bags to his car. Delhi was wonderful, and I saw and experienced so many amazing things, but I owe so much to my friend. He was my safety net in a different world known to house beggars and thieves and the one person I knew in my heart I could trust. In return, I hoped I had been a light to him, just as he was to me. Surri told me something that morning that just about broke my heart…that he realized I was his only friend. His life was only driving tourists and waiting outside the gates and then going home to a ramshackle hut filled with other drivers. He begged me to stay and didn't seem to understand why I had to go. When we arrived at the airport, he gave me a package of Indian incense that I had said smelled good when we were in Old Delhi. It must have cost him a day's wage, but he was persistent that I take it. He instructed me to always be careful on my trip as he grabbed my hand and held it in his. I removed my necklace that was one of my favorites with an abalone hibiscus and attached it to his rearview mirror. I saw a tear escape his eye as he touched the necklace and said, "I always remember my friend, Melissa…" I started to cry. Through all the language barriers, there was no misunderstanding the universal language of true friendship. This would be the last time I would ever see Surri. The impact he had on my life was monumental, and he was a part of the giant detour sign that helped me get on the right track. I'll always have a fond love for that man, and I pray whatever he is doing that he is happy and never forgot our wonderful time together.

Wanderlust Diaries: Next Stop, Goa

My flight to Goa was packed full of Israelis and Palestinians; apparently, this area was the prime vacation spot after their forced stint in the military, where they put down their weapons and headed south for a little R&R after years of war. At the baggage claim, they stood on opposite ends, and there was obvious tension among them. Being a novice traveler, I was unaware of the differences between the two groups but was informed that "maybe I should go ask an Israeli" when I obliviously asked a Palestinian girl if she wanted to share a cab to the northern beaches. I had never been surrounded by such a deliberate division of people before, and in the strange airport that doubled as a military airstrip, I opted to hitch a ride on a bus to avoid any more faux pas on my part with chatting up the wrong nationalities.

With my backpack snuggled on my back and cinched on my hips, I loaded up with the masses on the public bus. I felt like a chip in a Pringles can where every square inch of my body was squished against the next person. I was a whirlwind of emotions—excited to be completely on my own but sad to not have Surri by my side. I was anxious because I was not sure where I was going, and the close proximity to the other riders gave me no room to look at a map. I couldn't understand the bus driver who uttered garbled words that made no sense. I decided to get out where a few other riders exited and hope for the best. It appeared we were on a single dirt road frequented only by the clunky public buses and a few motorbikes with a jungle paradise to one side and the expanse of the Arabian Sea to the other. Once I could reference my map, I realized that I had prematurely gotten off the bus and was a long way from my intended destination. Along with me were two young men that needed to head the same way, so we decided to make the pilgrimage together. One was a quiet Palestinian boy; he stayed ten feet in front and didn't utter more than a couple of words to me. The other was an Israeli named Ohad. He asked me how I felt about the struggles between Israel and Palestine and stated how dreadful it was for the people because they were suffering terribly. It brought a new sense of reality talking to a human being that was actually living the nightmare of the Middle East. My pack grew heavy and dug into my shoulders as I walked with sweat cascading from the bridge of my nose like a fountain. We finally approached a small village that seemed promising but soon realized it only hosted a few shops and a small orphanage. Luckily for us, another dilapidated bus stopped, as we hopped on and traveled a few miles to the hostel.

My new home was exactly what I was hoping for—a stylish backpacker hangout right in the middle of the village. When I checked into my dorm, I met my new roommate, Emily. Emily was the epitome of the backpacker lifestyle, with breezy pants and plain T-shirt. Her wavy brown hair was tossed in a messy ponytail and the lack of makeup showed no concern of impressing anyone. She was a Canadian freelance editor and had the luxury to travel and work harmoniously at the same time. She was a seasoned nomad and taught me many tips that helped me throughout my travels. We walked to the beach and had dinner together with our conversations never missing a beat. I woke up in my tiny bunk bed and sauntered to the common area for a nice, simple breakfast that the innkeeper laid out; the fruit was infested with flies, so I stuck with a samosa and tea. Emily had some editing work to do, so I decided to pay a visit to the small village I passed the day before. I loaded up some children's books I found in the common area bookshelf that were hiding among the many copies of Lonely Planet guides left behind by travelers who wanted to lighten their pack. I chose a couple of old children's books that were the vintage cardboard style with the gold binding I remembered as a kid. I packed them in my rucksack and caught the next bus heading south to the village.

As I approached the small orphanage, the kids were walking around the open plaza while a lady watched over them. As I approached the gate, some children came running up to me as others kept their distance. I studied their faces, and something was not quite right. There was misalignment and disproportionate limbs on some. I noticed that the children that did not get up to greet me were confined to chairs because their legs were impaired, but they smiled from the distance. I would later learn from talking to the innkeeper at my hostel that this village was very remote and the villagers frequently married into each other's family. I could only assume that inbreeding was what had caused the ailments among the children. However, it would not be appropriate to ask, and most likely, the language barrier would cause a misunderstanding, anyway. I spent a few hours with the children, playing and laughing and reading them the books I brought. They spoke no English, only the village Konkani language, but they enjoyed looking at the colorful pictures and helped me turn the pages. What darling little children—so innocent. They did not replicate the children of Delhi that had already learned the fine craft of scams but laughed and enjoyed my company.

I eventually made my way back to my hostel and explored down a solitary dirt road with a couple of markets placed on the street sides and cows wandering about. At the end of the road was the picturesque beach that words could not describe. There were no tourists, resorts, or amenities, just sand, water, and palm trees. I made my way along the sand where the water met my feet. The only signs of other human influence were the few white stone crosses scattered along the shoreline from the Portuguese that spread Catholicism many years ago. This was my first time being completely alone—just me and the Arabian Sea. I let the hot sun and sea air kiss my face as I soaked it all in.

Wanderlust Diaries: Old Cities, New Friends

Back at the hostel, I met up with Emily, and we made plans to roam old Goa and the capital, Panaji. The hostel owner, Jai, offered us a ride to explore the capital in his open-top Jeep. Jai was quite a character with his wild afro hair and his lanky figure. He was a local but had traveled quite a bit, which was what gave him the idea to open a hostel to showcase the beauty and remoteness of the Goan coast of India. He was an intellect, and I found conversations with him intriguing as he made me want to know more. I was impressed by his entrepreneur mind and work ethic; needless to say, I started to develop an innocent crush on him. We piled in his Jeep and hit the road to see what the town had to offer.

Old Goa used to be the equivalent to Rome with a population that exceeded London and Lisbon, but a malaria and cholera pandemic wiped out the people, and only relics of the Portuguese grandeur and immaculate structures withstood the test of time. The population was reduced from two hundred thousand people to less than twenty thousand, and the city was walled off, and the capital moved to Panaji. The town showed the Portuguese impact of bringing Christianity to India, with many cathedrals and churches erected throughout the city. The architecture was quite different from the ornate mogul architecture of the temples in Delhi but interesting nonetheless. The churches were painted bright white every year, but the annual monsoons left a dirty hue to the exterior, and the interior smelled of years of built-up grime from the weather.

After a day of nonstop excitement in the open-air Jeep, with Jai's academic conversations about the history of Goa, I was famished. Jai took a few of us from the hostel to a relaxed restaurant, where a musician played the sitar and monkeys played in the trees overhead. I felt like I was in another world; just weeks prior, I was wearing steel-toed boots and a hardhat walking the piers of the shipyard—now I wore baggy harem pants while listening to strange music with people from around the globe. It was nothing less than thrilling, and the experience was intoxicating. I was becoming an addict, and I could not wait for what the next day had in store.

Wanderlust Diaries: The Scooter Gang of Goa

I had plans to explore some of the northern beaches with some Aussie girls I met, but the only way to get from village to village was to rent a motorcycle or scooter for the day. I was excited, considering the only skill I had on a motorcycle was a couple of dirt bike experiences with old boyfriends. The Aussie girls wanted to do some yoga before we set out, so I used my new scooter as an excuse to pay another visit to the orphanage I visited a couple of days prior. The children and their smiling faces had been on my mind, and I was eager to see them again. I had bought my friend a souvenir of old textile blocks for imprinting designs onto linen. I pulled an elephant and paisley designed block out of my pack. There was a box of free clothes in the "treasure chest" of the hostel, so I gathered a few light-colored items and set off for the orphanage. I remembered a demonstration when I bought the textile blocks about using nature as the dye for the fabrics, so with the help of the children, we gathered mango leaves and flowers to create various hues to play with. The kids were happy to see me; one girl ran to me with one of the books I had left, and insisted, I read it to her again. I left the children with the books and stamped linen bandanas we created; I hoped that my lasting moments with them were as important to them as they were to me. The stamps on the linen went deeper than the cloth as I realized the impression they made on my heart.

With the Aussie girls fresh from their yoga session, we headed out through the beach roads of the jungle with our scarfs flying behind us. I felt like the Red Baron going through the maze of cows, dogs, and pedestrians carrying wicker basket loads on their head. I had a few close calls. The buses always win with road rules, and they take up nearly the entire street—things got sketchy from time to time. My bike was beat to hell, and no gages worked, but it didn't diminish what a fantastic time I was having. We ended up at Arambol Beach, which was the big hippie hangout in its heyday. The beach was inhabited by people meditating or doing tantric yoga; the people watching was epic. Every night at sunset, the local hippies got together and played music while dancing to the rhythms they created with their bongo drums. The sunset was the ultimate symbol of celebrating life in their bodies; we joined in to the cerebral beat of the drums. It was such a great vibe—so carefree and nonjudgmental. I knew I had to navigate back to my hostel on my scooter with no headlights, but I was confident I would make it back with the help of my biker gang when the time was right. In the meantime, we just danced, hand in hand, on the edge of the sand. Our smiles were only seen by the light of the moon that shined on our faces as we all knew that, in this moment, all was right in the world.

Wanderlust Diaries: The South Beach of Palolem

Everything was slower in Goa. I had to adjust my mindset of sched-
ules and time frames and learn to just relax. There was no slower
place in Goa than the most southern beach of the region, Palolem.
When I arrived, I was greeted by the beach cottage owner, Raj. He
showed me the charming little beach shack that I was going to be
staying in. Every year in Palolem, the local people remove all huts in
preparation for the monsoon season. The sleepy little beach village
was lined with small huts made of bamboo or other simple materials.
My assigned hut had no frills, but I loved it regardless and was stoked
to have a mosquito net that cascaded down from the shallow ceiling
of a thatch roof. The gossamer fabric mosquito netting in my hut
made of twigs and palm branches made me feel like I was the Queen
of Goa.

There wasn't much to do except hit up the market and buy a
few spices. There was a nice table on the beach that was part of the
restaurant that Raj ran as well as the beach huts. He was quite the
entrepreneur, and I felt like he kept trying to keep me entertained as
I ordered a beer and sat in solitude watching the waves. I managed
to catch the perfect sunset as I sat at my little table decorated with
a single tea light candle and a stray dog at my feet. Raj would make
frequent check-in visits between his many handyman duties of fixing
up the beach huts. I didn't need the company, just the sound of the
waves crashing on the shore was all the interaction I needed, but I
was pleasantly surprised when a familiar form came walking along
the water's edge in front of my table. It was Jai, the hostel owner I had
met in the northern beaches. He was seeking some peace from the
hustle and bustle of hostel life, and it was nice to see a friendly face.

Jai took me to a nearby café where we shared some life stories
while crouched on beanbags on the sand floor. Jai left the business
world as a financial consultant to pursue his dreams, leading him to
opening a hostel in Goa. I truly admired his charisma and ability
to change directions to build something more meaningful, but he
cautioned me that things were not always greener on the other side
and that I should spend time soul searching before I made any dras-

tic changes in my life. Jai seemed so enlightened, and his advice on knowing what demons were troubling me were words I clung to for plotting the course of my next steps. He helped me understand that I couldn't change other people, only myself. I knew his words rang true as I recollected the many times I thought I could change people to my liking. I learned, in the end, the delicate threads I pulled to alter a person would always unravel the whole tapestry and be of no use. If I was burdened by the actions of others, I would face that same dilemma no matter what country I called home or what job paid my bills. He helped me learn that the path to happiness was completely an intrinsic thing, and even though his life might seem more glamorous than the life I built in Washington, it had the same snares. He had just figured out how to tame the ultimate beast—himself.

After dinner, I went for a solo walk on the beach under the bright stars. I loved walking where my footsteps flirted with the perimeter of the waterline. Sometimes a big wave would suddenly crash to the beach and my feet succumbed to the surf. As I contemplated Jai's words, I felt at peace. I retired to my little shack on the beach and curled into position under my mosquito net—it was a great day for the Queen of Goa, and many thoughts of life swirled in my mind under my imaginary crown.

Wanderlust Diaries: Goan Bliss and Bribes

The next few days were a blur as I made new routines of enjoying alone time under a giant mango tree at my favorite little café. The waiters had grown accustomed to me and would watch my belongings as I took breaks to cool off in the calm waters of the Arabian Sea. I made new friends with the dolphins as I would kayak the crescent-shaped bay while they played alongside me. I made time for myself, which was something I had failed to do in years, and resisted the urge to befriend anyone who crossed my path. I decided to write and reflect under my refuge of the mango tree. I always checked in with Raj and was entertained with his anecdotal stories about what broke that day and the ridiculous manner in which he tried to fix it with the materials on hand at this secluded destination.

I always looked forward to my time with Jai. When he offered for me to meet one of his old friends from a volunteer project he worked on in Guyana, I couldn't wait to meet them. Jai introduced me to Samantha, a pretty blonde that he had known for years who was in the area for holiday. I could tell by the glimmer in his eye when she spoke that he fancied her, but she had brought her boyfriend. The boyfriend seemed like a dud compared to Jai, and I wondered why she didn't end up with the better of the two. We had a lovely time together, and I felt like I had somehow found some of the most salt-of-the-earth people to call friends, but I knew I had to move on. The slow beaches of Goa immersed me like quicksand, and I was feeling too comfortable knowing that my time was limited; one day, I had to return to reality.

Jai was kind enough to offer me a ride to the airport in his open-top Jeep that he knew I loved. I said goodbye to my mango tree and loaded up in the back of the Jeep with Samantha while the boys turned up the radio and sat in the front. Our blond hair blew in the breeze as we grappled to hold on throughout the curves of the jungle road. Barreling down the Indian roads, I was still nervous with the way Indians drove, but I trusted Jai. It felt like it was one close call after another, but Jai knew the roads and wove us in and out of the obstacles with perfect precision. But there was one snag that Jai did not plan on as we took a turn and were signaled to pull over from a police vehicle. The cops staked out on the side of the road, and when they saw a "suspect" vehicle, they blew whistles and signaled the cars to the shoulder. Two blondes in the back must have seemed suspicious and was reason enough to pull us over.

Jai presented his paperwork and spoke the native Konkani language to the officer. As the cop examined the paperwork, Jai informed us that he was being accused of either kidnapping Samantha and I, or else, running an illegal taxi operation. It was complete and utter ridiculousness, but the truth of the matter was they were hoping for bribes to let us go. The cops were unbelievably corrupt in Goa. I would have felt safer asking a bum for help before I would have asked a cop, but here we were at their mercy. I tried explaining to the officer that Jai was my friend as I cycled through the countless photos of us on my phone, but it was to no avail—the cop didn't want the truth, he only wanted one of us to grease his dirty little palm. Jai was a man of principles and refused to succumb to their accusations and corruption. I started to grow nervous as the time passed, and my flight time was growing nearer by the second. The officer had Samantha and I step out of the Jeep and wait in his vehicle while Jai eloquently tried to explain and compel the officer to be reasonable. He avoided telling them I was about to miss my flight if they didn't let us go; that supported their illegal taxi theory and would only add fuel to the fire. In the end, the officer pilfered through my bag and confiscated two souvenir items I had bought for friends back home. It was so confusing, and my neatly packed rucksack was now spread all over the highway, but I was happy that he just let us go. The time delay of haggling with the police took away any sweet goodbye moment I could have with my friends as I grabbed my pack and ran for my flight. But the influence of Jai wasn't something I ever said goodbye to; his sprit became a part of me and something I carried with me for a long time.

Wanderlust Diaries: Slumming in Mumbai

When I arrived in Mumbai, my hopes of seeing Bollywood and belly dancers was replaced by the reality that this was just a huge city of smog and shantytowns. However, the hazy pollution filling the sky did make for a beautiful sunset. My taxi driver was a real sourpuss and was quite cranky that I did not speak Hindi. He kept blabbering on, and I would just repeat my hotel and say, "I DON'T UNDERSTAND YOU!" When I got to the hotel, I was so grateful when they decided to upgrade me to the penthouse suite for no particular reason at all. After the run-in with the corrupt police officer in Goa, the hectic airport, and the repulsive taxi driver, I was happy to have a nice bed and bathtub. I hadn't had warm water in India, and after sleeping in a thatch hut and hostels, it was going to be a great night's sleep that was much needed.

The next morning, I set off to catch a ferry across Mumbai harbor to the distant Elephanta Island. The ferry boats left from under a huge arch called the Gateway to India. At the harbor, a holy man approached and rubbed yellow marigold flowers on my brow and then planted a big red dot with paste on my forehead as he said a prayer. Prayers and blessings are always good, so I sported the Indian red dot. I wondered if the symbolism made me blend in any better—it didn't. Families approached me as I waited for the ferry and asked for me to take pictures with them and their children. It was like I was Cinderella at Disney World with the greetings I received; all this action, and it wasn't even nice o'clock yet. When I got to Elephanta Island, I observed the island was inhabited with thousands of monkeys. They were swinging from trees, along the pathways, everywhere...and it was mating season. It was Sodom and Gomorrah in monkey town—a big free for all. All the island visitors would watch and take photos of the monkey Kama Sutra while laughing, or else, look repulsed while they hid their children's eyes from the scene. The monkeys were smart too; if they saw an unobservant tourist, they would swing down and snatch cameras, purses, water bottles, whatever was in reach. Elephanta Island was known for the temples that were carved into the mountainside, depicting the many stories of Shiva, their god. The temples were carved around AD 450, and they were absolutely stunning.

When I got back to the mainland, I decided to try a walking tour of the old buildings that my guidebook recommended. Though the walking tour promised to show me grand architecture, what I really got out of it was the people watching. I watched the young children playing cricket, which seemed to be similar to American baseball. As I continued my walk, I realized I was in the slums, and it was here I witnessed some of the most extreme poverty I had ever seen. I realized that having a cardboard box was considered a perk, as most families lay out in the scorching heat on the sidewalks. I could do nothing but observe behind the shade of my sunglasses, trying to hold back tears from what I witnessed. There was a scene that plays out in my mind from time to time from this walk in Mumbai where I saw a young girl who could not have been older than two years old. I could see her parents were likely the two adults sleeping on the sidewalk nearby. I thought it was interesting watching this little girl in her dirty dress of tattered ruffles play in the street. Despite the impoverished situation she was born into, it didn't seem to bother her as she played in a little stream that was flowing down the sidewalk, jumping in the puddles and sitting in the wetness. I realized how odd it was for there to be water in this hot city as I scanned the surroundings to see where it was coming from. I was disgusted to see that it was not a stream of water, but instead, the trickle originated from a man that was urinating on the street; this little girl's play land was nothing more than filth. I was disgusted and heartbroken, but this little girl's face frequently played in the record of my deep thoughts when I think of wanting to change the world. I walked past bodies that were covered in flies, and I wondered if they were even alive. My tender heart had a hard time dealing with the realities of Mumbai, and I was ready to leave. Mumbai was host to many millionaires, but you wouldn't have guessed it from looking around. The only thing noteworthy was the million-dollar sunsets from the pier, only made possible by the atmosphere of smog and pollution from the lack of environmental controls in the new industrial processes.

Wanderlust Diaries: Thailand Transitions

My morning started by running like a madwoman through the Bangkok Airport. I only had fifty minutes to de-board my plane, make it through immigration/customs, check in with another airline, pass security, and then RUN across the terminal to make my plane to Phuket—I made it! Needless to say, I didn't get much sleep on my red-eye flight from Mumbai, so when I arrived to Phuket, I just bummed around the beach and fell asleep in the sand. I knew I was going to miss India, but I had brought one thing with me—the notorious Delhi belly. It must have been the last meal I ate in Mumbai, but something was churning my guts, and I just prayed that a little relaxation on the beach would calm down the washing machine-like effect happening in my stomach.

When I woke up, there was a man sitting rather close to me, not too close but close enough that it seemed like we were together on the beach as he sat perched a few inches from my towel. After a quick conversation, I learned he was Persian and on holiday exploring Thailand. The casual conversation seemed to be enjoyable as I agreed to join him for a motorbike ride into town. I hopped on the back of his bike as we took off through the busy streets of Phuket. There were so many stimuli to grab my attention—from the neon lights to the advertisements for the muay thai fights; it was a lot to take in. But there was something that could not go unnoticed—my stomach! I urged it to stop the gurgling, but as I sat on the bike with my new Persian friend, I knew I could not wait any longer. As he came to a stop at a red light, I had no other choice but to jump off the bike and run for the nearest bathroom. I would never see him again, but the memory of his confused face and waving goodbye as I dashed down the crowded streets and then disappeared into a restaurant will always live with me.

When I finally made my way back to my hostel, I was surprised to see the tiny young man that checked me in all dolled up and ready to party, but this time, he wasn't the sweet young man I remembered from the morning. I observed his rocking body filling out a gold sequined dress, stiletto heels, and bright red lipstick. He gave me a friendly hug, ignoring the fact that I might be processing such a huge change in his appearance, but I tried to hide my astonishment of his transformation. He was my first encounter with a Thai ladyboy, and I was shocked how I would have never guessed he was a man. He dominated that mini dress and high heels better than I could have ever dreamed; that strut was something I knew I would never master in all my years of being a woman. Downtown Phuket was a whirlwind of ladyboy cabarets and street side hustlers, trying to recruit patrons to watch the notorious "ping-pong shows." If you have never watched one, spoiler alert: the shows were not about ping-pong tournaments but pretty much anything and everything the women could shove up their lady bits for a show. Goldfish, live birds, rope, blow darts, cigarettes, if you can imagine it, I'm sure these uncouth women would do it for a buck. My transition from India to Thailand was a shock. I had shifted from a land of Hindi ideals and spiritual awakening to this wild land in Southeast Asia—a place where you could do anything, and tourists flocked to the well of debauchery like Pinocchio at Pleasure Island.

Wanderlust Diaries: Beach Please!

I left early in the morning for Phang-Nga, which had been nicknamed James Bond Island because of its appearance in the *Man with the Golden Gun* movie. It was stunning with huge limestone rock formations that created hundreds of tiny picturesque islands and caves. I kayaked through the caves and swam in the warm water. I started to learn that I hated tour groups. The masses of Chinese tourists with their selfie sticks was enough to ruin almost any heritage site, but this was the price you paid to see some of the most beautiful landscapes the earth had to offer. The tour groups consisted of a bunch of Chinese, a few guys from Kuwait, and a couple of other nationalities sprinkled in. The Kuwait dudes started playing some of their odd-sounding Arabic music on the loudspeaker, and I found it bizarre the catchy dance moves they liked to do. In America, the cheeky dance sensation at the time was the "sprinkler" or maybe even the robot, but for these guys, they liked to pretend they had an assault rifle and blow away their homies; it was definitely a culture shock. The group was amiable to me putting on some American pop and enjoyed the beats of Katy Perry and Lady Gaga instead.

The next couple of days, I sampled other beaches, such as Patong and Chalong, and worked on my tan while I learned how the locals harvested clams on the beach. The routine became the same with returning to Phuket in the evening. I would sit at a table in the street with my Tiger beer while I attempted to spot the ladyboys, only detectable by a slightly observable Adam's apple or sometimes by a sloppy tuck job. I felt I needed to get away from Phuket, which was very touristy and in-your-face excitement at all times. Some travelers had told me about a beautiful island called Ko Phi Phi, and with little planning, I hopped a ferry, ready to explore.

When I arrived, I was slightly disappointed with the fact it was by no means isolated, but what a place! The island contained all the fantastic ingredients for a perfect retreat: scuba diving galore, good food, and the best nightlife I have EVER been to. But all the scuba diving and beauty was not what made this tropical paradise so special—it also contained something else that was to seal in the wonder and excitement of the island. Her name was Ilka. She was from Prague, but after wanting something more than city life, she moved to Thailand on a work visa, where she was a dive master for a local shop. She had platinum dreadlocks that framed her beautiful face that hosted the cutest dimples I had ever seen. Her body was decorated in geometric tattoos that enhanced her perfect beach physique. She became my soul sister, and together, this island would become our utopia.

Wanderlust Diaries: Soul Sister

There was a time in my life when I almost sold my house and cars and was going to move somewhere tropical, buy a sailboat, and run a dive business. That idea sounded great in my early twenties after the Navy, but as time marched on, the dead-end jobs were enough to keep my head above water, and my roots in Washington started to tie me down. Somehow, that dream became only that—just something that would pop in my head from time to time or a romantic story I would share of what my life almost was. Then there was Ilka, the *yin* to my *yang*, who just said, "Fuck it" and did exactly what I had dreamed of. We spent every day scuba diving, where she showed me some of the hidden treasures in her underwater world. Sometimes we went for a hike where we summited to the viewpoint of the island with a 360-degree view of the paradise of white sand beaches and palm trees. At night, we would start by hanging out in a "locals only" pub that was in a tree house, where the locals and expats running the tourism industry would relax on hammocks and watch some comedy sitcoms on a projector screen in the treetop canopy. It was as if I had a pass to a hidden world with Ilka, and by evening time, we would stroll the beaches watching the tourists be entertained with the fire shows at each beachside bar.

Of all the beautiful things I witnessed on this island, the most memorable and real of them all was not the turtles or coral reefs but my friendship with Ilka. She helped me remember lost dreams and summon the tenacity in my soul that I has squelched to live a "normal" life. She reminded me that there was more to life than just paying bills, and money does not buy happiness. As I sat with the locals who didn't have much cash but were rich in experiences, I knew that I had stumbled on to a great awakening. Their pockets were empty, but they were memory millionaires; Ilka was one of them. She had given me a gift that most people never receive in the rat race of the adult world. I had a chance to see how spending all my time and energy making a living, did not equal making a life…or at least one I was proud to call my own.

Wanderlust Diaries: Next Stop, Bangkok

It was bittersweet leaving Ko Phi Phi. After Ilka and I celebrated the night before with too many buckets of beer, I scrambled to make my way to the dive shop to tell her goodbye, but she had already left on a boat tour for the day. My heart sank thinking I might never see her again, but she was too special for it to be truly farewell. The impression she made on me would change the way I viewed the world, and I was taking her spirit with me. I left her a note and then boarded my ferry back to the mainland. It was difficult leaving, but I knew staying longer would only make it harder, and there were other places on my list to explore. When the sun went to bed, I sat on the beach and watched families light paper lanterns and launch them over the sea. It was heartwarming watching a little girl giggle and dance around the paper lantern as her parents struggled to get it to fly. I enjoyed watching her whimsical silhouette dance against the lantern glow, contrasting the night sky. I listened to the pounding of the ocean waves, the melody of music and people laughing, and the percussion of the boom from distant fireworks over the water. I just sat there, enjoying my own private symphony.

The next morning when I arrived at the Bangkok Airport, I was surprised by how well laid out it was. I planned to tackle using the mass transit system of trains and buses to find my way to the hostel and around town. I was doing well. I found the airport rail system to downtown, figured out what direction to go (even though everything was in Thai symbols), but then I realized I had just royally made a big mistake. I looked down at my arm where my tote bag should have been; everything was going so well, and now I had lost my bag! My mind was racing in every direction as I contemplated where I must have misplaced it. It was a large tote I was using to lug around all the souvenirs I had bought in India and Thailand for friends and family, and it contained a lot of sentimental value despite not being essential. I was so mad at myself. I took a few deep breaths and retraced my steps. I remembered that at the baggage claim, there was a tiny Brazilian woman. She had big fake boobs, fake lips, fake hair extensions, and A LOT of luggage. She was struggling to get her huge suitcases onto a cart, so I helped her before I left the airport. I bet that's when it happened. I stood captive on the train heading away from the airport and my bag of goodies. I was very frustrated with my mishap as I got off at the next train station that was completely isolated. Only the train station attendant was around, and he approached me to ask why I would possibly get off at that stop. Of course, I had no idea what he actually was asking because he did not speak a word of English, but I tried to explain that I need to get on the next train going the other direction. He just gave me a puzzled look and kept making "whooshing" noises as he pointed down the tracks. I could only guess that meant the train did not stop here and just passed by. I crossed my fingers as I waited impatiently; a train arrived shortly after, and I hopped on to revisit the airport. I raced through the maze of escalators until I reached the baggage claim. There, a lone brown tote bag sat, right where I left it. I couldn't believe it! I expected it to be stolen or confiscated by the airport security. I never expected it would be as easy as waltzing over and reclaiming my bag I abandoned. I did a quick search to ensure no one planted cocaine or something crazy in there, but all was clear, and I made my way to my hostel.

Wanderlust Diaries: Hostel Life and Hangovers

The Hollywood Blockbuster movie *The Hangover* had just been released with the sequel taking place in Bangkok. I must have fell right into the idiotic fan base with my little dormitory room on the outskirts of the train station. I wanted Thailand to be more than bars and trying to recollect fuzzy memories from a night on Khaosan Road, so I purposefully chose a hostel that was slightly off the beaten path and close to the trains so I could get an early start in the mornings, but my dorm mates had other plans. From my first impressions of the group of five guys, I knew they were going to be a handful. They left the hostel room like a bunch of rock stars with clothes thrown everywhere and all their toiletries littering the communal sink. With their British accents and bottles of whiskey they chugged, they kept insisting I be a part of their wolf pack as they tried to force the liquor down my throat. I had had plenty of wild and crazy nights with men I respected and trusted in the Navy, and I would gladly drink to the foam with them, but these blokes were trouble, and I declined their offers to join their tomfoolery. Every morning I woke up, I expected the morons to have acquired a tiger from the antics I witnessed. Just like clockwork every night, I could hear them hoot and holler as they approached the hostel and clumsily made their way up the stairs into the dorm room. With complete lack of consideration for anyone else in the room, they would turn on the lights and howl at the moon like a bunch of heathens. My patience grew thin when they shook the bunk, howling, asking me again to join their wolf pack for the millionth time. I tried to remind myself of the stupid things I had done when I was younger as I just wished they would pass out.

After two days of this monkey business, I was at my wit's end the final night. As my idiot dorm mates returned to the hostel at daybreak after a long night of drinking, I could hear their sloppy British commentary coming closer. But there was something different this time… I heard a woman's voice. It wasn't just any woman's voice, but the giggle and high-pitched squeakiness of a Thai girl. I could hear the drunken assholes loudly whisper "SHHHHH" as they unlocked the door and stumbled through the threshold. The dude that was sleeping on my bottom bunk threw the girl onto his bed as they began to grunt and pant like dogs in the street. Banging a hooker in a dormitory on my squeaky bunk bed was not something I was going to tolerate. Despite my hatred of sexual tourism and trafficking, private rooms were only a couple of dollars more—my bunkmate was not only a predator but a cheapskate as well! I jumped off the top bunk like the Wild Woman of Borneo and chastised the hooker until she left. We all leave travel destinations with different things. I had hoped to leave with photos and a few souvenirs while the British jackasses were likely leaving with empty wallets, a hangover, and maybe a couple STDs, but they were also leaving one little thing extra—I peed in their aftershave bottle and howled like a she-wolf while I did it.

Wanderlust Diaries: Hidden Gems of Thailand

Bangkok had many wonderful things for the novice traveler to indulge in. I had started to enjoy the feeling of being lost. There was gratification in the uncertainty and slight fear that can rival the opposite feelings of optimism and reason when you have a goal to reach. The city was my puzzle of locks, and it was up to me to find the keys. I had the goal to reach Chinatown to get some yummy street food, but every time I would walk in one direction, I would ask in my completely broken Thai, "K or a-pai, yoo tee nai Chinatown?" I received a lot of arm gestures pointing me different directions, but when I would walk a little while that direction and ask again, I would receive arm gestures the opposite way. I knew I was close, and I felt like waving down a taxi was cheating in the exploration game. Finally, I rounded a corner and gazed upon streets of red-and-gold decor and paper lanterns—I made it! The feelings of suffocation when I was struggling to find my way was overcome by the brightness of making headway, and it was a high I enjoyed. I reveled in the streets full of vendors to sample the different fare. For twenty baht (less than a dollar), I could indulge in a plate of the different peculiar food. I decided to try a bunch of different delicacies, such as the infamous curry at Jek Pui Curry house, the Thai oyster omelet, and Chinese dumplings—I even tried fried crickets. I put miles on the soles of my shoes as I explored deeper into the belly of Bangkok.

I discovered the canals and the shuttle boats that transported passengers from place to place for only fifteen baht (about fifty cents). But there was a catch—the boats were wild. The boats didn't stop per se, more like crash into the pier while the masses of people jumped on and off, shifting Thai money from palm to palm. The canals were where most Thai people lived and you could spot them having tea, doing laundry, or just living life in their small houses on the water bank. In the early morning was when all the merchants took their small wooden boats and bartered for fresh foods and materials to sell for the day.

Another adventure I partook was when I woke early to catch a train to Ayutthaya. Ayutthaya was the old capital of Siam and was about a two-hour train ride north of Bangkok. In its heyday, it was full of merchants and glittering temples, but constant wars and a final losing battle with Burma left the place ransacked. However, there were plenty of ruins to explore, and I could only imagine how magnificent it was in its era. Ayutthaya tried to preserve its heritage by developing elephant sanctuaries and finding useful purposes for elephants in the modern world. For a little bit extra than a tuk tuk,

I cruised around the ruins on top of the mighty back of an elephant and helped support the program. I played with the elephants for a while and fed them snacks of corn and long beans.

A different day full of adventure, I paid a visit to a famous temple, Wat Pho; it was more than just a temple but home to the largest reclining Buddha. The Buddha was almost too big for the ornate temple it was housed in. I visited the Wat Phra Kaew and Grand Palace, which was mainly known for the "Emerald Buddha." The stories behind all these fantastic monuments were beyond words. The Emerald Buddha, for instance, was thought to be nothing special and covered with plaster as just a run-of-the-mill Buddha statue in the fourteenth century. It wasn't until the plaster began to fall off that a beautiful jade green hand-carved statue was evident. I found symbolism in the beauty around me. From the reclining Buddha teaching me to take it easy and focus on peace to the Emerald Buddha teaching me that appearances on the outside are not always as they seem, true beauty was beneath the surface for those willing to look. All these wonders exhibited the most ornate and detailed decor that showcased the grandeur of the places; it was wonderful to experience such art and architectural genius. Every night before I retired to my shitty little hostel by the train station, I would partake in some of the wildness of Khaosan Road, but it wasn't the cheap drinks that I flocked to but rather my favorite five-dollar massages. I would ignore any groans coming from the adjacent beds and just enjoy the feeling of the tiny Thai women abusing my body with the wicked body contortions and stretching maneuvers they mastered in the name of health.

Wanderlust Diaries: Unleash the Tiger

I started by visiting the floating markets. It was so cool to float around in a little rowboat and buy breakfast from the merchants that had their whole set up in these small vessels. It was insane to see locals with burners and pots for making full fried noodle dishes while others peddled simpler things like fresh fruit. I traveled to a small town called Kanchanaburi, which was host to historical significance during WWII. A "death railway bridge" was built by POWs of Japanese forces to deliver ammunition and support from Thailand to Burma, but Allied Forces destroyed the bridge. The history of the old railroad trestle made me imagine the gruesome things that those channels of steel witnessed.

My final stop in Thailand was at the Tiger Temple. After signing a waiver stating that I wouldn't sue the temple if the tiger ripped my face off, I was free to explore the temple that was inhabited by these beautiful felines—all doped up on opium and sprawled throughout the lavish courtyards. I walked in stride with the mighty cats as I stopped to pet them and take photos. The head caretaker was ironically from my hometown in Washington, and I found it crazy that we would cross paths at this exotic place an ocean away. He had decided to boycott the USA because of his hatred of the new president and the cheap cost of living in Thailand. As we visited among the tigers, I knew that my time in the States wasn't the same story as the expat I shared coffee with. As we visited and I shared the details of the homeland while he shared his exotic travel stories of his new life in Asia, I realized that I could see that the grass was not always greener on the other side of the ocean. I saw parallels with the tigers; even though the cats were free, their mind was clouded with drugs, and it was a false reality.

This trip had shown me so many things and exposed the stripes of my inner tiger that I could no longer hide. I had learned the power of understanding the human condition, and how in the end, all people of all walks of life just want to be loved and accepted. My friendship with Surri was a testament to ignoring the labels society places on people but evaluating individuals by their inner worth and merit. The caliber of a person was not held in their fancy home or car but in the integrity of their heart. I learned the value of finding a purpose worth driving toward, and hell-or-high-water, making it happen, just like Jai in Goa. Jai taught me that when a dream seemed too big, it didn't matter; as long as the path you are on was progressing ever so slightly closer to your purpose, you couldn't be faulted. My kindred spirit, Ilka, let me remember the vibrance and tenacity I once had and rekindled that fire in my soul. I would never let the rat race take that away from me as her beautiful face with dimples that only God could create would be a daily reminder every time I looked in the mirror and channeled her energy and spirit. Even the idiot dorm mates, my wolf pack, taught me a lesson or two about how having a good time is great, but if you cannot remember any of it, what is the point? By avoiding the wolf pack of heathens, I explored some of the most beautiful sights Thailand had to offer, and even though I did not have someone to share it with, I was able to lean on my own strength and abilities and grow as a person. My tiger stripes no longer could be hidden as I felt unleashed and ready to take on the world again with my eyes open and head clear.

PROLOGUE

SOUTHEAST ASIA

With new goals and a fresh outlook on life, I returned home to Washington, but I wasn't the same girl that I was before. In India and Thailand, I had found missing puzzle pieces and started putting my broken life back together. I finished the bachelor's degree I had put off for years and started to work on improving myself and setting goals. I started a small business that was more aligned with the purpose I had started to discover on my last adventure. With the craft brewery business booming, I had decided to take the chance and open a craft cider house to compliment the growing beer industry. My goal was not only to produce my favorite drink, but also a way in which I was going to tap into the community by offering a vessel that could contribute a percentage of profits to the local causes and global organizations I deemed worthy. I knew as one person, I could only do so much, but by creating a thriving business, I could possibly be drilling a well that would not run dry. I still had to maintain my job at the shipyard, but I cut out the toxic people and found a new position that did not have me working long hours and allowed me the bandwidth to continue my progress. I had cut many ties but mended broken relationships with the people in my life that stood by me, knowing I was a work in progress.

After a duty rotation in Japan working for the naval shipyard, I decided to take advantage of being across the Pacific Ocean and make a detour through Asia before I headed back home. Looking at the map, I thought a circle loop through Vietnam, Cambodia, and Laos would be a great plan for another good adventure—and it was indeed!

Wanderlust Diaries: Hanoi

Since I was in Vietnam, I could officially use the line "what can I get for ten dollars?" Well, in my case, I got a room, breakfast, two shots of liquor, and unlimited beer at the hostel for five bucks, so I can only imagine what an extra five would get me. Hanoi was chaotic but full of life. The motorbikes whizzed by me like a swarm of locusts. The only way to cross the street was to give my full trust and hope that walking slowly and steadily across the busy road, the stream of buzzing engines didn't clip me—it was a rush! Sometimes in the horrendous traffic, I would use a drafting technique coined from too many years of watching NASCAR with my uncles. I would walk directly behind a local with no more than an inch between our bodies and follow them through the swarm of vehicles.

My hostel was great, except for some reason, my dormitory had an odor that reminded me of a collaboration of wet dog and dead rats; it was a shame because other than the smell, the place was great and hosted other fun fellow travelers. I walked about town, taking in the chaos that was Hanoi. As I sat on a bench enjoying a beautiful view of a lake, a tout (scammer) approached me. I was used to their game and gave the normal "no," but this fella was persistent. He proceeded to pull a bottle of glue out of his bag and slop it on my boots. *Really?* I thought. The man just threw glue on my boots—it looks like someone just jizzed all over them, and now he wanted money.

I roamed around for a while, but honestly, the stimulus of the bustling city was quite overwhelming. I started my quest for the perfect banh mi sandwich, finding one that was good but not quite as good as the one I had found back home, so the search continued. As I squeezed my way through the tight alleyways where vendors crouched on the streets, selling their wares and the motorbikes unapologetically zipped through the narrow corridors, I noticed so many odd cuisines cooking on the tiny charcoal grills. As I examined the types of meat that a woman was cooking, I gasped as I saw the resemblance of what appeared to be a dog, all curled up on the tiny grill and only identifiable by the jaw and teeth that was unmistakably canine. I just kept walking, trying to put it into perspective that I was not in the United States anymore, and this was just what they did here. I expelled the visions of my fur babies at home from my head as I made my way back to the hostel. It was nice to be able to take a shower to alleviate the sweltering jungle heat. At the hostel, they really tried to accommodate travelers. Free beer and shots lured in the hostel rats as we sat on the rooftop bar, introducing each other to new drinking games and stories of our travels. Today was great and a wonderful start to the journey.

Wanderlust Diaries: Junk Boats of Halong Bay

I could barely sleep, awaiting this next adventure. I woke up early and watched Hanoi wake up and come to life. The village women gathered ingredients and started prepping raw chicken and pork while squatting in the streets as wild roosters crowed to start the day. I headed out to Halong Bay—the karst rock formations that sculpted the coastline made for a completely jaw-dropping landscape. I booked a ride with the "party cruise," so it was no surprise my boat-mates were all beautiful young people that were full of life. We set sail into the jagged rock islands and sat on the sundeck, mesmerized by the beauty we were surrounded by. We kayaked the coast while exploring some caves as we jumped off the boat into the warm water of the Gulf of Tonkin. We let loose of any inhibitions inside the hull of the junk boat, allowing the sails to plot our course through the dazzling panorama of rocks and ocean.

My fellow travelers were spirited and exuberant, and funny enough, my roommates were three very handsome young men. I felt like such a cougar, but it was ridiculous the way my travels played out with our four tiny twin-sized beds all stacked beside each other in the berthing compartment of the boat. I dialed back the odometer of my true age and indulged in the most ridiculous drinking games with my fellas as we even assigned animal noises to one another to signal it was time to retreat to the berthing room for some sneaky shots of the smuggled hooch we had onboard. The stuff was four dollars a gallon and might make you go blind, but damn, it was potent. The bittersweet part of traveling was that I met some really amazing people. I got to know them, and as soon as they came into my life, they were gone. Just like the cycling tides of Halong Bay, I was cast ashore to find the next adventure and left with only photos and fun memories of my handsome men in the junk boats of Vietnam.

Wanderlust Diaries: Buses, Bulls, and Bullshit

I got used to speaking in broken English to communicate, but there were some conversational exchanges that left me speechless and laughing uncontrollably on the inside. For instance, when I booked a bus to my next destination, Hué, the Vietnamese staff asked me, "You want romantic bus?" I just stood there, a little puzzled. I wanted to make sure this "romantic bus" did not include sexy Vietnamese boys jumping in my bunk bed (yes, the buses here have beds). I decided to roll the dice and see how it played out. Riding on a bus in Vietnam, you see some crazy stuff. Remember in the movie *Wizard of Oz* when Dorothy woke up in the twister and looked out her window and saw cows, knitting grandmothers, and the witch riding a bicycle just casually swirling around in the cyclone? Well, the bus ride felt like that. I saw families of five on a scooter, naked little boys swimming in ponds, and even a guy pulling a trailer containing a mule on a motorbike while holding a bouquet of helium balloons. It was never dull; my eyes got tired from the nonstop stimulus of realizing "This is Vietnam!"

So on the LONG bus journey from Hanoi to Huế, I settled into my little sleeper bunk. I was hoping to relax and have time to think, but what I didn't realize is that I must have booked a seat on Satan's chariot, and it was a white knuckling ride from hell. The driver took corners through gravel roads like he was driving in the Baja 1000, and there was no sleep to be had when he wailed on his horn nonstop. It felt more like a roller coaster and I was captive in my little tuna can. Throughout the night, we stopped frequently, and the driver would meet some locals and pick up brown paper bags—drugs I wondered? As I lay awake, the driver made a sudden and unexpected swerve, and then a loud BANG, CRASH, THUD ensued. *What the hell was that?* I thought as I looked out the window to see that the driver had actually swerved to miss a bull that was crossing the road, but the jolt caused the luggage compartment on the bottom of the bus to become unlatched, and we were leaving a trail of luggage and havoc behind us. Motorbikes were splitting the luggage trail like the parting of the Red Sea, but the driver apparently was oblivious to what was happening. "Sumimasen!" I yelled, realizing that I was no longer in Japan and he had no clue what I was saying, so I just started yelling, "Stop! Stop!" The other travelers awoke to the madness as we pulled over and helped gather the bags off the side of the highway. The bus ride was a saga of bulls and bullshit, but I loved it all the same as I tried to write down every detail in my notebook inside the refuge of my little tuna can bus bunk.

Wanderlust Diaries: I'm in love with Huế!

Just when I was thinking it would be difficult to top Halong Bay, I met Huế. When traveling, my guiding compass was intuition and trust; this had sometimes gotten me into trouble, but overall, holding to these pillars worked for me. As I got off the fourteen-hour overnight "romantic bus," I stepped out into the grand city of Huế. The city was once the capital and had so many places to see. I could not wait to explore. This was when I met Thao. He had a kind face and was not the typical local that was pushy and made me uncomfortable. He offered me a ride on his motorbike to my hotel. I had the choice to say no and get a boring cab, walk with my big backpack until I found a hostel, or just roll the dice and trust him. He strapped my backpack to the back of his bike, and away we went. He asked if I wanted to grab some coffee, so I accepted the offer after I picked a hostel and threw my bags inside. What went from a day with no set agenda turned into one of the most memorable days I would ever have. We didn't stop at coffee; we toured all around the city on his trusty steed. This was the way to experience Vietnam...with the warm wind in my face, a silly pink helmet that was too small for my dreadlocked head, and a cute sundress. We just explored the town with not a care in the world.

Thao showed me all the hidden gems of the city—royal tombs, the royal palace, pagodas. He even drove me outside the city limits where I met his parents and they showed me their rice plantation. I had no idea how rice was even harvested, but we went out into the fields as he showed me the tedious method of how you harvest and how important it was to the local villagers. Another thrilling adventure we embarked upon was a brisk hike through the demilitarized zones (DMZs)—of course, watching out for landmines! On the hike, we found old American bunkers high on a hilltop, overlooking the Perfume River. The vegetation was starting to take over this little piece of history with the vines weaving through the bricks and mortar, causing the weaker structures to succumb to the test of time and become nothing more than rubble among the foliage. As we walked through old prisons and bunkers, I could only imagine the horrors that took place inside those walls.

As Thao and I walked through the town, locals would giggle and say things to Thao in Vietnamese. After we passed, he would let me know what they said, which normally was teasing him about walking around with a Western woman, or sometimes about my crazy hair. After passing one fella, I asked Thao what the man had said and for a change wasn't about me! The man was giving Thao a hard time about not coming to karaoke; this piqued my interest because I liked to think of myself as a karaoke diva and LOVED to sing. After we finished seeing all the hot spots of Huế, we met for dinner at a place where only the locals go. Thao invited two of his best friends, Li and Phon, and we spent the night drinking cheap beer and talking. At the local restaurants, you didn't just order beer; they asked if you drank beer, and they brought you a full case and a bucket of ice. You chilled the beer yourself and drank what you wanted, crumpling your empties to the ground. In addition, it was considered rude if you just casually drank before toasting "yo!" to each sip! I could not get use to the nonstop toasting, but I caught on as my pile of empty cans grew like an aluminum can army at my feet. We made it to karaoke, which was just the four of us in a box together. Li and I giggled and talked about what American men she thought were cute as we tried to sing Taylor Swift and her favorite Vietnamese songs.

What a fantastic day! I don't think I could have asked for more. It is the small blips in time that pass much too quickly that make up your life, and I realized that the small moments of hiking in the DMZ or sitting in the street drinking cans of Tiger beer were priceless. I had planned on heading south the next day, but my time with Thao changed my course in Vietnam as I agreed to join him on an adventure cruising on his motorcycle through the mountain jungles and the infamous Ho Chi Minh trail. In the end, we only regret the chances we did not take. This was my adventure story.

Wanderlust Diaries: Welcome to the Jungle!

A long time ago, I would have never guessed one of the most epic days of my life would be riding the Ho Chi Minh trail on a motorcycle with a Vietnamese boy, but I guess that was my new reality—random curves, swerves, and unexpected encounters made up the essence of what became my life. Thao and I set off early to explore the Ho Chi Minh trail. It was the perfect day with the sun beating down on us as we cut through the jungle on his motorcycle like a hot knife through butter. It was the most beautiful vision. I felt as if I was actually watching our adventure in an out-of-body experience. As we got deeper into the jungle, Creedence Clearwater Revival's Vietnam classic, *Fortunate Son*, kept playing over and over in my head as our soundtrack.

To ease the long bike ride, we pulled over to a side trail. As I dismounted the bike, I wondered where we were headed, but I trusted Thao. We made our way down a narrow path. I was in flip-flops, but I did my best to keep up. I was stunned to see where he had led me. It was a gorgeous waterfall with an emerald pool just waiting for us. Without any hesitation, I jumped in and let the water engulf me. After a lot of skillful pleading, Thao finally jumped in as well. The fish seemed to be attracted to my milky-white skin and nibble my legs. I think Thao thought I was crazy as I would be midsentence and squeal as the underwater residents spooked me from below. As we played in the water, I looked up to see a teenage boy that appeared to be holding a rifle staring down at us in the lagoon. I gestured to Thao, but he remained unalarmed. When you get deep into the mountains, they called the village people the "minorities." Most of them do not speak Vietnamese and were considered poor and lead a very simple life. I watched this boy make his way down to us. He walked past my heap of clothes and purse, paying no mind to them. He then proceeded to strip down to his undies and dive into the water. The gun was actually a fish spear that from a distance resembled a .22-caliber rifle. I watched him plummet in and out of the water, searching for fish. More and more minority children arrived—I guess we were in their swimming hole. After I wiggled back into my shorts and tank top, Thao and I continued on our journey through the jungle.

The only regret I would have for the day was that I chose to wear shorts and a tank top in the jungle heat of Vietnam! I lathered on sunscreen all day but to no avail—the only true sunscreen would've been to bathe my body in concrete to avoid the powerful rays. From my body placement on the back of the bike and my outfit choice, I looked like a red-and-white candy cane. We continued carving our way through the curves of what was left of the Ho Chi Minh trail; it was now called the Ho Chi Minh Duong because a road was paved over most of where it had been. Throughout the day, Thao and I learned a lot about each other as we would stop for coffee or a bite to eat to break up the ride. I remember very specifically asking him the day prior about his views on the Vietnam War. I did not want to commit to two days of exploring the war zone with a North Vietnamese boy, and I thought I remembered him telling me that Huế, his hometown, was a supporter of the South. As we dug deeper into conversations about our families and life, I mentioned how my dad served in the war, and he replied about how his dad and grandpa were in the war as well…for the Việt Cong. Wow. So here I was, having lunch only about three hundred meters from Hamburger Hill in the mountains of Vietnam, on the Ho Chi Minh trail, with the son of a Việt Cong. Did it get any more poetic?

We stopped at a local market where I filled two grocery bags full of cookies and bags of balloons. Thao mentioned that toward the end of the day, we would stop at a minority village and there were many children and I wanted to be prepared. As we continued on, the sound of thunder struck louder than I could ever describe. Out of nowhere, our beautiful sunny skies turned gray and opened up on us. Just like in the movie, *Forest Gump*, I remembered how Tom Hanks eloquently described all the different types of rain: big ol' fat rain, stinging rain, rain that blew in sideways—it was like a monsoon! We stopped in search of a safe haven and took refuge in a tunnel, hoping for the worst to pass. We were drenched but still laughing from sharing jokes about our pathetic drowned rat appearances. Finally, we just gave in and continued on. When the roads got wet, I learned that the most dangerous thing was avoiding the cow shit. The cows wandered the roads freely, and with the extra rain, the cow patties were like banana peels in the Nintendo *Mario Kart* game. The rain did not stop, but it did not stop us from a break at the next community. We made our way to the minority village and as I took off my bike helmet, the children took turns touching my platinum dreadlocks and giggling at me. When I opened up the bag full of cookies, the children were like moths to a flame with their hands out pleading for me to bestow a chocolate gift to them. It was a really great time saying hello to the children, but we had to head out to check into a guesthouse that was expecting us.

The lightning strikes and thunder crashes grew in strength; eventually, all the lights in the village went out, and it was just us sitting by the light of my smartphone playing silly card games. We somehow got a hold of some crazy "happy water," which was spirited rice liquor with infused roots of some sort inside. We played simple card games that didn't take much effort to explain, and the easiest game was ironically "WAR," which was bizarre given our circumstances. As I lay in my bed with lightning flashes casting eerie shadows on the wall and the curtains dancing from the wind tunnel of the rickety windows of the guesthouse, I felt at peace. I had a friend that was born to family of the Viêt Cong, and we had ridden the trails of the most horrific scenes humanity had ever seen, yet we swam in lagoons with the locals and drank rice liquor in a dark guesthouse while playing a card game of WAR. There was no need for white flags or peace talks—all was well in the world.

Wanderlust Diaries: D'Nang and Beyond

Today was bittersweet. I found a new friend with Thao, but I knew I must part ways soon and his frequent chatter about how I should move here and be an English teacher wouldn't change that. It was very serendipitous that I even met him, and I was so thankful because he made the biggest impression on my time in Vietnam. We had breakfast together and headed out again on his trusty Honda motorcycle. This time, I dressed more appropriately. I would have worn a burka if I had one because the awful sunburn I had was no joke. We throttled through the belly of Vietnam and made our way to the gorgeous coast. The roads consisted of hairpin turns but it was worth the adrenaline-filled ride to gaze upon the unspoiled golden beaches of D'Nang and beyond. The movie *Top Gear* was filmed on the path we took. As we twisted and turned through the corkscrew roads, the foot peg scraped the pavement, sending chills down my body as we leaned through the curves.

Once in D'Nang, I walked the beach on the sun-filled day with not a cloud in the sky. D'Nang was historically known for being the beach American troops took over during the war to give the soldiers some much needed R&R but was widely known for beer, BBQ, and bud to take their mind off reality. The next city on the coast was Hoi An as we continued our journey. I was admiring the adorable colonial-style town, but the hard part was saying goodbye to someone that became a good friend. Thao kept asking me if I could stay in Vietnam longer, but I knew I had to prepare for Saigon. I needed to get back on track and plan my new route after spending the extra days traveling with him that put me off course. As he unloaded my bags off his dusty motorbike, he pulled out a small sack and handed it to me. As I opened it, I began to tear up because he remembered me mentioning how much I loved Vietnamese coffee. I will always remember our frequent coffee stops in the sweltering heat; inside the bag was a coffee set with the contraption to make it and some local grounds from his hometown. Such a thoughtful man… I couldn't wait to share stories of our adventures and explain what a great person I was blessed to have met. Despite any language or cultural barrier, there was no misinterpretation of friendship. In history, I would learn of the great wars that were won, the battles that were lost, and the great men who fell in the trenches of that sweltering jungle we explored. There was never a division based on country or creed but a bond based on camaraderie and our kindred spirit. We rewrote the saga of our forefathers with a happy ending in the jungles of Vietnam.

Wanderlust Diaries: Moonlighting in Hoi An

If you have ever traveled anywhere in Southeast Asia, you will inevitably have heard the phrase "same same but different." That's how they described things there, but I finally truly understood the meaning. As I explored the quintessential little town of Hoi An, I meandered aimlessly through the colonial era streets and alleyways of the town. I bought some souvenirs for friends, sat and enjoyed beers for four thousand dong (nineteen cents), and sampled some street food. It was great, but then as I looked at the time, I knew I had to get back to my hostel. The phrase "same same but different" must have indeed came from someone, such as myself, playing the oh-so-fun game of trying to find a hostel while slightly tipsy through the streets that all look the same...but were indeed quite different. The shops were all selling the same things, the buildings all generally the same color, the touts trying the same scams...but different. It was like I was inside a giant hamster maze; it was a little awkward feeling, but I'll admit it was a good technique for exploring the city. Once inside my hostel and free from the mental drain of searching for my sanctuary, I was able to focus on more important things...like my lobster red skin! My clothes dug into my tender flesh, so I changed into my bathing suit and headed to the beach for a late-night dip. Fifty thousand dong for a motorbike taxi, my swimsuit, shorts, and a small cash stash, and I was off.

The water was fantastic. I made a local beach hut my personal oasis, and as long as I would buy a coconut every once in a while, I could stay under one of their palm tree huts between dips in the perfect Gulf. As I was out enjoying the waves, in came a gaggle of Australian boys. With the ambiance of the moon and stars, they stripped down, shedding their shorts on the beach, and diving into the water. I will never forget Sam. As some of the others made their way to the beach bars they had been frequenting all day, naked Sam and I chitchatted, and I was charmed by his silliness and free spirit. It was shortly after the topic of how "you have never really lived until you skinny dipped in the Gulf of Tonkin" that one of the funniest things happened. The beach was pretty mellow with only a couple of people lounging around or having a beer, but all of a sudden, Sam came to high alert and started yelling with that blustery bold Aussie accent, "Those bloody fucks are taking my clothes! Piss off! Piss off!" I briefly saw some movement on the beach, which apparently was some locals escaping with Sam's wallet, phone, and ALL his clothes. As he ran toward the beach, the vision of his white backside enhanced by the light of the glowing moon like a scene from *Baywatch* would forever be etched into my mind.

I slowly made my way to the beach from the water. I laughed hysterically as poor Sam stood there, so vulnerable, holding his private parts with a sheepish look on his face. All I could muster up the courage to say was "So how do you feel about skinny-dipping now…alive?" We both laughed, but I felt somewhat bad for him. All I had to offer was my denim shorty shorts that came nowhere close to fitting him. He wiggled them on as much as possible with lumps and bumps hanging out in all directions. Those were the only shorts I had with me for my entire trip, so I told him that I had to have them back. After a few vain attempts to locate his fellow hammered Aussie buddies, Sam's buzz wore off and he was left with the reality that he had no money and was wearing loaner daisy dukes on a beach in Vietnam. I had enough dong for a motorbike taxi, so I told him he could catch a ride back with me if he wanted; it wasn't like he had much choice. I flagged down a motorbike, and you can imagine the driver's face when he looked at both of us—what a hot mess. When we got into town, he made his way to his hotel and returned my shorts. I never got his last name, and I doubt I will ever see him again, but Sam and his moonlighting in Hoi An, Vietnam, will always make me laugh.

Wanderlust Diaries: Beach Bliss

After noodles for breakfast, a Vietnam specialty, I headed directly to the beach. I found my new little haven, ordered a coconut, and did absolutely nothing—it was fabulous. One of the biggest highlights of the day was washing my dreadlocks in the sea, and after removing the fishtail braid I had been wearing for five days, I found my lost shipyard-issued earplug that had gone missing. I remembered losing it a couple of days earlier when I was staying in a hostel with two guys that were snoring in harmony with one another. The snoring symphony wasn't really that amazing when I was missing my earplugs, so I was quite happy to find them. When backpacking, especially in Vietnam, there was no sense in getting all dolled up. I hadn't opened my makeup bag because the heat would just melt the foundation right off my face and the ease of dreadlocks kept my morning routine ridiculously simple.

While lying on the beach, a few familiar faces appeared. There was Elizabeth, the cute blonde from Ohio that I met on the bus ride from hell, and there was Rick from England that I met at the hostel in Hanoi; backpackers often wash up in the same places with some of them only confined to how many days were left on their visa. Our travel stories left us all flabbergasted as I shared my encounters with Thao on the Ho Chi Minh trail and last night's skinny-dipping tale with Sam and the moonlight; the others filled in the gaps of their itinerary since we had last seen each other. We laughed so hard, and the punch lines of our misadventures left us speechless, yet we were all the best storytellers that night as we downed our Tiger beer. Traveling by myself, I was rarely alone, and old travel buddies were always a delight to see. I made my way back to the city to hook up with an Aussie fella and a Kiwi girl that I had met at breakfast. We proceeded to make our way down the Boulevard to seek out the short supply of four-thousand-dong draft beer; it was the freedom festival for Vietnam, so cheap beer was in short supply. We would crash a bar and drink till we blew the keg, then make our way to the next bar and repeat.

After assessing my travel plans, I realized that my goofing off and beach bliss days had put me behind on my travel plans—my next stop was Saigon. I packed a bag and headed out—no time for lollygagging around on a twenty-hour bus ride. I rolled up to the airport with my wet towel and swimsuit strapped to my bag, a ridiculous boho outfit that matched my crazy dread head and my sunburned feet. If you have sand between your toes, messy hair, and sparking eyes, you must be doing something right!

Wanderlust Diaries: Midnight in Saigon

I was not sure why my brain conjured the idea to leave laid back Hoi An for Saigon on a midnight flight, but I did. I made my way into the heart of the high-octane city that was still bubbling with celebrations of the night. Ironically, this American girl chose to enter the city on the very day of the forty-year celebration of US troops pulling out of Saigon. Historically, I thought I remembered in history class being told that the Vietnam War was a draw, but that's not the story here. This night, they celebrated their victory over America and forty years of freedom. I decided to let them have their fun as I made my way to my hostel.

The next morning, I meandered through the scorching hot city. This three-hundred-year-old metropolis boasted timeless traditions and culture with monks praying and artists showcasing their work, but as I walked through the streets, a beggar grabbed my arm, reminding me that I was indeed still in a developing country. I was so lucky to have met new friends from the hostel. At breakfast, I met a beautiful crimson-haired Dutch girl, Michella. Within one hour, our group expanded to seven people, and we set off in a pack to tour the city. A must see in Saigon was the war museum. As I walked through the exhibits, I couldn't even begin to describe the gut-wrenching feeling from reading the stories and seeing the photos. I had to remove my bandana from my head to stop the tears pouring from my eyes. One thing that really bothered me besides the horrible atrocities was that I felt so uneducated about all of it. I did well in grade school, and never were any of these things discussed. My father was in Vietnam, and I will by no means ever downplay our troops and what all they suffered and witnessed, but I will say that the Vietnam War was not what I learned in textbooks as a child. There were so many evils of this war, and my heart goes out to anyone who was affected by it.

Wanderlust Diaries: Sai-gonna Get Robbed!

After an emotional trip to the war museum, my newfound buddies and I really just wanted to hug a bunch of puppies to lighten the mood, but instead, we settled for banh mis and cheap beer. We made our own activity of a walking tour through the city. I would love to embellish a wonderful time, but this city was quite possibly the roughest I had been to at that point. The heat literally made us melt as sweat poured off our bodies like the Roman Trevi fountain. Perspiration cascaded off the brim of our noses while we constantly tugged our disgusting damp clothing away from our sweaty bodies.

At restaurants, they padded the bill, which caused chaos in a group of backpackers who were trying to watch every dime to make their travels go further. As we sat in the streets, hanging out with our cheap beers, one friend looked away from her cell phone for one minute, and like a magic trick, it had vanished. The touts here were quick, and they were watching from a distance, just waiting for a vulnerable moment. As my friend pleaded with the bar staff about the whereabouts of her phone, a young Vietnamese boy, with a greasy ponytail and soulless black eyes actually raised his fists and pushed her away, yelling at us to go. Surely, the missing phone was probably in the hands of shady bar staff, and the couple bucks they would make off a black market phone would never replace the months of memories of my friend's travel pictures. We walked along the highway to a different district. With the chaos of the experience still in the air, a motorbike rider swooped in beside us and snatched my other friend's phone that was tightly clutched in her hand as she tried to take a photo. We saw it coming, but our shrieks were not quick enough for the skilled thief. We went to a safe haven where we could just hang out and dance, but it was hard to dance when I was clutching my purse as if it was the Holy Grail. We managed to have a wonderful time together and made the best of a potentially sour evening. The next morning on my way back to the hostel, I crossed the street, just like I normally did. It wasn't a horribly busy intersection and I had plenty of space. Out of nowhere, a motorbike sped up from around the corner; he was so close that he actually ran over the half inch of extra room at the top of my flip-flops. It all happened so fast, but I saw a switchblade, and the rest was a blur as he tried to rip and pull at my purse to free it from my body. The attempt was not successful, and he sped off just as quickly as he appeared. In Saigon, keep your friends close, and your wallets closer.

I went with my friend to the police station to help her file a police report for her phone so at least her insurance would replace it. The police were actually worse than the beggars and thieves in the streets. The police officer sat in his chair playing games on his phone, smirking and obviously annoyed with our presence. We are the outsiders and on our own. Later, I met up with two beautiful ladies from Canada that had quickly become my friends. We grabbed lunch, and they decided that this city was for the birds and changed their plans to join me in Cambodia. Traveling was not always easy… There were times when I was on top of the world and times that I almost lost faith in humanity, but it was all part of the experience. You take the good with the bad and don't let the rough times spoil the wonderful memories that will happen. So onto Cambodia! Goodbye, Saigon. I'm not Sai-gonna miss you!

Wanderlust Diaries: The Border Crossing

Passports are precious; they are your everything when in a foreign place. They are your identity… Your ticket into new wonderful places and out of bad ones. The next adventure starred me, Charlotte, and Ava on a bus to Cambodia. These girls were a riot, and my new Canadian comrades blindly tagged along, hoping I would figure out the plan for all of us. As we made our way out of Ho Chi Minh City and approached the border on our bus, things started to seem a little sketchy.

Charlotte was normally quite boisterous, but she had not been sleeping well and took some pills to help her pass out. When we got to the border, all three of us girls were sprawled out in awkward bus positions like Tetris pieces to catch a quick snooze. Suddenly, the bus driver stopped, and we were wrangled through the immigration process like cattle. Poor Charlotte was completely out of it from the sleeping pills, so Ava and I dragged her lifeless body from one checkpoint to another as she struggled to keep one eye open. This process was bizarre, to say the least; they took our passports, and then some random guy hopped on a scooter and took them away in a plastic bag. We then frantically had to jump on the bus, and I do mean "jump." The driver would start rolling out before all the passengers were on. We scurried as fast as we could, carrying Charlotte, and literally hopped on the bus. It would have been nice to have understood what the hell was going on. We later got our passports back just to get them taken away again with no explanation. I hated feeling so naked and vulnerable without my passport. We stopped at a weird roadside restaurant that I could not stomach eating at—filth covered the streets, and the place smelled of rotten meat. It might have been the rancid smells of the street meat or the anxiety from the border crossing, but I felt nauseous. Ava and Charlotte were getting nervous at the whole process, and I felt like I had to have answers to things I was completely in the dark about. Finally, after loitering around for about half an hour, our driver arrived, carrying a plastic bag full of passports. We had our passports back in hand, and all was well.

We arrived in Phnom Penh, Cambodia, and I was so excited to see what this country had to offer. We made our way with our heavy packs to the Mad Monkey Hostel, which was actually a great place. Eclectic artists painted the hallways in different whimsical themes. My dormitory was called the "canopy room" because it was basically on the roof and felt as if I was in a jungle. Apparently, the shower room shared a very flimsy wall with the bar. As I washed away the sweat and grime from Saigon, I heard chanting from the adjacent room from a game of beer pong as I was serenaded by the drunken hoots and hollers and blustering laughter as I cleaned up. So far, I was in complete elation with Cambodia. The Khmer people had been unbelievable warm and welcoming. Life was good, and I was so happy to be on the next leg of my journey.

Wanderlust Diaries: The Killing Fields

I'm not sure how it is possible to walk around in one-hundred-degree jungle heat but still have the chills. Ava, Charlotte, and I set off on a bumpy tuk tuk ride to the infamous Killing Fields. It was actually really hard for me to write about it because it was very difficult to witness. The dusty roads we walked upon had human bones, making their way to the surface. I tried to avoid them out of reverence to the victims of Pol Pot's regime and the horrendous genocide that took place at the bloody hands if the Khmer Rouge. Watching the movie *The Killing Fields* gave me a glimpse into the atrocities but did not do justice to what evils took place on the grounds I walked that day. I didn't understand how a whole country could be influenced to completely wipe out teachers, scholars—even if you wore glasses, you were murdered in cold blood. The awful executioners would not even waste bullets but massacre millions by the blunt edge of whatever tool was nearby, *and why?* I walked beside the massive grave sites of the countless Cambodians that gave the ultimate sacrifice for a cause that was in vain. The evil that took place here sent shivers down my spine as tears poured down my cheeks. There were trees that had blood and brains from where the repulsive Khmer Rouge would smash babies against the bark before they threw them in a pile of other rotting flesh. They would sprinkle skin-melting chemicals on the bodies to keep the stench down even if the people were still alive. They would play the revolutionary music through loudspeakers to drown out the screams of the victims being thoughtlessly tortured and murdered for no other reason than for sport or potential threat to a horrible leader. Woven bracelets and trinkets were pinned throughout the trees, but nothing could ever mask the transgressions that occurred. I saw the Killing Fields from the atrocities of the Khmer Rouge. My heart was heavy, but I was glad to have witnessed it.

So this was the start to my trip to Cambodia. With the Americans shoveling in bombs for the Vietnam War and then the whole Khmer Rouge ordeal, I was in amazement of how the people could be so kind. In other countries, I felt like I was always being swindled, but in Cambodia, it was different. The only thing I could offer in return for their kindness was buying an extra bottle of water or plate of street food to offer to the homeless kids in hopes that they would be the change for a better world one day. One of the most touching moments I have ever experienced happened as I visited the night market that afternoon, I noticed a skinny young boy who couldn't have been over five years old. He watched us gluttonously eating plates of street food. As he made his way closer, I motioned for him to take one of our plates of spring rolls. He cautiously made his way to us, and as if he was afraid we would change our mind, he quickly grabbed the plate and disappeared into the crowd. I realized how this one-dollar plate of street food that was completely in excess for us would quite possibly be the only food that he had eaten in a while. I bought a few more grilled meat sticks and experienced a touching moment when I gave a young girl with ratty clothes and a dirty face a few kebabs. She gratefully accepted, but as I watched her and her skeletal figure depart, she did not greedily devour the food like a feral animal but brought it to an elderly man that was sitting on the out-skirts of the crowd. His limbs were severed, and he was nothing but a bag of flesh covering his bones; he had not moved from that space in the crowded market in a while. Today was a hard day to stomach. I was humbled and so unbelievably grateful.

Wanderlust Diaries: Phnom Penh, Cambodia

If you take the time to explore beneath the layer of garbage, you would find one of the most authentic hidden treasures on this earth and some of the kindest and gentlest people I had ever met. My new friends and I were in a nonstop whirlwind around the city, exploring in every mode of transportation we could find. For a couple of bucks, a tuk tuk would buzz us around to see the sites. As we passed some shantytowns, the stench was almost unbearable from the garbage riddled with open sewage spilling into the streets. We took a cruise down the mighty Mekong River to see the way of life of the river people. We even took four-wheelers for a day, skirting through the dirt roads and villages. As we would enter the villages, young children would run out of their huts as fast as their bare feet could carry them just to say hello and give high fives as we motored by. I bought some snacks and was delighted to give them away to some of the village children. They would look at me with the brightest sparkling eyes, put their tiny hands together while they bowed and gratefully accepted the treats I brought them. Some children had never seen White people in these remote villages, and as we rolled up on our four-wheelers covered in mud, some children would run away, crying and clutching at their mother's skirt.

We puttered into some temples that eerily seemed to be abandoned and in somewhat disheveled condition. When we stayed long enough, young boys with their shaved heads and bright orange robes would appear to satisfy their curiosity. The young monks were very shy but would give us bashful smiles when they understood we were friendly and just roaming the countryside. After a day of exploring, covered in mud but filled with complete joy from the day, we stayed for a bit, having beers with some locals and our tuk tuk driver. The locals would smile at us, and the brave ones would come over and introduce themselves and sit with us to share a beer. "To Kampuchea!" we would cheer, and we toasted our cans of lager. They would call their families over to meet us. We had a wonderful time learning about them, their families, and way of life. Our tuk tuk driver, Sitar, actually took a side route to introduce us to his family at his home. He was genuinely charismatic and wanted to share with us the people who were important to him, just out of the goodness of his heart.

One of the grandest sites of Phnom Penh was the palace grounds. The architecture was completely astounding and left me with my jaw dropped and in complete amazement. The stupas, gold trimmed pagodas, and the statues with the most ornate detail were unlike any I had ever seen. This was Cambodia! I had to say goodbye to my friends as they headed back to Vietnam and I planned to continue my journey north to Siem Reap. The street food finally caught up to me. I knew I couldn't dodge that bullet forever, but it was unfortunate that it was on a long bus ride with no bathroom. I guess I had to power through it, or else, shit my pants—either way, it was a good story to tell.

Wanderlust Diaries: The Powers of the Cobra Venom Liquor

When traveling in third-world countries, you are always gambling with the extreme likelihood of contaminated food and water. I was a little too loose with the gamble on street food, and it finally caught up to me. I checked into my hostel, and when I wanted to just curl up on my bed, I powered through and decided to go out and try to eat and at least see the town. I saw one of the hostel workers sitting down after his shift was over at a little outside food pavilion. I walked over to say hello. He wanted me to try this weird-looking beef kebab he had, but with my stomach still twisted on knots, I kindly rejected the offer, admitting my stomach was upset. "You need cobra venom wine," he said, explaining that this was a remedy Cambodians used to treat illnesses. The idea sounded preposterous as he quickly rattled off some Khmer commands to his friend that worked at the food joint. His friend returned with a dusty bottle that contained a snake with a scorpion trapped in its fangs engulfed in a liquid that I assumed was strong liquor. I thought to myself, *What the hell! It can't get much worse.* As I opened the bottle and lifted it to my lips, I started to reconsider the idea; after, all it was a snake and a scorpion inside. *Was this a good plan?* As my stomach churned like a washing machine, I didn't care anymore. Down the hatch, and there she went! I took a big swig, trying to forget the slightly rancid smell that escaped as I took the lid off. I felt the firewater make its way past my lips, over my tongue…all the way down my throat as if I had swallowed lava rocks. *Oh. My. God.* I had partaken in habu sake in Japan, and this was no comparison. I sat and had a cheap beer with the group, and then…I felt better. This was the night I killed "Pete the Parasite" in Siem Reap, Cambodia.

So now having renewed strength, I headed to the hostel to grab a map. It was time to explore! One of my dorm mates had just checked in, and after a quick conversation to make sure she was not a weirdo, I asked her if she wanted to join me. Being a little gun-shy about the street food, we stopped into a restaurant and were pleasantly surprised to be entertained by traditional Cambodian dancers as we ate. We walked the streets to check out the night market and Pub Street. The next morning, I intended to wake very early to catch the infamous sunrise at Angkor Wat. So there I lay, dreaming of snake liquor in Siem Reap. The name actually undiplomatically meant "Siamese defeated…" I thought of how I felt victorious defeating Pete the Parasite and knew that the next day was going to be one for the books… I couldn't wait.

Wanderlust Diaries: The Temples of Angkor

This was the biggest reason I wanted to visit Cambodia—Angkor Wat. The temples of Angkor were the largest religious monument on earth, and the huge complex of shrines was an architectural dream. So with the early morning chimes of our cell phone alarms, it was time to start the bucket-list day. Alice, whom I actually met a while ago in a hostel in Hiroshima, joined me in Cambodia for this adventure, along with my dorm mate, Julia. Very rarely did I see Americans traveling solo, but it was really fun to have these two American girls in tow. At 4:45 a.m., we were off to see the unparalleled beauty of Angkor Wat at sunrise. Angkor Wat was complete heaven on earth; the temple was the ultimate expression of Khmer genius, and seeing the sun make its accent over this beautiful place was a vision. We had bought a very detailed book that explained every carving, symbolism, and purpose for the parts of this grand complex. After Angkor Wat, we didn't stop there but hiked around nineteen other temples, totaling fifteen miles of trekking before we decided to call it a day. My favorite temple actually wasn't even the renowned Angkor Wat, but instead a temple that was allowed to be kept in its original unrestored form, just as the French had found it many years ago. Ta Prohm was a complete Indiana Jones fantasy. Scenes from this temple were used in the *Tomb Raider* movies because of its uniqueness. Throughout the years from its creation in 1186, birds would perch off the temple walls. The seeds carried in the bird poop would seep into the cracks of the rocks. Trees would start to grow from within the cracks, and after hundreds of years of abandonment, what was left was a true poetic representation of how man can create, but nature will inevitably take back. The temple walls and impressive structures were caught in the muscular embrace of the monstrous tree roots that engulfed the structures. These trees were gigantic and dwarfed the temple that had at one time been a place of grandeur. I walked around the mazelike shrines in complete awe, snapping pictures as if I was paid by National Geographic for this thrilling contribution. The place was so photogenic; every part of it screamed for attention. When we finished exploring after a very long day in the scorching heat, we found our tuk tuk driver lying in a makeshift hammock inside his carriage. What a trooper!

We made our way back into town to celebrate the day. Sometimes I realized how I felt I was in love with places I had never been to before and with people I had never met. I had no idea what Cambodia would bring me, but I felt drawn to it. Here I have met some of the most wonderful people that will forever be a part of memories of the most gorgeous places on earth. It was a bucket-list day that I happily marked complete.

Wanderlust Diaries: Temples, Tuk Tuks, and Land Mines

Siem Reap had been a wonderful time, and it was very serendipitous that I was able to meet up with my two American travel buddies. With two full days of exploring the incredible temples and still battling food poisoning, it made for a very busy stop. Come to find out from a nurse that was traveling and became a dorm mate, apparently, the VA had messed up my medications. My new nurse friend informed me that the pills I had been taking for travel sickness was actually malaria medication, and the VA must have mislabeled my pill bottles. I recovered, but no thanks to the VA.

Julia, Alice, and I made a fantastic trio. We would explore during the day and at night head to the main drag for some fish spa pampering and three-dollar massages. We visited a land mine museum that was run by a child soldier of the Khmer Rouge. I was entranced listening to him explain his tragic story of having to battle his own family who all perished, and he later defected against the Khmer Rouge to serve for the Vietnamese army. He had made it his life's mission to make Cambodia safe again for his people and had been working on clearing these awful devices that were impregnated everywhere. Hundreds of Cambodians died every day because of land mines, and 1 in every 250 residents had been personally a victim to these sneaky death traps. The museum that he started was very small, but the mission was to give insight and fund his duty for land mine removal and caring for the victims. As I took a brochure and the contact info of that inspirational man I had just met, I knew that I was at a point in my life where I could contribute to his cause. When I was to return home, this day became more than a memory as I concocted a cider recipe that would give reverence to this noteworthy aid of land mine removal. I would call this cider the "land mine," and the flavors of peach and ancho chili peppers would do more than provide refreshment but provide a small contribution to a global cause.

So now about those tuk tuks! The infamous tuk tuk was just a motorcycle that pulled a small carriage, and in Siem Reap, they were everywhere! The tuk tuk drivers had to get very creative to get your business. I had seen a Cambodian man do a sexy dance, tell jokes, and even lift his shirt to show a permanent marker writing "Tuk Tuk?" on his chest. As I walked the streets, absorbing in the way of life, I accepted that the tuk tuk drivers were every bit part of the culture here as the monstrous temples. They had a routine and would ask me in rapid succession, "You want tuk tuk? You want weed? You want boom boom? Aah…you so boring!" From the war museums, to the great temples, to curing food poisoning with cobra venom liquor… Cambodia was anything but boring and captured my heart.

Wanderlust Diaries: BO, Bugs, and Weiner Sightings

So hoping to avoid a dreadfully long bus ride into Laos, I had booked a quick and easy plane ticket, not so easy if the airline decided to take a week off flying from Cambodia and canceled my booking, but this was the joys of traveling. I flew into Bangkok and went standby from there. The plan worked with the only awful part of the whole ordeal being a few backpackers on the small plane into Vientiane—THEY SMELLED AWFUL! I understand roughing it—hell, I hadn't even opened my makeup bag the whole trip, but I could barely stomach the ride. I think the smelliest one, I will call him Stinky Joe, sat right beside me. The best way to describe his odor would be to imagine if a bear shit out a big bag of rotten onions—it was bad. He would casually talk and try to engage me in conversation, but it took every bit of concentration to not vomit. At one point, he lifted his arms to wave at his buddy, and I barked at him, "OMG, put your arms down! You smell!"

When I arrived in Laos, I totally realized how laid back this country was. I was able to get a visa, go through immigration, customs, and pick up my bag faster that I could swat a fly. I made my way to the hostel and took a quick shower to rinse any Stinky Joe particles that might have become airborne. Unfortunately, this place was a little bit of a shithole. As soon as I started to get settled in, I saw a bug crawl across my sheet. Bedbugs were a backpacker's worst nightmare. They would infiltrate your pack and were like stalker ex-boyfriends who would follow you everywhere you went. After my bedbug discovery, my dorm room became a frenzy of backpackers frantically looking for the little creatures. It was like winning a bingo game when someone found one, and everyone would run over to the bunk and compare their bugs to the latest find. As everyone scurried about the dorm, the sick part of me found entertainment in quoting *Wikipedia* from my phone of the feeding habits and techniques of the bedbug…of *how they insert their mandible into your unsuspecting flesh and dig deep until they find an adequate blood vessel to feed on.* My twisted humor was enough to make everyone completely paranoid and feeling bugs all over their body. We went and talked to the manager while I showed him the showcase of the bug photo shoot on my phone. He was appalled and moved us all to a new dorm room that seemed never have been used and was bug-free. The new room was a sprawl of bunk beds in the top floor of the building, and despite a lack of ambiance, the fact it was bug-free was good enough for us.

My dorm mates were quite fun, but this was where the story got interesting. I was pretty tired, but some nonstop chatter had kept me in a partial sleep throughout the night. The dormitory was big with a span of bunk beds side by side, reminding me of barracks from boot camp. I did have the luxury of a curtain that spanned the circumference of my lower bunk for privacy. All of a sudden, I heard a crash and some giggling, so I decided to check things out. Apparently, I found myself in love shack dorm with two guys that were coupled up. My bunk mate was crawling down the ladder to meet his "friend" in an adjacent bed just as I had decided to pull back my privacy curtain. What I got was an eye full of furry man meat right in my face as he scurried down the ladder of my bunk…naked. *Why did he choose to get naked and crawl down the bunk? Why wouldn't he just wait till he got to his friend's bunk? Why didn't they get a damn private room? And why did I open my curtain*! These questions would probably always remain unanswered, but what a ridiculous first night in Laos.

Wanderlust Diaries: I'm NOT Madonna!

Vientiane, Laos, the verdict was still out on this place. My first experience involved a ramshackle hostel with bed bugs, but that happens, so I started the morning with a brisk walk through town. It was pretty similar to Cambodia; the people were poor but unbelievably kind. While walking, I always tried to stay alert and observe my surroundings, especially people. I watched their patterns, and if something didn't look right, I paid close attention. I had noticed a Lao lady— nothing really special about her, but she had nice long black hair and seemed to be a little older. I noticed her as I walked toward a monastery, and strangely enough, as I made my way back to the hostel, I saw her again, watching me. I kept her in the corner of my eye, and after a few blocks, I noticed her cross the busy road to my side of the street. I slowed down to let her pass me, but she suddenly stopped. "Bob Marley," she said as she touched my dreaded hair and as she started a casual conversation. The lady did not appear to be a threat and was actually very kind. She told me her name was Ana (that did not sound like a Lao name, but sometimes people gave themselves names that were easier for English speakers to pronounce). We spoke for a few minutes, and she was very sweet, and as we parted, she kept saying she hoped she would meet me again.

I spent the rest of the morning at Vientiane's main attraction, the Buddha Park, which was a park with hundreds of beautifully carved Buddhas and other deities. The park was very magical, but as I made my way back to my hostel, I was surprised to see Ana. She joyfully came over to me and said she knew we would meet again and asked if I wanted to go to the morning market with her. I didn't have any other plans and I liked her, so off we went. At this point in my trip, I hated every thread of the clothes I had packed; they were gross, and the sweltering heat made my clothes stick to my clammy body like a banana peel. Ana had a stall at the market and attended to her business while I shopped around. I found some breezy fisherman pants, and as I started to pay for them, I felt a presence over my shoulder.

I turned to see Ana, but she wasn't alone. With her was a young girl, probably not older than fifteen. She was wearing tattered rags to cloth her emaciated figure. Her face and hair were dirty and held in her arms was a little baby. It was so hot outside, and the baby was wrapped in a blanket, and I could see where dirt from the market floor covered the sweat on his brow. The young girl looked at me, and after we locked eyes, she quickly came in close and passed me her baby. Before I could reject the offering, the girl vanished, weaving into the masses of people at the market. So there I was, holding a child in one arm and fisherman pants in the other. *What just happened?* Ana explained the girl was her granddaughter and they had no money to care for the baby as she pleaded for me to consider taking the child back to America. So apparently, blond White women must all be like Madonna and take in third-world babies as their own.

My heart was crushed... I had so many emotions. I felt heart sick that this was Ana's best option, but I felt mad because I wondered if I was being scammed. I felt guilty because my thoughts circled around how even if I legally could take the child, what an inconvenience it would be. I gave the baby back to Ana as I held back tears. I explained that I could not help her. Maybe it was the ultimate scam, but the dirty face of that baby and Ana's pleading eyes would be burned into my soul. I was still in disbelief, and I could not bear the thought of seeing Ana again, so I opted to hop on the next bus out of Vientiane. You never know what will happen in Laos—maybe you will come home with fisherman pants...or maybe a baby. I'll take the pants, please.

Wanderlust Diaries: Paradise City

Vang Vieng, a village surrounded by a karst mountain range with a lazy river that trickled through the countryside had become a backpacker's mecca. On the bus from Vientiane, I met Celeste, a beautiful French girl who was also heading to Vang Vieng like myself, and we both booked the same hostel. This city was incredibly fun, and the boom of backpackers was the lifeblood to the town. All the open-air restaurants were filled with lounge beds instead of stuffy tables with episodes of *Friends* or *Family Guy* playing on overhead TVs. Every backpacker seemed to have the routine down: wake up whenever, float the river, get trashed, get food, go to the bar, and crawl back to the hostel. Seemed like a pretty easy life, and you could identify the veteran backpackers by how many woven wristbands they were wearing, signifying how many times they have tubed the river. Celeste and I had a wonderful time. We danced the night away on the rickety dance floor of Sakura, which was a bunch of rotting two-by-six boards piled on the ground with a wild dance party that ensued regardless, led by the DJ wearing glam rock leather pants and a bandana over his wavy hair. In Vang Vieng, everyone dances. It didn't matter if you were good at it, but everyone's sweaty bodies moved in rhythm to the loud music that seemed oddly out of place for this sleepy village.

The next day of tubing the river was a blast. The river was lined with pubs, and each one had a different game to partake in. At one of the bars, we were all playing volleyball when a swarm of flying black ants attacked. All backpackers ran to a water spring as we huddled together, picking ants off one another. At another stop, I saw a hand-printed wooden sign that said "caves" with an arrow. This piqued my interest, and I took on the hike barefoot with a Swedish man, Liam, whom I had met and became fond of. When asked what the craziest thing I did on my trip, the cave trek might be the cake topper, but it was worth it. The climb to the caves wasn't easy, and topped with being barefoot made it even more daring. The cave was an unspoiled wonder with few backpackers leaving the hedonistic river scene. The caves were completely enchanting by the light of Liam's flashlight as our bare feet clung to the slippery rocks. The site had a history with the Vietnam War. Captives were held here, and on the cave walls were handprints—legend has it, they were the bloody remembrances of the victims.

Back on the banks, we continued on, letting the lazy river sweep us away without a care in the world. We had separated from the masses of backpackers at the last bar, where they tirelessly played beer pong. As we continued, it started to get dark. The twilight outlined the peaks of the mountains while fireflies danced around us like a ballet of twinkling lights—this was paradise. It was complete peace as we floated on and the noise from the last bar faded into only the symphony of frogs and crickets on the riverbank. It was somewhere in this Zen moment that we all realized it was much too peaceful and dark. We overshot the takeout spot. We finally floated and saw a distant light from a house. We made our way to the bank to find a dirt road. We had no idea where it led, but inner tubes in hand, we made our way up the path. Every once in a while, we would pass a house and ask the people, "Vang Vieng?" We followed the direction they pointed us to, and finally, after over an hour, we approached an old Pepsi sign on the side of the road—it was written in Lao, but it did have the distinct words "Vang Vieng." *Hallelujah*! We were headed the right way!

As me, Celeste, and Liam made our grand entrance into town barefoot, in bathing suits, while sheepishly carrying our tubes, it was quite the scene. There was no escaping the main road to return the tubes, and we were on parade in front of the other backpackers who had long been off the river. We were welcomed with high fives and boisterous laughter…and a somewhat annoyed employee that was relieved to see us and get his tubes back. Wiped out, we had dinner together, a beer, and called it a night. It was days like this that make life memorable and fun. I loved every minute of it.

Wanderlust Diaries: The Quest to Find the Blue Lagoon

The lure of the revered blue lagoon piqued my interest. The locals and veteran backpackers talked about this beautiful place, so it became the quest for the day. Liam and I set off on his motorcycle with directions written on a napkin from my hostel owner. The view was spectacular, with lush green trees and rugged mountains as far as the eye could see. The dirt roads were riddled with potholes, and staying on the bike was often a challenge as we explored deeper into the countryside. When we finally saw a tiny handwritten sign directing us to the lagoon, we were excited to see what was in store. Three little kids stood watch at the makeshift entry gate that consisted of a rope strung across the road, preventing any entry from visitors that did not throw the kids a few bucks. I dug in my bag and handed the children some spare change as we made our way to the lagoon.

As we approached, we noticed we had the entire place to ourselves, but it was not quite as spectacular as described. The blue lagoon was more a murky shade of brown with stagnant water that was riddled with mosquitos. There was a remnant of a tree swing that looked like it had not been used in years and likely would not hold any weight. As Liam and I gave each other befuddled looks, we knew that there was no way we were going to put a toe in the nasty lagoon. I saw the prying eyes of the three little boys peeking at us from the distance. I realized we had just been tricked, and it was not the sacred lagoon after all. We gave the little boys one last giggle as we motored past them, and they laughed at how they swindled us out of a couple bucks for their backyard mud pit.

A few miles down the road, guided by my cocktail napkin directions, we found the actual lagoon and created a spot by the banks with the other backpackers. The lagoon sparkled a radiant hue that could only be compared to a million sapphires twinkling beneath the water's surface. Some swung from the vines of the giant tree that seemed perfectly placed to jump into the cool waters. Some smoked weed with their friends, and some basked in the sun like a rotisserie while periodically lathering on some sunscreen. And then there was me...who sat on my airplane blanket that had doubled as a towel for my adventures countless times and now marked the spot on the earth where I got to sit and just enjoy God's bounty. This wonderful not-so-secret blue lagoon was refuge to a handsome Swede, and blonde American and countless other nationalities that turned the lagoon into a multicultural soup and were willing to go the extra mile to be a part of something beautiful.

Wanderlust Diaries: Into the Boonies-Authentic Laos

I don't think I have ever felt as uncomfortable as I did this day, but I didn't choose to backpack three third-world countries solo to be comfortable. I left the forever memorable Vang Vieng. I could have stayed so much longer there, but that place sucked people in. The pure bliss of tubing the incredible river escorted by fireflies, frolicking in the blue lagoon and dancing all night in thatch tiki huts in the middle of nowhere was surely only a dream, and I was afraid to wake up. It was one of those places that was so unbelievable. I did not want the memory to be tainted and remain perfectly intact. The few days I spent in perfect harmony dancing with beautiful Celeste or saddled to the back of a motorcycle with my handsome Swede, Liam, was nothing short of magical.

My goal was to get to a small village on the outskirts of a town called Sayaboury. That was really as much as I knew, but I was thankful for a GPS smartphone app that allowed me to have a map based on satellite location despite not having Wi-Fi. I took a bus to Luang Prabang and then hiked across town to find a bus station that would take me southwest. There was only one bus that went there, and when I saw it, I was very close to just renting a scooter. This bus had busted headlights and desperately needed a face-lift. It was so confusing if I was even headed in the right direction. Nothing was in English, and all the other passengers consisted of farmers carrying large bags of different fruits, veggies, and dead animal products. We would stop at every village to pick up more locals. The stench from the different aromas mixing in the stagnant air of the bus cabin was something I would always remember.

I must have passed out for most of the ride. I awoke to everyone scurrying off the bus with their totes and loading them in the back of a large pickup truck. *Where were the tuk tuks? Where was I? Should I get in the truck too?* It was so bewildering, and I only had a moment to choose to hop in this truck or pray like hell a tuk tuk might show up that was highly doubtful. So I hopped in the back with my big backpack and told the driver the village I needed to go to. He seemed to understand me, and off we went. It was me, a few locals, bags of rice, mangos, durians, and one cage of chickens; you can imagine how well I fit in. Sometimes I would catch the Lao people sneakily comparing their skin color to my tan forearm. They didn't like to be dark, and seeing that a White woman was darker than them made them giddy as they would point it out to their friends.

During my brief planning of the trip, Sayaboury seemed like a decent-size city, but in reality, it was merely a small trading post; the village I was headed to was a dot on the map. The guesthouse I had hoped to stay in had long since been closed, and the village consisted of just a couple of blocks of houses. Knowing I was out of options, the driver took me to a house that somewhat functioned as a guest-house, meaning, that they were willing to take twenty-five thousand kip (about three dollars) in trade for a place to stay for the night. I hadn't eaten since the morning before, so I was absolutely starving. I laid my bags in the room they showed me that was obviously normally occupied by the daughter of the household. I walked around the couple of small blocks of the town to realize that this was not like any other place I had been on my travels so far. I was so far off the beaten path that any hopes of food or convenience of any means were not available here. In authentic Laos, the villagers got their food early in the morning from the markets and made big pots of soup for their families; there were no restaurants, stores, or vending machines. I walked back to the guesthouse and sheepishly asked for food, making the gesture to be eating soup. The lady motioned for me to sit at this little table they had on the porch; shortly thereafter, the whole family had joined me. I desperately wanted to make conversation, but since the only word I knew in Lao was Saibadee (hello), I didn't have very much material to work with. Finally, the rice noodle soup was ready, and I was given a bowl of noodles with broth and a plate of what looked like dandelion greens. As I ate, I watched the different cultural exchanges take place. I wish I could've understood what was happening, but watching the dynamics of a traditional Lao household was interesting, to say the least.

There were still a few hours to kill before I tried to sleep, so I asked if they had a shower. After a few confused looks, the lady of the house directed me to outside in the back of the home. There sat an extremely large pottery jar with a giant ladle. I quickly undressed and took a Lao shower, hoping not to get any surprise visitors. After a shower and putting on some conservative clothes, I sat with the family. They had one TV that looked like it was from the eighties and gathered around it, watching a show. As they all would laugh at the antics of the show. I would try to fit in by giving a laugh, but I think that drew even more attention to me. I felt like I was a blond circus freak that was crashing their party. I finally called it a night. The next day, I would trek to the Elephant Camp; this was the highlight of my trip I had been waiting for!

Wanderlust Diaries: The Trek to Elephant Camp

Traveling, I always woke up early, but lying in someone else's bed in their home in a foreign country was just a weird feeling. I examined the coloring book masterpieces tacked on the wall and plush stuffed animals that kept me company on the tiny bed; they were likely belonging to the little five-year-old girl of the family who probably was wondering why a stranger was in her room. I waited until I heard movement about the house as a cue to make an entrance. "Saibadee," I said, excited to be able to use the only word I knew in Lao. I needed to go to the market to buy some fruit to sustain me on the trek, but I really wasn't in the mood for the confusion and language barrier. But I was in the middle of nowhere Laos. This was the way of life, so I grabbed some cash and made my way to get some fruit. Besides, this village never saw Westerners; to be shy and aloof would not be the best impression of the American woman that had infiltrated their home. I said goodbye to the family as the father helped me load my bags in the back of his pickup. I needed to go to the Elephant Camp, and he seemed to be helpful with getting me there. After about twenty minutes in the back of a truck on a bumpy dirt road, the road ended at an old sign with an elephant. I guess this was my stop.

So there I was with my backpack and my smartphone that led me deep into the palm tree jungle via a GPS app. A stray street dog was my only companion as he trotted beside me down the dusty path. I was happy for the company, but when he would bark and snarl at the tree line, I would often wish I was by myself. If I was going to be attacked by a tiger or wild beast, I would rather not have warning. It was starting to freak me out and play tricks with my mind. At one point, I cursed every unnecessary item that was buried in my pack—lotion, jeans, sweaters—every extra ounce was digging into my sunburned shoulders as I trekked further and further into the tropical jungle. Finally, after a couple of hours and drenched in sweat, I arrived at the ranger station. The ranger spoke English— hooray! He was quite surprised to see me entering the park this way. As he called the owner, he informed me that they would have gladly picked me up at the Sayaboury bus station. It was too late for that, but nice to have a safe place of refuge while I waited for the safari jeep to pick me up.

To access the camp, I was dropped off at a small hut, where I waited for a couple more travelers who were accessing the park. The camp was completely hidden, and no roads could take you there. We boarded a rickety old boat and finally made our way to the destination. From the coast, I could see a small line of bamboo bungalows disguised in a thick palm tree forest, but as exciting as that was, it wasn't even the best part. Bathing in the water were four beautiful elephants, trumpeting their trunks as they splashed about in the sea. I had arrived!

Wanderlust Diaries: Wanderbliss at Elephant Camp

I had always loved elephants, even before they were popular. I always thought of them as my spirit animal. I loved their eyes—how they appeared so old and seemed to tell a story. I loved their bristled and wrinkled skin and their big floppy ears. At the camp, I learned about their personalities and got to truly interact with them. This camp was not for tourists. The whole mission was to provide a safe haven for the dwindling population of Asian elephants and protect them from poachers and abusive hard labor in the lumber industry. The camp tried to educate the tourism business of the perils of exploiting the animals, and I realized how some of my experiences in the past might have accidentally fallen into the trap of abuse to my spirit animal, which saddened me. There was only solar energy at the camp, and no amenities were offered except for a mosquito net; I was in heaven. When I learned about the mission of this conservation camp, I was intrigued, but now I was completely in awe at the heartfelt endeavor of the young men who started this. It really made me want to think bigger and do more. I realized global issues like this spoke to my heart; I knew I would figure out a way to marry my cider making with supporting this cause of protecting these beautiful pachyderms.

The elephants were not captives, but free to be elephants, with only mild guidance from their trusted mahouts. During my time at the camp, the mahouts taught me how to mount an elephant with no assistance from the ground and ride it bareback. The touristy carriages that some places offered were painful for the elephants, and it was no problem for a person to just hop on and ride them bareback through the jungle—it was a crazy feeling. Riding the elephants, I had to position myself above the shoulder blades. With each step, I felt the muscular movement as the elephant lumbered through the jungle. I fed the elephants sugarcane and watched them bath in the sea as they joyfully played together, in harmony with man and the nature around them. I learned about the proper care of the elephants. This facility hosted the only real elephant vet clinic in Laos. At night, I would escort these beauties to their safe resting place deep in the jungle and, afterward, meet up with the mahouts for a late-night swim in the sea under a beautiful neon pink sunset. I loved hearing the stories from the volunteers that had chosen to give up their careers to stay here and work with their passion. I loved every minute at this camp. I loved choosing to sleep under the stars in a hammock above the beautiful elephants that I spent the day caring for. I loved watching fireflies compete with the moon for who could create a more dazzling light show. I loved that the only noise I heard for miles was the playful squeal of my friendly beasts that were contently settling down for a peaceful night. If heaven were on earth, it would have been in the middle of nowhere Laos with the big beautiful elephants that I had grown to absolutely adore.

Wanderlust Diaries: End of the Road, Laos

The final destination for Laos was Luang Prabang. The Lao laid-back lifestyle was evident here, and it was easy to get in a routine. Celeste, my close friend from Vang Vieng, washed up here as well, so it was wonderful to have a travel buddy. During the day, I would explore some of the beautiful natural wonders. Kwang Si Falls was like stepping into the Garden of Eden with lush foliage and multitiered menthol green pools. We swam in the lagoons while tiny fish nibbled on our toes. One evening, Celeste and I hiked up Mount Phousi to watch a glowing sunset over the Mekong River and the mountain range and let twilight envelop the city. The night market was the best I had seen on my travels, and I would pass the time perusing the local fare until my group of friends from the hostel was ready to meet at Utopia. Utopia was probably one of the coolest bars I had been to with a complete Southeast Asia feel of tiki huts, a volleyball court, and hammocks—a tranquil oasis to spend the night with like-minded travelers.

For some reason, this city closed down at 11:30 p.m., and the only place to hang out was a dreadful little bowling alley. All the travelers from Utopia would load up in tuk tuks and haul down dirt roads, blaring music while trying to hold on to their Beer Laos, the local lager of choice. The bowling alley was nothing special, but for some odd reason, EVERYONE went there and partied until the wee hours of the night. With Celeste being French, all the Frenchies would surround us, and many of them did not speak any English. I found myself frequently in circles with a bunch of Frenchman trying to talk to me, but the only expression I knew was from *Moulin Rouge*, which unfortunately I learned meant "Can I please take you to bed tonight." This fun phrase scored me some free drinks, but it wasn't very helpful when Sammy the Frenchie was brokenhearted when I tried to explain to him that no, he could not actually come to my dorm and must go home...but in charades because he didn't speak English! Ah, the joys of language barriers!

In the morning, I would wake before sunrise to watch the monks make their daily walk through town. Business owners would sit on the streets and give the line of young monks offerings of rice and food for the day. My hostel was great, and the owner was a sweet Lao lady that would always stop me in my tracks to ask for a quick English lesson; trying to explain verbs, nouns, spelling, and pronunciation in quick fifteen-minute intervals was quite challenging. The journey through Laos had been wonderful, and I had been so blessed to have met Celeste; her carefree spirit was the perfect complement to this beautiful place.

Wanderlust Diaries: Reflection—End of a Journey

I was trapped somewhere between nostalgia for the familiar and a compelling thirst for new experiences. I was excited to be coming home to my beautiful cabin with farm animals and the ones who loved me. As I sat there on the Boeing Dreamliner headed back home, I found myself with teary eyes and a full heart. The emotions weren't sadness because the trip was over but pure joy that it had even happened. Trips like this made me appreciate life and become grateful for the simplest things that were often overlooked.

I was grateful for the fresh air of Washington, but I now realized how lucky I was to live in a wonderful place, where the streets were not covered in garbage, and a smell of sewage did not cling to my nostrils as I strolled the nicely groomed walkways of my Evergreen State. I was thankful for good food and craft beer. Throughout my travels, I had seen villagers cooking dogs, rats, and any other vermin imaginable just to feed their families while, in my world back home, I was spoiled with weekly dinner parties, local breweries, and endless options at my fingertips. I didn't have to worry about contaminated food, water, or parasites that would leave me ill for weeks. I was thankful for my beautiful land of rolling hills and maple trees. During my trip, I had traveled through war zones that were still riddled with land mines from previous conflict. I couldn't imagine a world where I would be scared to let children play outside or go for a hike because of unexploded ordinance that was littered throughout the countryside.

I was thankful for my friends back home—the friends that knew me for my faults but loved me anyway, and every few days, I didn't have to give the same old backpacker introductions. I had collected friends on the road like playing cards on the greatest poker run of my life. I had been so unbelievably lucky to have met those fun, spirited, beautiful people, and there would likely not be a day that went by that their smiling faces would not appear in my mind. We traveled the exotic places together and made the greatest memories that I would carry in my heart forever. With travel friends, you don't have to deal with drama—you take people for who they are, or else, you move on. You don't have to be burdened by grudges of the past, but with each new place comes an opportunity to prove to yourself who you are and what you stand for to people you have never met. This was a world where we were all equals, traveling a circuit together. It didn't matter what part of the world you were from, what job you had, or how much money you made—what mattered was your character. Maybe they would love you or maybe not, but it was the ultimate freedom to create the true person that you saw in yourself.

I was very proud of my adventure. I seamlessly traveled through three countries, connecting in friendship, dodging close calls, and experiencing things that would become immortal in my soul. As I finished my journey, I realized there are many roads in life. Some paths will take you far from where you started, some paths will lead you somewhere wild and exotic, some will take you somewhere unexpected and change your perspective from the people you meet, and some will lead you home. I was finally home from my adventures on the roads of Southeast Asia that had led me to a world I had only known in my dreams.

PROLOGUE

ICELAND, SCOTLAND, GREECE, AND ITALY

ℒ ife was starting to become more of what I had envisioned. My daily routine became working my normal job at the naval shipyard, but then coming home to my farmstead that was now bustling with pigs, goats, chickens, ducks, rabbits, and my two beautiful fur baby dogs that were more like my children than house pets. I had been promoted at the shipyard and loved my new job working as a project manager for the Nuclear-Guided Missile Submarine Program. Despite my obligations to the Navy, I still had a duty to ensure my vision of opening the cider house was not neglected. My cidery was doing great and growing with wholesale accounts, where I distinguished my business with supporting charitable causes, such as the ones that called to me in Southeast Asia. My motto was "Micro Cidery, MACRO Cause," and it was my contribution to the world despite keeping me unbelievably busy.

Throughout my genuine attempts to adjust my head and put it on straight, there was one person who stayed with me throughout it all—Joel. He was not only someone I loved dearly but my best friend. He had become a partner to help me with the vision of the cider house and was the one person I could always depend on. I had never gone on an adventure with another person and secretly loved the thrill of backpacking solo, but I knew that my wanderlust was a part of me, and I wanted to share it with my best friend. Joel agreed to join me through Europe, so we packed our bags, and I hoped Joel's patience and sense of adventure was as strong as our friendship to survive the next few weeks.

Wanderlust Diaries: Iceland — the Journey Begins!

It was amazing to think that an ordinary day that started snuggling on the couch with my blue-eyed fur baby, Kaya, could end up halfway around the world in a rented SUV loaded with backpacks and a makeshift bed in the back. My first impression of Iceland was one I would never forget. I was glad to share this adventure with Joel. Iceland was a wanderluster's paradise. After leaving Reykjavik, the countryside was bountiful with free-ranging Icelandic horses and sheep. Every so often, a young sheep herder was spotted with their herding dogs rounding up the white fluffy sheep that scurried along the roadside. It took all my restraint to not jump out of the car, chase one of the billowy creatures, and bestow a big hug. There was not much that this country was lacking. In our first day after pulling an all-nighter on the plane, we had seen natural geysers that put Old Faithful to shame and waterfalls that were omnipotent in their natural beauty. While driving, I noticed there was rarely a stretch of highway where the surroundings did not have a few waterfalls resembling bridle veils cascading from the craggy green cliffsides.

We were driving the Ring Road, which was a road that completely encompassed the entire country; with each turn, there was another marvel. I tried to imagine Icelandic legends as we made our way throughout the diverse surroundings. Sometimes I imagined we were in a lush valley inhabited by elves, and then as we turned a corner down the winding road, I envisioned a cave of ice giants that dwelled on the icy slopes of the snow-covered majestic mountains. Each part of Iceland was unique and full of adventure. A short hike through a black path from the volcanic residue led us to an ice blue glacier—an untouched paradise. Every night, we would pull off the road and crawl in the back of our SUV while I cracked open a cider and hoped to catch the northern lights. Iceland was our utopia ready to be explored.

Wanderlust Diaries: Iceland...or Another Planet

Sometimes driving down the one-lane roads of Iceland felt like a bizarre different world...with the Icelandic tongue singing on the radio and the outrageous scenery that was unlike anything I had ever laid eyes on. In one turn, it changed from a lush pastoral setting with distant waterfalls and grazing sheep to a black sand desert that created a wasteland from destruction of receding glaciers and eventual landslides. The fjords were a zigzagged wonderland that curved along the Atlantic. Myths of trolls and elves were backbones to the local folklore, and it truly felt like another world until a brief interruption from the latest of Taylor Swift on the radio brought us back to reality.

Joel and I pretty much had the road to ourselves. Every once in a while, we would see another car, but on the east side of the island, it was completely remote and speckled with a few farms. Sometimes we would pass a freakishly large truck, equipped with monster tires, lifts, and snorkels—seriously Iceland at its extreme! We found an ancient Viking village perched on a beach with impressive mountains towering above. It was creepily picturesque and a wonderful setting to insist on Joel pose for the camera. Despite his deep sighs, I knew he secretly loved every minute of it. His beard was made for this country, and I loved watching the locals look at him with envy as he personified a true Viking in this magical place.

After a long day of driving, we pulled over somewhere in the North Country. As we lay in the back of the SUV, I read Joel silly ghost stories to pass the time. I don't think he really enjoyed it, and my childlike imagination was grating on his nerves, but it seemed to fit the setting. Just as I was about to drift off, out of the corner of my eye, I caught a glimpse of something. This was it—the moment I had been waiting for! As the blustery winds blew the clouds around in the night sky that was highlighted by the brilliance of a full moon, I saw the most dazzling colors emerge. It was as if I had beckoned a portal open, and as the silhouettes of the midnight clouds slowly dissipated, the aurora borealis appeared. Neon pinks and greens filled the night sky like a scene of lightsaber battles from *Star Wars*. The night was complete, and I truly think it was possible I might be on another planet.

Wanderlust Diaries: Icelandic Language, Lunch, and Lights

The Icelandic language was very interesting. All the words made me feel like I was a Viking, but Joel insisted I sounded Japanese from trying too hard to nail the dialect. All the towns had names that were a reflection of the geological traits of the area—having fjord, vic, hofn, or lon as a tag to the words. It was apparent that the locals LOVED their "hot pots." Hot pots were the geothermal hot tubs found throughout the countryside. They could range from a horse trough with hot pipes to a fancy infinity pool in the middle of nowhere overlooking an ice field. We happened upon the coolest hot pot I could have ever imagined—it was a menthol blue cascading lagoon heated by the natural hot springs and in the middle of a lava canyon. This was a perfect way to relax and take a break from the long drive.

Another Icelandic word that was imperative to learn was Vinbuo, which was the only place to get beer, cider, etc. These tricky spots were rare, and they seemed to close at random hours of the day; if we found one, it was like winning the lottery. Iceland would not be complete without discussing the hot dogs—this was a staple in the country and for good reason. Iceland was expensive, and rather than blow fifty bucks on a plate of whale, roasted puffin, or lamb (which were mostly only around to cater to tourists), we ate like the locals and grabbed hot dogs at the petrol stations. They weren't your average hot dogs—they had ground lamb and all the fixings you could imagine. I would have never thought that I would have traveled over a country and an ocean to crave hot dogs at gas stations, but it was a real thing.

I was a little disappointed when I checked the aurora borealis forecaster and for the entire country, there was only one tiny dot that represented clear skies and a chance to see the northern lights. It was as far north as you could possibly go on the tip of a mountain with a fjord down below and a stone's throw from the arctic circle. So we were off—chasing the infamous lights. We headed deep into the isolated north, through single-lane tunnels bored through the belly of the giant mountains. These tunnels had an effect from the earth crunchers that bore them that made me feel like Jonah in the belly of a great whale. The tunnels had a sort of framing that looked like we were traveling through a giant rib cage in cavernous darkness. It was creepy, and my imagination would not let up. As we tracked a spot, searching for clear skies, the hunt got even more perilous when the only pull-off location on the mountain roads was a narrow construction site. We angled the car off the road as I gathered rocks from landslides to chock the tires to keep us from plummeting over the cliff while we slept. I had an emergency stash of some Icelandic beer that we sipped as we waited. Joel gave up and retired to bed, but I kept watch, like a vigilant soldier who was maintaining the midnight duty.

Suddenly, they appeared. I squawked at Joel to get up, popping our air mattress in the frenzy. The aurora activity could sometimes only last a matter of minutes, so timing was crucial. There in the sky was a sweep of neon green that joined other streaks. It was magical to watch the atmospheric gases make such a show—it was like a symphony with no sound. The streaks would burn bright, then dim away, only to return more triumphant and brighter minutes later. New additions of light would join in as swirling beams of energy in a cauldron of the arctic sky. Eventually, the swirling lights would seem to grow heavy and cascade in spirals like New Year's confetti downward toward the ocean and our isolated car perched on the cliff. Words truly could never describe the experience, but if only one word was allowed, it could only be described as "magical."

Wanderlust Diaries: Sagas in Wonderland

One day, I will look back on this diary entry and remember how I was camping in the back of my car, listening to the waves crash on the cliff as I was parked on a lava field—I don't make this stuff up. The plan for the day was to chase down the relics of old stories handed down through the ages that had completely identified the Icelandic culture. We made good time on the Ring Road, so we had time to spare to truly get off the beaten path.

We found a stunning gully that was the home to a beautiful troll princess. Here, the locals took their trolls pretty seriously because they could guard your bridges or else demolish them. Trolls couldn't go into the sun, or else, they turned to stone; you could oftentimes find pillars of stone that were honored as the remains of one of the mythical creatures. But don't dare say that any of this was a mere fairy tale; 85 percent of Icelandic people truly believed in elves and other "hidden people." We found old churches made of stone with relics from Nottingham and hiked through lava fields to find sacred wells that were believed to dispense holy water or ale—whatever you needed at the time.

The Snæfelnes Peninsula was home to the famous sagas and eddas that are still taught today, and we gazed upon the scenes that depicted theses vivid stories. Jules Verne even wrote *Journey to the Center of the Earth* based on this indescribable place. To get to all these oddities, I drove the rental SUV like a scene out of *Mad Max*, full throttle down a single dirt path through the lava fields. The landscape was nothing but giant craters and sinkholes from broken lava tubes, and the earth's crust had bubbled and split like a flesh wound desperately in need of stitches. It felt like we were driving the SUV on the moon, and it was thrilling—what an adventure!

Wanderlust Diaries: Journey to the Center of the Earth

The Snæfelnes Peninsula was extraordinary in what it could offer the adventurous soul. An eerie mist dominated the first day of driving, but it added to the authenticity of the experience. We blazed through lava fields in our trusty 4×4 steed blaring the top 40 of Iceland's best pop tunes. The Icelandic history was amazing. Around every nook was something different, whether it be an elf church or supposed ruins from a troll kingdom. The highlight of the day was taking an F-road to the tip-top of the Snæfellsjökull glacier—it was unreal that a path like this could ever exist and that we would be lucky enough to take it. The Snæfellsjökull glacier was the setting for the famous novel, *Journey to the Center of the Earth*, and for good reason. When the mountain erupted, it spewed molten lava for miles and collapsed into itself, making a deep cavernous pit—surely, a portal to the earth's core according to the author, so who was I to question the logic? The ride was wild and unbelievably picturesque; lucky Joel got to be the subject of my shutterbug frenzy. He complained at first, but when I gave him sneak peaks of how dashing he looked shirtless with his long beard blowing in the breeze in a setting fit for a Viking warrior, he changed his tune.

The weather could be unpredictable, and in a matter of seconds, we got swept up in a sleet and hailstorm. We were hiking around the glacier and didn't even have the SUV to take refuge in. The hail was beating so hard I could not even see a foot in front of me as the icy storm assaulted our faces. We trotted down a trail as fast as our legs could carry us and spotted a cave that was dug into the side of the mountain that would be perfect shelter. As soon as we entered the cave, I realized we weren't alone—I shrieked! My imagination had been running wild with folklore of elves and trolls, so apparently, I spooked easy. On the receiving end of my high-pitched alarm was a solo trekker seeking refuge from the storm as well; hell, maybe it was Jules Verne himself! It was another amazing day for the books.

Wanderlust Diaries: Don't Burp!

If we were rating places with the best cuisine, Iceland would not be a competitor. Everything was really expensive, so unless we wanted some fine dining, the best we were going to get was hot dogs (Pylsa) from the gas station, which was surprisingly delicious. There were, however, a few signature dishes that I had to try when in Iceland. Needing no introduction is Hákarl, or as Joel and I called it, Hot Karl. Hot Karl was a slab of Greenland shark, and in our dictionary, putrid shark meat. This shark urinates through its skin, and the only way that it was edible to humans was to let it rot outside for a while. I really didn't understand why it was so popular, but it was best eaten quickly and then drowned out by a shot of brennivin. Brennivin was birch licorice schnapps that was almost equally as disgusting, but at least it took my mind off the fishy death meat in my mouth. It was just as awful as it sounded and not recommended; hence, don't burp because the last thing you ever want in this world is to experience it twice.

We also tried some other Icelandic dishes that were quite memorable in Reykjavik, the capital city, and one of the only places we found any other sustenance, not at a gas station, on the isolated Ring Road. We had some arctic char, roasted puffin, reindeer tartar, and even a lamb doughnut. In the spirit of Icelandic food sagas, one morning, we drove out to a sleepy little fishing village and came across a small café at the harbor attached to a fishing net factory. Tourists were rarely seen here, so the owner and his gray-haired fishing buddies spoiled us with stories of their family's fishing victories and the biggest hauls brought in by the local fishing boats before it became more regulated. On the walls of the café were names inscribed of the fishermen and women who brought in the biggest catches every year. Scrolling through the names, I loved the way Iceland chose a completely different way to name their people, with "dottir" or "son" tacked on to the end of a reference to the parents' name instead of the normal family naming style. The simplicity was lovely as I read the names and knew that Olafdottir was "Olaf's daughter…" and apparently, she was a hell of a fisherwoman. The jolly owner brought out plates of pickled herring, salmon, eggs, veggies, toast, and jams for a "fisherman's breakfast," which was delightful among the fun-loving local company sharing stories of their ancestors.

Iceland was definitely worth an honorable mention in the craft beer scene. With some of the purest water on the planet, we tasted some amazing brews. At a whole-in-the-wall brasserie, Joel asked the barkeep for a good IPA that had lots of hops. The young man looked at Joel and coyingly grinned as he exclaimed that he had only sold one other bottle before, but it could be classified as "melt your face off hops" with 1000 IBUs. Joel took him up on it, and it was pretty tasty. So in synopsis, if you were looking for fancy food, Iceland may not be tops, but if you like weird stuff, good beer, and the option to grill your gas station hot dogs on a geothermal-heated lava rock, this might be the place for you!

Wanderlust Diaries: The Blue Lagoon and Beard-i-Locks

Aah…imagine a lagoon filled with aquamarine silica-rich waters in the middle of a lava field—far away from anywhere or anything. There was nothing to do but float around and rub silica masks on our faces as we enjoyed complete serenity. The day was very indulgent, but after a week of sleeping in the back of a frigid SUV, it was okay to splurge. The lagoon was a wonderful oasis to reflect on an amazing trip thus far. With an overcast day, steam would rise off the turquoise water and converge with the mist in the air, creating an eerily beautiful scene. The Japanese tourists would flock to the silica mud mask troughs and slather it on their body as they waded about the pool, undoubtedly carrying their selfie sticks and posing in every corner of the lagoon. It would be quite entertaining as we would see a figure emerge from the steam canopy and lumber toward us with a ridiculous amount of white mud on their face. It looked like a horror scene out of *Swamp Thing*.

After a relaxing time at the lagoon and exploring the capital, we knew it was that time—time to retire to our safe haven, our freedom and our bed, our SUV. Nights usually consisted of parking in a back road or lava field, blowing up the air mattress, turning the heater on full blast for a few minutes, and then snuggling to keep warm all night. With it being shoulder season for tourists, most guesthouses were closed for the season, especially with no reservations, so car camping was our best bet. Inevitably, the fun and adventurous part of that can sometimes be overcame by many factors: when you have to get up to pee, it is windy, FREEZING COLD, and now the car was an ice chest, the air mattress was flat, I couldn't find my shoes, and Joel's beard smelled like a hot dog—*catch my drift on the romance here?* The night following the adventures of the Blue Lagoon was especially theatrical come nighttime as we tried to get some sleep. With dreadlocks, I was very picky about what products I put in my hair—white girl dreadlocks were finicky, and the wrong product could wreak havoc. After the lagoon, I opted to avoid the recommended hair conditioners and wash my locks with plain water instead. As I lay down on the deflating air mattress, I was startled by the sound that was best described as Cheetos being broken in half with a very discernable crunch sound. As I lifted my head, I realized the blue lagoon minerals had turned my dreadlocks into little statues that were one by one breaking off. I panicked as I tried to mend my locks but ended up spending the night erect in the passenger seat clutching my head to avoid contact with the headrest. Joel's comfort endeavors were quite a comedy act as I watched him try every position possible in that SUV and was never content. The backbench seat was too squished, so he moved to the driver seat, sprawling his long legs over the steering wheel as if he was in a gynecologist's exam chair—that was not comfortable—so he went back to the back seat. Another notable mention of the night's escapades involve "where" we chose to pull over. As I got out of the car for a late-night pee break, I saw a big warning sign; it was written in Icelandic but had an English translation. Apparently, this area was used for ordinance testing, and there was likely still unexploded ammunition in the lava field. The sign instructed to use caution, and if you saw ordinance to avoid picking it up. This was our last night in the car—what memories! Iceland would always be an experience we would never forget!

Wanderlust Diaries: Scotland and Chasing Marty Moose

As we got to the rental car counter after landing in Edinburgh, the young lad must have found some humor in renting us a little VW Polo with an insurance premium as much as the daily fee; honestly, it wasn't that bad, but the manual transmission and right-hand drive in this tiny beast made for quite an adventure. With Joel doing his best to navigate, we made our way out of the city after a late flight. The next morning, we enjoyed an absolutely fantastic Scottish breakfast complete with blood pudding. This black gelatinous patty was actually a savory delight despite the thoughts of the pork blood and fat it was made of.

So we were off in our little tuna can on wheels. I did quite well behind the wheel. Joel had never driven in the United Kingdom before, so we thought it was best I drove. I tended to drift left and end up with the passenger side skirting the nonexistent shoulder of the carriageway. Joel set up some code words for how close I was to the edge as he would squeal like a schoolgirl when I would drift too far to the left. It was such a thrill, zipping around the tight corners on the single-lane roads through the Scottish Highlands, enjoying the beautiful greens and rolling hills broken up by quaint little towns made of stone buildings. I did mess up a little bit. In an attempt to make an evasive maneuver in search of a Scottish Highland cow, I must have misjudged the shoulder, and suddenly, BANG!... there went the hubcap! I made a pretty noteworthy dent in the wheel, but at least I knew I was getting my money's worth for the ridiculous insurance premium I paid on the rental. Now we were driving a hoopty through the country with no hubcap.

We found our way to the home of Nessie in the Loch Ness area, which was beautiful with the mountains that plunged into the deep cavernous lake, where legends and imaginations ran rampant with sightings of the infamous sea creature. We hurried to make it to the Isle of Skye, which was quite a haul, to a castle that had relation to Joel's family. Just as we got there, they closed! (Marty Moose No. 1). We managed to find a dirt road that actually led us right to the belly of the castle, free of charge and no crowds. We continued our journey out to the tip of the Isle of Skye in hopes of finally having a late dinner and beer at a renowned brewery. After a long days drive, with our lips parched and tummies rumbling we finally made it to the tip of the Isle, to see a dark building and a big closed sign (Marty Moose No. 2). It felt like we were the cast of *National Lampoon's Vacation*, and the sly Marty Moose was always one step ahead of us when we encountered so many closed signs. Fortunately for us, the excitement wasn't in the destination, but the journey of broken hubcaps, delicious food, and the legends of Nessie in beautiful Scotland.

Wanderlust Diaries: The Greek Sample Platter

If I could sum up Greece in a nutshell, it would be Acropolis, relaxing over drawn out dinners in open-air piazzas and exploring the islands. Coming to Greece, it felt like watching the evolution of men at war as I took note of the ruins compared to the modern-day disheveled city. Seeing the ruins at Acropolis left me imagining what these beautiful temples were like in their prime. The marble and meticulous sculptures dedicated to the gods left the mind to only imagine what it would have been like so many years ago, before wars and time ravaged them to what lay there today. I found myself contemplating an interesting thought wandering through these ruins, reading the stories of how so-and-so invaded, and war crippled a monument, and then the next temple was destroyed by another conflict, but then I saw historical treasures riddled with graffiti—the modern man's war on society. I expected to see Athens as a mighty city that history books could not correctly describe the culture in text; instead, I found a small hill of ruins and a giant sprawling city with trash on the streets and citizens on the verge of riots as the economy continued to decline. Despite the graffiti and the economic issues in this country, there were so many treasures to explore, so we decided to head south.

Santorini was iconic. Cascading cliffs terraced the landscape with bright white stucco buildings adorned with blue dome roofs. We rented ATVs, which was perfect for exploring every nook and cranny of this little wonderland. We sampled every beach that varied in color of silky sand—from lava red, heavenly white, to charcoal black—each beach was unique. This country was different from others I had visited because it moved at a different pace. The tempo was slow and relaxed; you had time to breathe. Mornings, the villages slowly woke up as we began our daily wanderings. I never really knew what time it was in Greece. When we were hungry, we ate; when we were hot, we swam; when the glowing sun would start to dim, we headed on our ATVs to a private cliff to watch the most unique sunset of a rainbow of glowing colors that decorated the bay. Time stood still for us in Greece, and it was nice to slow down and relax.

We spent a couple of days exploring some smaller islands. One island, Hydra, did not allow any cars or engine transportation of any sort, so everyone got around on donkeys. This island was lovely, and I could imagine living on a hillside with my little goats and peddling milk products in the market every day. Riding my donkey down the cobbled streets, I would exclaim "Kalimera!" as I greeted the locals. I daydreamed the life that was possible here with my wonderful bearded man by my side.

Wanderlust Diaries: Italy — What an Introduction!

After landing in Naples after a very relaxing time in Greece, we were introduced to the Italian culture rather quickly. We crammed into an airport bus departing to the heart of the city in the same fashion as in Japan during rush hour at the Ginza station. There was not a square inch between us and the other passengers. Joel and I managed to squeeze into the bus with barely enough room to close the door; it was like being stacked into a human Pringles can. That didn't stop an Italian woman who missed the bus from wrapping on the bus door with her umbrella, yelling curse words at the driver. It was like being in the setting of a comedy show as the driver yelled obscenities in that beautiful language of love. We explored the city of Naples and even checked out the archaeological museum that housed pillaged art and pieces of history. There were antiquities of old erotica made from mosaics, like an aged Hustler magazine for the ancient civilization. The next day, we walked for miles navigating through the archaeological treasure of Pompeii and Herculaneum. These cities were completely buried after the eruption of Mount Vesuvius in AD 79, and there were even full skeletons that were discovered, huddled together in crumpled masses. It was a sad sight to be seen, knowing what an awful death these people suffered through. These hidden cities were absolutely amazing to witness—and sort of like a real maze! Joel and I even squeezed in a few rounds of hide-and-seek, evading one another through the ancient hallways and streets and taking refuge in what once was a house with the walls and pillars intact and even terra cotta vases placed on the tables—it was unreal.

Wanderlust Diaries: Just Rome-in Around

I think my head almost exploded from how much history and culture we crammed into a short couple of days. We roamed the city, thinking of how this magnificent place had once been the world's superpower. The city had seen so many things—the Middle Ages, Dark Ages, Renaissance, and after all of it, so much remained to be seen with a little modern styling. Priceless art and sculptures were housed in the Vatican Museum. What I remembered from art classes made the experience of seeing the pieces in person all the better. Every damaged marble sculpture was even more perfect knowing what these relics had been through. The Sistine Chapel was everything I thought it would be, and if it wouldn't have been for all the pushy tourists, I could have stayed for hours looking at each colorful portrait that symbolized something special. St. Peter's Basilica was so lavishly ornate that my eyes could not even focus on one thing—it was all too much exquisite golden decor to take in. The Colosseum was a travertine historical masterpiece despite the chunks of limestone and concrete that were missing as I thought about the gladiators that must have fought in the amphitheater; the way it was set up for beast fights and even aquatic battles blew my mind. The games would last one hundred days and nights, and about five thousand animals were slaughtered in the arena.

Besides the conventional art, there were other art forms we explored—the food! As a coffee and wine lover, some of the biggest issues I would have in a day did not come from getting lost but the decision on when it was appropriate to switch from the roasted perfection in a cup of espresso to the lovely red vino served in an elegant stemmed wineglass. Joel and I made stops at the local markets for prosciutto snacks while he drooled at the legs of pork hanging from the rafters in the conventional meat markets that cured not only bacon but also our insatiable appetites. There is a point in a woman's life where you stop counting your birthdays just as there was a point in the trip where I stopped counting my glasses of wine. Each glass was paired with delectable dishes of pizza, pasta, or gnocchi and was exquisite. Rome was a perfect pairing of history, sights, and food with my own personal gladiator to share it with.

Wanderlust Diaries: Pisa and Cinque Terra

Just a short train ride took us from the cultural headquarters of Rome to new exciting places. Pisa was a pleasant stop, and actually seeing the leaning tower put things in a new perspective about this marvel. The tower settled wrong on the soft earth and was over five degrees off vertical. The beautiful marble tower was a complete spectacle to see, and pictures did not do it justice. As we sat down for lunch and enjoyed a carafe of vino, the skies opened up and started to pour over the piazza. Hordes of tourists flocked to shelter and ran around like chickens to escape the downpour. Cuddled dry under a canopy, we sat drinking our wine, enjoying the view of that astounding architectural art piece.

Our destination for the night was a charming village on the Italian Riviera coastline called Cinque Terra. I had never heard of this place, but it was absolutely the postcard view of what Italy represented. These five little seaside villages carved into the mountainside had no cars that ran through the cobbled streets. Steep rugged stairs were the arteries of the village, and the buildings were stacked on top of each other like colorful pastel Legos that overlooked the sea. Forgetting about the other tourists, the peeling paint and bristled fishermen made the place completely authentic. I was in complete awe when the innkeeper escorted us up the never-ending steep steps to our apartment. Our room could not have been more perfect. We had a wall that opened up over the gorgeous blue Mediterranean Sea with a view that was lost into the horizon. When I look at postcards from the place, I can see our room...in that beautiful little seaside village of Riomaggiore that stole our hearts. We spent the evening exploring but enjoyed dinner on the balcony of our beautiful little piece of the world, followed by prosecco and grappa, an Italian liquor made from remnants of wine stems and pumice. We drank and laughed as we watched Italian cartoons and MTV videos. What a postcard day!

Wanderlust Diaries: Firenze, Amore Mio

When traveling, sometimes you find a spot that resonates and you think to yourself, "I could live here..." Florence was one of those places. Walking the cobbled uneven streets and perusing the open piazzas, I could feel the Renaissance Era. Ornate sculptures surrounded us, telling stories of the gods and iconic citizens of the proud city. As I looked at the beautiful art I was surrounded by, I wished that we could have this feeling in the United States. Even though we don't have the age that these countries do, why couldn't we have this beautiful art filled in open parks and piazzas? I enjoyed every second of this Tuscan beauty as I set my sights on a long to-do list: the Duomo, the Galleria dell' Accademia, and the Uffizi Gallery, to name a few. Joel was along for the ride as I escorted him to the beautiful galleries, and I would relate the masterpieces to the proper Teenage Mutant Ninja Turtle when he wanted to know where the next stop was. It was more fun to say "Red Bandana," and Joel would filter through his recollection of which turtle related to the artist; like a silly trivia game between the two of us, he would eventually decipher what iconic site we were headed to next. I must say that I had no idea how impressive Michelangelo's statue of David would actually be. He was marbled perfection, even the veins in his hands appeared lifelike and how he captured the realistic effect of every muscle in the human body—it was unreal. Florence had captured the gold medal for food on our trip. We walked along the streets, found a pasta bar, and ordered a formaggio spinach stuffed ravioli with a sage citrus sauce and a cocoa boar sauce pasta dish—it was absolutely delicious! Florence, you captured my heart… Amore Mio!

Wanderlust Diaries: Ducati, Pick-Pockets, and my Big Mouth

Bologna, home to Ducati, was a highlight that we prearranged on our trip to privately tour the factory and go to the museum. Joel was in heaven looking at the motors as we made our way through the assembly line. Joel seemed even more knowledgeable than our guide on some of the processes and specifications on the bikes, being that he was a true gearhead and motorcycle enthusiast. We saw the impressive winning bikes from throughout the decades of history with the Ducati name. After dragging Joel through all the art galleries, it was nice to see Joel scamper around the bike museum like a kid in a candy store.

On our way back into town from the factory, we hopped on a local bus. I knew it was the pick-pocket's playground; the scavengers preyed on tourists that were more concerned with understanding the foreign language and bus stops than protecting their valuables. We sat in the back. I guarded my purse like a fortress. They weren't getting into my Teflon mesh-lined purse with a steel-embedded strap. I was like a bank vault, but I grew very cautious when I saw a group of Nigerian immigrant men hop on the bus. These men seemed to be prevalent in the big cities and were usually peddling knockoff designer bags, souvenirs, or else, the scammers with the woven bracelets in the crowded piazzas. They had a gimmick to find a tourist, quickly tie a bracelet on their wrist while making awkward conversation, and then the tourist was obliged to pay them while they were attached by the wrist as the con artist watched the tourist go through their wallet. I watched them like a hawk as they entered the bus. With precision, I observed the last man quickly and calmly walk past an unsuspecting Indian boy that was sitting toward the middle of the bus. The Nigerian dipped into the unsuspecting boy's jacket pocket, pulling out a small trifold wallet. With no hesitation, the Nigerian man slipped his new loot into his pocket and continued down the bus aisle. *Did I really just see that happen?* This thief was smoother than a hot knife through butter and had the sleight of the hand trick on par with a magician. As fast as it all went down, I could not control my uncontrollable mouth. I hate thieves. They can ruin the life of innocent people, and I just witnessed it happen right in front of me. I barked, "HEY! I just saw you take his wallet! I SAW YOU!" as I alerted the other bus riders. I didn't back down as he glared at me in disgust. He pulled a wallet out of his pants pocket and pointed to the little pink zippered polka-dot change purse—that was NOT the wallet I saw him steal, and now I was one hundred percent validated in my accusation. The rest of the ride was tense. The Nigerian man would lock eyes on me, knowing I saw what he did. We all got out at the last stop, so Joel and I hustled from the bus station. We were going to throw away a glass water bottle, but after my bus escapades, Joel kept in in hand in case it was needed to smash someone's head. That Indian boy never got his wallet back to my knowledge, but at least I know I wouldn't lose sleep from doing whatever I could, and I was glad Joel and I didn't get jumped. My mouth sure had a mind of its own!

Wanderlust Diaries: Last Stop, Venice

We became quite the pair of travel buddies. I knew that Joel would be secretly happy if I found a coffee shop that did not only serve espresso but had an option of hot chocolate for him. I knew that even though it was more appropriate to stand at the coffee bar counters, standing in a busy café made him anxious, so we would always find a place to take a seat as we started the morning people watching while sipping our warm morning beverages. Joel knew that even though it was frivolous, I liked to always buy bread crumbs from street vendors to feed the scavenger pigeons as they flocked to me and perched on my arms like the old lady in Mary Poppins—sometimes I would even sing the chorus *Feed the birds, tuppence a bag* just to give Joel a chuckle. I knew that Joel's stomach was a never-ending black hole, and no matter what time of day it was, his eyes would scan the endless cicchetti stands for the perfect snacks. We would load up our tiny plates with the delectable finger foods that we washed down with a refreshing glass of wine. I knew if Joel was starting to get grumpy, a cicchetti would usually do the trick. As I watched him prep a giant piece of bread with what appeared to be a big hunk of mozzarella, his face turned ghostly as he realized it was a seafood paste of creamed catfish. That flavor would taint his cicchetti memory as his mustache reminded me of his fishy exploits from the lingering smell.

We poetically finished the trip on a gondola ride in the canals with a bottle of Prosecco. I had never taken on a backpacking trip with someone I loved before. I had always worried that I would feel "tied down" instead of free. With Joel, I found a partner that made me feel at home but on an adventure at the same time. We did not spend the trip gazing at each other but looking at beautiful things in the same direction. I think he started to understand my wanderlust, even if the style was not for him. He knew that the only way to keep me happy was to keep me wild as he was able to see firsthand how much I loved the thrill of a new place. Good friends will listen to your adventures when you get home, but only best friends will be a part of them. As we headed home, I couldn't help but reflect on the wonderful journey we had experienced together. The countless photos would always be an instant return trip to the memories we created as we danced through four beautiful countries together.

A LITTLE EUROPE, AFRICA, AND THE MIDDLE EAST

I truly hopscotched the globe with this trip. It all started innocently enough with just the scholastic endeavor to head to cider country in the heart of England, but I figured since I was already across the big pond, why not make an adventure out of it! I had never seen Africa, and if I was going to explore the world, I needed to experience the wilds of this untamed continent. Logistically, it only made sense to pepper in a couple of Middle Eastern countries and a return flight from Spain.

Life on the home front was going great as my shipyard job was rewarding and my cider house continued to grow. I had finished my master's degree but looked to expand my mind further with classes on advanced fermentation and control that could only be found in England. I saved up my vacation days at the shipyard by working extra hours, knowing that one day I would use the time for an adventure. Now was the time to cash in on my investment. With my backpack full and heart open, I set off on another thrilling ride.

Wanderlust Diaries: Airplane Scare-Plane

We were halfway across the Atlantic on a brand-new Boeing Dreamliner. I had managed to get a great seat; in fact, the perfect seat near the middle exit of this huge jet with lots of leg room. I watched the monitor tracking our progress into London, and I was happy I didn't doze off as I started to notice a beautiful horizon. The sun would soon be rising in Europe, and it was a new day full of possibilities. Just as I started to enjoy this inner peace of flying toward the light and away from the night, the plane changed its course. The new light of day turned to black as we headed back west. *How odd!* I wondered if I was mistaken, but the airplane monitor proved the direction change to be true. Why would we turn around when we were halfway across the Atlantic? I looked out my window, imagining what the problem could be. As I examined the starboard motor, I found some peace in seeing a Rolls Royce sticker on the engine. *Surely, it wasn't mechanical?* I passed the time with my ear to the window listening for strange noises…as if I would have any insight to the mechanics of the plane!

As we headed back to Canada, the air in the cabin seemed to turn quite chilly. I got up to ask the flight attendant for a blanket. I then understood what the reason for the turnaround was—it wasn't the engines, lack of fuel, or any other crazy thing my mind had conjured up. As I spoke with the flight attendant, she quickly grabbed me a blanket as she continued her conversation with the doctor onboard. Apparently, toward the rear of the cabin, a man had suffered a heart attack. The unknown man would not have made it to London, so we headed back to North America as the crew made preps for an emergency landing. The flight attendants shuffled the other two passengers on my row to somewhere else on the plane. My "perfect" seat was apparently the best option to relocate the unknown man for close proximity to the exit once we landed. The extra leg room allowed access for the flight attendants and doctor monitoring his condition.

My hopes of catching a nap to be fresh for London vanished as I spent the next couple of hours next to the unknown man and nurse that tended to him as he would go in and out of consciousness. The man was traveling alone. I wondered why he was headed to London. *Was it to see family? For vacation? Possibly for medical treatments?* I wondered so many things about this unknown man as I sat next to him, watching him suffer and feeling utterly helpless to ease his pain in any way. As I watched the airplane monitor make progress toward the mainland, I felt hopeful that despite the detour, a life would be saved; when compared to that, my few hours lost roaming about Piccadilly Circus seemed quite insignificant.

The captain announced we would be making our emergency landing in Happy Valley Goose Bay, in the New Foundland territory. The sun was starting to rise over New Foundland. It was quite possibly the most gorgeous sunrise I had ever seen in my life with vibrant pinks and a hint of neon orange painted over the sky and spreading light over sleepy Canada. There was snow on the ground and a photogenic dusting of white powder over the evergreen trees. Even a reflective stream capturing mornings first light made an appearance on the rural countryside—Norman Rockwell himself could not have painted a better picture. I looked over to the unknown man and gently whispered into his ear, "Do you want to see the most beautiful sunrise over Canada?" He lifted his eyebrows, and despite his labored breathing, he turned his head to look out my window. He opened his eyes that had been squinted in pain to acknowledge God's magnificence outside the window of the Dreamliner. "It's beautiful," he grunted as he passed me a smile and returned to his position. I was very glad I shared that moment with him. He would not be making his trip to London—to see family, have that last vacation, or whatever was his intention. In fact, he wouldn't even make it to the rural Canadian airport. The unknown man died twenty minutes later on the floor of the Boeing 787 Dreamliner…right beside my extra legroom.

Wanderlust Diaries: White Knuckling Into Cider Country

Meandering about foreign lands alone might seems brazen, but to me, this was nothing compared to the feat that was inevitable—driving in London. I toasted the town with a pint of cider, I had eaten my fish and chips, and I had snapped some photos of the iconic landmarks. It was time to go to the cider heartland, and to get there,

I must drive! I didn't have the best track record for driving in the United Kingdom. I was thankful I had only lost a hubcap and dented a wheel in Scotland, but it was hard to drive on the right side when all your instincts said it was wrong.

I had planned to rent the car in the suburbs of London to avoid the traffic, so as I got behind the wheel of my fancy Fiat, I programmed in the address of my new friend I met on Couchsurfing, and I was ready to go, except the fancy car with its push button ignition would not start. *Bloody hell...what now?* I circled the car and scratched my head. Finally, I figured out the magic trick to this contraption, and I was off—headed to Cider country. I was a little alarmed that my navigation system kept directing me into London, but once I hit the gas pedal, I did not question the directions. I just listened to the sweet little British accent on the navigation system (I named her Linda), and as long as I kept the motored beast inside the white lines, I just kept on moving...farther and farther into the heart of the city. I wanted to question Linda, but as traffic got more and more congested, I didn't dare take my hands off the wheel to fiddle with the computer. *Damn it, Linda, where are you taking me*! I knew something was askew as I started to recognize some landmarks, but the constant roundabouts and chaotic buses were unyielding and kept me pressing onward. As I idled in a sandwich of red buses with floods of smartly dressed pedestrians scurrying about the streets, I had time to question Linda. I quickly pushed a few buttons, and just as I feared, this cheeky broad led me into the heart of London! Apparently, when I was fumbling around with the ignition before I started the journey, the GPS defaulted back to the last saved destination—the Waldorf Hotel, dead center London! "LINDA!" I exclaimed as I realized what a pickle I was in. I managed to whittle my way through the narrow streets with giant open-top buses and white knuckled my way out of the city. Whew! That was ridiculous, but I made it out with all my hubcaps.

As I continued onward to the Midlands, I was hesitant to stop for anything. I was running on nothing but espresso and last night's fish and chips, but I was hopeful that possibly a convenient gas station would appear for a bathroom break. I refused to detour, afraid that I would end up on another wild goose chase into the big city. I realized that driving on the motorway really wasn't that bad…as long as I kept going straight. Somewhere after I was unable to merge to the service station in the city of Reading, my bladder was about to burst. I pulled over onto the shoulder and spotted a railroad a few feet beyond the guard rail—perfect pee spot. I couldn't help but think of the Monopoly man shaking his finger at me with disapproval as I took a whiz on the Reading Railroad. Catch phrases of "No Free Parking" and "Go to Jail…Go Directly to Jail" circled my head as I laughed at the irony.

So back on the road, the scenery changed from city suburbs to green rolling hills with speckled deciduous trees rendering gorgeous fall colors. Sheep grazed on the hillsides, and the four-lane motorway transitioned into simple country roads that carved through rural farmlands. Linda led me into the quaint town of Ledbury, where I would call home for the next few days. The town consisted of one main street with a few sprawling side roads and cute brick houses spread neatly in rows. As I approached the address, I realized that house numbers were different from what I was used to, so I started to worry that I might have some difficulty in finding the residence. I was staying with a man named Jack that I had made acquaintance with through an interesting way of travel called Couchsurfing. He had offered to host me, but without Wi-Fi, I had no way to contact him for better directions. As I tried one last row of houses, I saw an interesting sign; printed on some notebook paper, I saw "Mel, you're almost here" posted on a fence line. I followed a few more signs that were decorated with arrows and smiley faces, and finally, I found the last one: "Welcome, Mel, my Yankee friend!" I made it to Cider Country!

Wanderlust Diaries: Couchsurfing Easy Sailing

This means of travel might not be everyone's cup of tea. You never know what is behind the door you are choosing. You know at least you will get a place to sleep, but the rest is up to chance. The host could be a complete weirdo with a teddy bear fetish, a pervert with cameras mounted everywhere, or else, they could be the perfect gentleman…like Jack. Jack greeted me with open arms to his quaint little house in Ledbury, England. Jack was an amazing person that shared the thirst for travel and a lust for life that I had really only seen in myself. Four years prior, Jack had a near-death experience from a car wreck. Actually, he medically died, but after months of being in a coma, intense brain surgery, and a metal plate in his head, he was a living and breathing example of YOLO (you only live once) and had worked his way around the globe meeting new people.

Jack and I didn't have a moment of awkward silence and managed to tackle the most obscure and personal conversations that usually took years to trust another person with, let alone a stranger. Jack told me of his crazy couchsurfing experiences of hosts that were Thailand ladyboys who loved his English accent, and I shared some of my misadventures that had become the most entertaining of tales. Jack was a kindred spirit, and I knew it was serendipity that our paths had crossed. After a full day, Jack asked if I would please come meet his parents. They wanted to meet their son's Yankee friend that he had been talking about. Jack told me that his family would not approve of couchsurfing; *after all, what respectable English gentleman would let a complete stranger into his home?* He casually had a fantastic story preplanned that would be more suitable, so I obliged his request. However, I teased him with threats to make up the most embarrassing stories if he made me lie to his folks. From the simple life Jack led with minimal possessions, I didn't expect the night I had in store.

As we drove into the next hamlet where Jack lived as a boy, I couldn't believe this was his upbringing. His home was on a huge working dairy farm, with hundreds of cows, sheep, gigantic barns, dozens of tractors, and even its own lodge where the men would gather for their annual pheasant hunts. The words to describe this place were nothing short of a farmer's paradise. As we arrived, Jack's dad rolled up in his brand-new Case tractor from working the farm all day and took me inside where his mum was making us tea. I felt I was in a movie complete with children building train sets in the living room, a sibling rivalry between Jack and his sister, and even a homemade traditional dinner of Yorkshire pudding, roast beef, and enough food to feed an army. Jack's mum wanted to make sure I had some real English food, but she didn't realize that the food wasn't what provided the warmth at the table—it was the feeling of the love and hospitality emanating from these strangers that welcomed me into their beautiful home as if I was their own daughter.

I spent the evening talking to Jack's numerous family members and trying to keep them all straight. I tried to make a good impression because most Americans didn't have the best reputation. They seemed to be quite taken with me and even invited me on a fox hunt the next day—*seriously, a fox hunt*! After I showed the kiddos how to make an amazing marshmallow smore in the firepit, I realized how blessed I was to be in this spot at this moment with these people— my new English family. Every once in a while, I think I am just living an ordinary life, but I think of all the wonderful people I meet, I realize it indeed might be a fairy tale.

Wanderlust Diaries: For Business or Pleasure?

Jack and I arrived to the Huntsman's Private residence early in the morning. The fox hunt was actually banned in England, so the gathering among the elite of the Shires was kept *hush hush*, and only a few were invited to the rendezvous point. The Huntsman used the legal decoy of blaming the pesky rabbits that plagued the farmers as a "Pest Control" loophole, and with England lawmen turning a blind eye, the hunt was on. With coffee in hand, Jack and I trampled through the dew-laden pasture filled with horse trailers and eager participants dressed in their finest attire. We spotted Jack's mum, all decked out in her tan riding pants, tall boots, tweed jacket, and fancy cap. She was a sight to behold perched on her remarkable speckled gray mare; the spirited horse was giddy with excitement from the serenade of the hounds wailing in the fenced courtyard. Jack's sister was busy getting her two small kiddos mounted on their ponies; it was their first hunt, and despite the early hour, they were anxiously awaiting the event.

Obviously, I was absent of the proper clothing for this tradition, but I managed to mingle with the "Terrier boys." These young chaps worked for the Huntsman and rode the trail on a four-wheeler quad. I hitched a ride deep into the forest, chatting up the fellas about their role in the sport. Attached to the rails of the quad was an aluminum box with holes drilled into the side. As I ran my hands along the box examining the odd enclosure, Phillip, the older of the Terrier boys, warned me to not stick my fingers in there. "Why?" I asked with genuine curiosity, making sure they were at ease with my questioning considering the legality of the sport. Phillip then opened the silver box ever so slowly; as I peeked inside, there were two small black rat terrier dogs. The dogs trembled as they fed off the frenzy of the trail ride and the howls from the hounds and bugles sounding in the distant forest.

Eventually, the anticipation of the hunt drew to quite a morbid action-packed finale. Phillip listened to the sounds of the forest, and like a seasoned hunter motioned for me to hop on the quad; we motored over a few clicks and staged ourselves in a thicket, where two trails merged into one with a grassy knoll on one side. "Shhh… they're coming," Phillip warned as I anxiously awaited the action. Then over a log appeared a furry little beast, wide-eyed, and in full sprint through the thicket and onto the trail. Busting through the brush, hot on its tail, was a pack of the hounds. I could see a group of riders traveling quickly behind, navigating the brush and trotting to follow the hounds to the poor little fox. I lost track of the fox, but I knew something was odd as I saw the hounds bellowed and pawed the earth. Phillip then gave me a devilish look and tipped his cap to me as he opened the box on the quad. With fervent energy, the two terriers exploded out of the crate and hit the ground running. "Where are they going?" I asked. Phillip explained how the only job of the terriers was to track the fox if it went to ground. And that they did, and so ended my naive childhood memories of watching the *Fox and Hound* and expecting a Disney ending to the event. To protect the exclusivity of the sport, I won't describe the ending, but it wasn't pretty.

The rest of the day consisted of cider meetings with orchard managers and some impromptu business discussions with some successful entrepreneurs that were intrigued with my cider venture. I could talk forever on the amount of information I had gained in those past few days—my head felt like it has expanded so much with new ideas and knowledge that it might explode like an overstuffed tick. I was forever indebted to Jack. His connections had helped me in ways I wouldn't have been able to accomplish on my own. One day, I met the granddaughter of Bulmer's cider. The largest cidery in the world that was currently owned by Heineken. I met the Polish and Bulgarian immigrants that tended the fields, and they showed me the techniques of the harvest. I even had high tea with the owner of a green energy plant that had dealings with orchards and pressed fruit and used the pumice for the creation of biofuel to power the electrical grid. I could not wait to bring my new experiences and knowledge back home. From fox hunts to high tea with wealthy CEOs, a mind expanded from new experiences and knowledge can never go back to its original dimension.

Wanderlust Diaries: Just "Milling" About

One thousand liters—I washed the apples, milled, and pressed one thousand liters by traditional old-time methods that day. The stodgy professor, sporting his white lab coat and balding head, seemed to enjoy challenging me on my untraditional methods that idealized breweries instead of English cider houses. How dare I answer quantity calculations in barrels—it was liters in the cider world, and to use a culinary apple instead of a bittersharp was something that I must repent and never mention again. The class was very in-depth with refreshers on fluid dynamics and laboratory techniques that remind me of Navy Nuclear Power School. I did not realize that I needed steel-toed shoes for the class. Thank goodness, I was able to borrow some of Jack's size thirteen clown shoes, for boots were not included in my packing list. A poor Swedish man was chased off-site for not wearing his steel-toed boots, so even wearing the ridiculous clodhoppers was worth staying out of the professor's cross hairs.

I was learning a lot, and after a long day at the mill, I was ready to kick back a few ciders myself. Jack had offered to throw a load of my clothes in the wash, so after a day of fox hunting and days of trampling through orchards and milling apples, all my clothes were covered in mud and apple pumice; I was thankful for the offer and gratefully accepted. However, I was ABSOLUTELY mortified when I pulled my Fiat into the driveway. Gentleman Jack had done my laundry while I was at school, but I did not realize that he did not have a clothes dryer. As I walked up the sidewalk, there were all my clothes neatly hanging on a clothesline—panties and all! Jack's hospitality was beyond measure, but I never would have agreed to him hanging up my underwear for me. As we headed off to the local pub for a cider, the topic of my bra size or color of my undies was never mentioned; Thank God, but that's Gentleman Jack, and even though he was quick-witted, he never crossed the line. Tomorrow would be another challenging day at the cider school, but secretly, I loved the opportunity to push my mental limits and try new techniques. Besides, a smooth sea never makes a skilled sailor, and it was always a great day to learn something new.

Wanderlust Diaries: A Day of the Yankee Bird

The past few days, I had fallen into quite the routine. I woke up early and grabbed coffee and breakfast from the shy Polish immigrant worker at the local bakery. I then continued to the Orchard Center on the small single-lane carriage road and enjoyed hours of cider lectures and practical exercises for the craft that I loved. When I returned home, Jack and I would walk the cobblestone road into the village and grab a pint or two from the smiling barkeep that now recognized me. "Ello! Anotha cida," she sweetly said as she opened her tap to pour me a drink. The town was like living in a postcard, and calling it home while I explored the cider heartland had been amazing.

Jack's family became an extension of my own. They insisted I had dinner with them and participate in some of the activities on the estate, including the infamous "shoot" the boys were always talking about. Jack's family had their own lodge that hosted a fancy pheasant hunt, and since it was a private affair, I didn't need a license. Over the past week, the fellas of the club had shot hundreds of birds and were selling them for a mere fifty pence a head, so letting me join in was not only offered but insisted upon. To the gentlemen at the club, I was the rare "Yankee Bird," an endearing term coined by Jack's dad. With a mountain of birds to process, I joined the womenfolk to help cook. Jack's mom and sister traditionally prepared the pheasant and some partridge while I made myself an integral part of the assembly line by removing the bird shot.

As we sat around the table, the conversation never dwindled. Tilly, Jack's niece, would keep me entertained with her childish banter and attempts at a Welsh accent. She knew I loved the way people from Wales spoke, and her impersonation was always spot-on. Jack's brother-in-law always wanted to talk politics and hear my thoughts on our options for the American president. Jack's mom always liked to hear about my travel plans and cautioned me to be careful—just like moms do. Jack's dad was a man of few words, but the words he spoke were profound with intelligent predictions of the dairy market resulting from Brexit (the plan for England to leave the European Union), and he showed a genuine interest in my career and business plan for the cider house.

As I said my goodbyes to this wonderful family, Jack's mom offered her home if I could ever visit again, and I offered the same if they ever visited Washington. I really did not feel the chapter in life has closed with these people, and I honestly knew I would see them again. Just as Jack and I were headed out the door, a casual mention of how I wanted to grab a good traditional English breakfast in the morning led Jack's mom and sister to harass us enough for me to promise to return in the morning so they could teach me how to prepare the dish and join them for one last meal. With promises of bringing the black pudding and bread from the Polish baker the next day, I was excited that I got to spend another day with them.

What was so unbelievably bizarre was that, coming to England, I had no expectations outside the cider school—that was my focus. I was thankful to be able to stay with Jack, but I had no idea that meeting him and his lovely family would change the entire flavor of the trip. Some people cross your path and change your entire direction.

Wanderlust Diaries: Leaving Ledbury

I graduated cider school! For many years, I had attended trainings and schools based on my nuclear background or for my degree program, but this one was different because I pursued it because I wanted to and to build my business. The morning started with the last stroll into Ledbury. Jack and I picked up some fresh-baked bread and some black pudding (blood sausage) from the local butcher and baker, and we headed to his parents' house. As we pulled up the driveway, Jack's mum was tending her garden to pick some fresh tomatoes for breakfast. She took off her dirty gardening gloves to greet me with a big hug. Her warmth reminded me how much I was going to miss them. As we scurried about the kitchen, I relished in the moment with the family. Jack's sister and I prepared the breakfast as she showed me some tips, and I teased her about their floppy bacon compared to the crispy kind preferred in America. Maybe I was just not accustomed to a family like this, but the faces that had surrounded me were faces I wouldn't soon be forgetting, and their hospitality and kindness was an amazing and unexpected way to start my trip.

As I said my goodbyes, I had one last cider stop. I had arranged a private meeting with the owner of Oliver's Cider and Perry. The name of this place might not be recognizable, but the man who runs it was far from ordinary. He was the band sound manager for the Proclaimers (that's right folks, I would walk five hundred miles band!). He had just returned from the United States on a tour, and even though he wasn't open, he said he would love to show me around. He also had attended the same cider school I had graduated from years before and was excited to show me uniqueness can dramatically differ from the textbook. He gave me a glass and dug around his cellar to find me some of his special varieties. As he sifted through the dusty bottles, I was in awe at this old farmstead and the character it held. Musty rooms with light peeking through the rafters were filled with barrels holding his cider with only a chalk marking on the wood to tell of its contents. He shared his unconventional methods with me as he explained the flavors that swirled around in my glass. I could have stayed all night jabbering on with this man—such charisma! I was hoping that possibly the Proclaimers might pop in, and I would get a private show, but as the clock kept ticking, I knew I had better go. I loaded up a box of cider to be shipped back to the United States and hit the road.

It was back to London for me. Sadly, this part of the trip was drawing to an end, but the sadness was quickly replaced by all the wonderful memories and friendships I had made. As England's top 20 played on the radio, I reflected on what experiences I had managed to take part in: the cider school, the business meetings with CEOs and orchard managers, drinking with the band manager of the Proclaimers from dusty cellar bottles, the fox hunt, the gatherings with Jack's family. This could not have been ANY more perfect. As I navigated out of the quiet villages, a less enjoyable memory flooded my brain as the carriage roads turned into a four-lane mega motorway as I approached London. I sat in a complete standstill of a sea of crimson brake lights and realized from the commercials on the radio that London had been hit by a massive outbreak that was causing the traffic on the M25. Only this time, it was not the plague but rather Bieber Fever. Apparently, Justin Bieber was performing that night, and I was caught in the thick of a massive traffic jam. Well, onto the next chapter. England, you have treated me well. Cheers!

Wanderlust Diaries: Opulent Dubai

Everything was first class in Dubai—from the giant pillars in the airport to the monster structures that promenade the skyline. Dubai didn't play small. I got in early on the red-eye flight from London, and first on my list was the Burj Khalifa, the tallest building and man-made structure in the world. There seemed to be something off with the vibe. Places were open, and there were more than enough service workers opening doors and shuffling me through elevators with their pressed suits, but *where were all the people?* I had the number one tourist attraction in Dubai completely to myself, and I had wondered if some sort of apocalyptic event happened while I was in transit and I hadn't caught on to it yet. I peered out from the lookout of this grand structure. The Persian Gulf as far as the eye could see in one direction and desert wasteland in the other, but you wouldn't know that from the looks of the city. Man-made turquoise pools populated the view with fountains only rivaled by the Bellagio in Vegas.

I walked along the boardwalks, exploring the nooks and crannies of the city, but I still found myself basically alone. As the sun continued to rise high in the Arabic sky, I knew I needed to find a watering hole. I wove through the bottom level of the streets, planning my traverse routes through areas where the skyscrapers would block the ball of fire in the sky that was beating down on me and gave me some shade. I made my way to the metro, and just like opening a magic door, I found all the people of the city! Very few people walked around the city streets—it was too hot. Instead, they made their way from metro station to their destination via above-ground walkways, like a modern-day hamster maze. I rode a train that dropped me off near the beach. I was trying to be conservative with my clothing in this Muslim nation, so a bathing suit was not packed in my day bag. I found a nice spot on the beach and unrolled my recently acquired fleece airplane blanket, which did the trick of staking my claim on the beautiful golden sand. I didn't have any other choice than to strip to my undies with a tank top. I would have thought this would have been completely out of the question, but as I found myself surrounded by hundreds of bikini-clad foreigners, I figured it would be acceptable. I splashed around in the surf, trying to avoid getting my hair and bra wet. Backpacking created difficulty with cleaning clothes, so I wanted to try to be cautious because I had a lot of traveling ahead of me. As I splashed around, admiring the shoreline, it looked as if the waves crashed onto the silky golden sand beach and out of the earth grew the monstrous sandstone skyscrapers, perfectly matching hues to collaborate the serene oasis with the giant bustling city. In the distance was the notorious Burj Al Arab, the sailboat sail-shaped building that towered over the beach horizon and showcased modern man's triumph over boring engineered structures—it was a masterpiece.

As I tried to bob about the surface avoiding the waves, I finally gave up and embraced my inner mermaid and dove into the water, drenching myself and quenching the dry heat. Oh well, in the end, my clothes and dreads would dry, but the memory of splashing about in the Persian Gulf would last a lifetime.

Wanderlust Diaries: Turbulence

As I sat in the airport, I was completely exhausted but anxious for the next leg of the journey. I had flown into Johannesburg, or Jo'berg for short, and was waiting on a small plane to arrive to take me to Zambia. Jo'berg wasn't fairy-tale material. Just minutes of being in the airport, I had a man offer to "help" me with my passport—*no thank you*. It was almost mandatory to wrap my luggage in cellophane to deter the pilferers from rummaging the valuables out of my bag.

I screened the other travelers waiting in the holding area. There was an assortment of joyful Japanese tourists, some Africans ornately dressed in colorful robes with geometric designs, and a Caucasian man that looked as if he was straight out of Texas. There was an open seat beside him, so I followed the pungent aroma of Old Spice and took a seat. There was something about that smell that I found comforting; it made me think of growing up in the South and a familiar scent when I would see my uncles that fancied the fragrance. As I struck up a conversation with him, I learned his name was Bill, and he was an American expatriate that now lived in South Africa. He wore a plaid button-down shirt and pressed denim trousers. His cleanly shaven face reminded me of a typical Southern gentleman. He would travel to Zambia and the Zululand to pick up trinkets and bobbets to sell at a higher price tag for profit in South Africa. He exposed to me his secrets of wearing as much of the swag as possible to avoid paying higher taxes when he arrived at customs with declarations. He rolled up his long-sleeve plaid shirt to reveal hundreds of woven bracelets and charms. As we started to board the plane, Bill continued our pleasant conversation until we were stopped to show our ticket and passport. As we approached, Bill said something quite peculiar to me that would make sense later as I learned more about him. He whispered under his breath, "Watch, they are going to stop me. They always do." As I quickly passed through the checkpoint, I looked back to see that Bill was right behind me.

Once at my chair, I was assigned an aisle seat next to some parents consoling a squalling baby. I was sure the distraught parents were hoping to have the row to themselves, so as the plane finished boarding, I switched seats to an open spot next to Bill. We chatted away, and it helped keep my mind off the disturbing turbulence as the small aircraft struggled to make its ascent. I was a frequent traveler, but there was still something unnerving about sitting through a rough patch of turbulence. As the flight attendant made her rounds, I happily accepted a couple of glasses of Shiraz red wine poured from my individual bottle to take the edge off. Bill joined me with the vino as my excitement grew for the impending destination. The scenery changed from white billowy clouds to far sweeping plains. I broke out my earbuds to play a song I had preloaded on my iPod—"Africa" by Toto. I shared an earbud with Bill as we giggled in our attempts to sing the verses, and with fervent passion, we would belt out the chorus—being that was really the only part of the song we knew.

Maybe it was the wine, but Bill later revealed to me why he said what he did. As we violently thrusted our way through the turbulent sky, Bill leaned over and put his hand to his lips to tell me his secret. He explained that he was glad that the airline security thought we were together and he wasn't traveling alone because he was treated differently and not stopped. As he finished his story, the last words lingered in the air like fall leaves floating to the ground as our plane twisted and turned in the balmy Zambian sky. Bill continued, "I've got a lot of hash I'm bringing." I could see it now on the headlines: "South African Airways Flight Number SA48 Went Down Today Carrying Forty Japanese Tourists, One Blond American, and Bill… the Smuggler Carrying Seventy Handcrafted Bracelets on His Arms and a Pound of Hash Up His Ass."

Wanderlust Diaries: Unspoiled Zambia

To be honest, the town itself wasn't much to look at. Livingstone was Victoria Falls's sister on the Zimbabwe side. The difference between the two being that the Zambian side wasn't built for tourists, but it could accommodate them. Livingstone was settled by the Whites who built walls around their houses to try to make malaria-free camps.

The hostel I was staying at was one of those camps, but the walls now served for security. I tossed my bag into my dorm and quickly set off to the national park. Outside the walls were a couple of disheveled blue taxi cabs from the 1970s, so I picked the driver that seemed to have an honest-looking countenance and kind aura and hit the road. The national park was so much different from anything you would see in the USA. A small group of thatch roofed shops lined the entry with groups of men, young and old, trying to sell trinkets, necklaces, and various African souvenirs. I bought a bracelet from one of the vendors who told me stories of the goddess of the Zambezi and how I must wear it; two hours later, it had already broke. I scurried past the tall dark men that were six-foot pillars of innuendos. I could hear the words "Mzungu," for White person accompanied by many catcalls to get my attention.

The parks were no more than a narrow cobblestone path that led to various viewpoints of the falls. I bridled my angst to go directly to the main observatory and chose a rather challenging trail down to the belly of the falls, called the "boiling pot." This trail was no joke with a very steep descent. I only passed one other couple that was making the return trip up the cliffside, and the haggard and exhausted looks on their sweaty faces made me not look forward to the grueling ascent that was a necessity of the hike. As I made my way down, I listened to the sounds of the jungle. The few birds that inhabited the canopy, the leaves that crackled as the lizards and chameleons maneuvered the crannies of the jungle floor. But then there was a noise that made the hairs in the back of my neck stand on end, and I knew I wasn't alone.

The noises got louder and louder as I heard something coming through the bush. With nowhere to run, I waited for what was to come. Finally, I realized that the primate of concern was not human but, rather, a troop of baboons coming to investigate. I'm not talking a couple of baboons but hundreds of these curious creatures emerged from the thick of the jungle. Some carried tiny babies, some groomed one another, and some sprawled out on the pathways, making it nearly impossible for me to pass on the narrow goat trail. I was cautious not to step on any tails or get too close, but the largest one of the group did have a lesson in manners that day. I watched the big fellow make his way down from the treetops by the populous jungle vines, and as he got closer, he lurched at me and grabbed my bag. I quickly analyzed my options and filtered my next action into what was less likely to result in a monkey bite. Looking back now, I'm not sure I would have chosen the same thing, but I settled for a masculine and strong "No!" and spatted his curious little hands as I stood my ground. I remember asking myself in a slight moment of panic, "*What would Jane Goodall do*?" It worked, and I continued my trek down to the boiling pot.

The view was magnificent. It was just me and the swarms of baboons enjoying this whimsical and enchanting place. There were no humans for miles, and the only noise was the thunder of the waterfall and the various grunts of my furry companions. I enjoyed this moment as I reflected on what a blessing it was to be here, sitting at the foot of this might waterfall in unspoiled Zambia.

Wanderlust Diaries: Life on the Edge

Maybe it was the scorching heat, or maybe it was the couple of ciders I drank with my hostel homies, but I woke with a little headache, but that was not going to put a damper on the incredible adventure I had planned. The infamous Devil's Pool had piqued my interest from Google searches about Victoria Falls, and despite the risk factor, this was a bucket-list item that had to be checked off. The Devil's Pool was a small low-current eddy with a natural ledge that could only be accessed by taking a boat to a small island and swimming across to the Devil's Pool where you were at the crest of the mighty Victoria Falls. This could only be accessed during the dry season and only be safely maneuvered during one month of the year—lucky for me, this was the month. As I anxiously awaited my boat to arrive, life could not be any more perfect as I sipped my coffee and watched four elephants playing in the river and munching on reeds.

After the boat ride and a small hike across Livingstone Island, I was finally there. The waterfall was calling my name, beckoning me to test that fine line between sanity and adventure. As I stripped down to my bathing suit, I knew there was no turning back. I slipped into the unforgiving Zambezi River and swam like hell to a small embankment that provided refuge from the river and entry into the Devil's Pool. I held my breath and jumped into the pool, leaving behind any fears or worry about the implications. It was absolutely one of the most exhilarating experiences I could have ever imagined. Lying on my belly, I lifted my arms into the air as I let the water escape around my body and plummet to the depths below. All around me was the grandest of waterfalls, a symbol of nature's fury and majesty, and then there was me in the middle of it, smiling and taking photos like a complete mad woman. A rainbow intricately displaying all the hues hung like a well-positioned picture frame over this blissful setting. I could have stayed there in that magic place for hours, but other adventurous spirits were trickling in, so I headed back to allow them to enjoy this impressive oasis.

On the ride back to the hostel, it was like watching the *Lion King*—a whole gang of mongoose scurried about while two warthogs kneaded the ground to root up some earthworms. Impala casually roamed along the grassy sidewalks grazing without a care in the world, but then towering above them all were four beautifully spotted giraffes. I jumped out of the car, camera in hand, and trudged through a few mudholes to admire them up close. They were not bothered by me but seemed to just stare at me with goofy looks on their face. With almost psychic abilities, the giraffes grouped into the perfect poses for my photographs—what beautiful and elegant creatures!

When I got back to the hostel, I was a little alarmed when the front desk worker came running over to me. "Meleeesa, I have some good news for you," she said with her adorable accent. I figured that possibly she had found a refrigerator magnet of Zambia for me to buy. I collect them, and with Zambia not being a tourist stop, I couldn't find any for a souvenir. But this was not her news. She informed me that the request I had posted on the travel bulletin board had received interest that day, and two other girls wanted to join me on my journey to South Africa. Sometimes life really has a way of coming together. Life can show you difficult things but replace it with God's beauty and unimaginable grandeur. Life can also put people in your path to learn from and experience amazing adventures with. I couldn't wait to meet the wonderful girls, and I hoped they were ready for a life on the edge.

Wanderlust Diaries: Establishing my Tribe

Deborah was a contract emergency room nurse that was Canadian by birth but was working in Saudi Arabia when her contract ended, so she came to Zambia to explore the area. She was obviously intelligent and could speak a little Arabic. She had a simple look with medium-length brown hair and medium build. She was mild mannered but seemed to be good company. Michella, or Mik for short, was a middle-aged New Zealander. She had short blond hair and the most intoxicating Kiwi accent. She had lost the love of her life the prior year, and with the passing of her beloved husband, she set out as far away from home as possible to avoid the painful remembrances of her partner and to forge a new path. Her children were grown and living their adult lives, so she set out to try to remember how to live life again on her own. Talking with her, I could feel the palpable pain she was still feeling from her heavy-laden heart as she showed me her memorial tattoo to her husband. This was the beginning of my tribe—a Saudi nurse, a Kiwi looking to heal a broken heart, and a blond dread-headed American leading the pack.

The plan was simple—there really was no plan, just an intent and a general direction to plot our course with the ending point of Johannesburg. I had previously looked into a travel company and even made a deposit in case my plans fell through to join a tour, but I hate organized tours. There was nothing worse than being stuck on a bus with a group of rude tourists, diminishing the experience by polluting the picturesque scenery with selfie sticks. However, I did get a copy of the day-by-day itinerary that the grassroots tour company used for a nine-day tour, including where to stop for the night and safe campsites. The starting point was across the border into Zimbabwe, where we would pick up the safari overland truck and set out on our journey. So we were off, backpacks heavy on our shoulders, sun beating down on our pale skin, but we all were smiling and excited to take on this epic adventure together. The border crossing was interesting, to say the least. We exited Zambia and walked across a long and expansive bridge that spanned the gap between the two countries. As we snapped a couple of photos of the geological marvel of the steep canyon and the roaring falls, we witnessed a young man bungee jump off the bridge, bellowing the whole way down as his voice echoed through the canyon. The bungee tightened to snap his body back up as he bobbed in the air of this beautiful place.

A quick thirty-dollar visa later, we wandered to a rest camp where we were to camp out and pick up the truck the next morning. I can say that my African safari experience was far from the luxury white linen camps that are seen on TV—for five bucks a night, I had a rustic canvas tent that looked like it had survived through a couple of world wars and a tattered brown sleeping mat. After we set up camp, we headed to the market to pick up some groceries for breakfast the next morning. Along the way, we met a kooky older lady that was obviously starving for some conversation from someone who could speak English and not hassle her to buy bracelets and bowls from the street peddlers. Her name was DeeDee, and she was sixty-nine years old and retired. She was from Canada, but apparently, she whimsically booked a trip to Zimbabwe from her travel agent and was incredibly lonely and bored. She felt unsafe traveling alone and thought there would be more tourists to meet along the way. She was thankful and very happy to see this odd group of "muzungus" (White people), and she was inquisitive about what we were doing. She became fascinated about the nontypical way we met via a posting on a hostel bulletin board and the journey we were about to embark upon as she joined us for our shopping and dinner that night.

We treated ourselves to a nice meal at a local restaurant where we ordered crocodile and impala steaks, and I had a warthog schnitzel, perfectly paired with a South African wine. A group of young men dressed in their elaborate costumes delighted us with some traditional songs and dances. I admired these athletic young dark-skinned boys as they sang the songs of their nation with such pride and enthusiasm as I sipped my wine. I thought of how the passionate kicking and twirling reminded me of the American line dance, *Copperhead Road*; instead of cowboys in tight denim jeans with enormous belt buckles and pearl snap shirts, I was watching these gyrating African boys wrapped in leopard skin hides with their bare feet kicking high into the heavens.

With DeeDee dropping hints about the solitude she was experiencing and how happy she was to meet us, I still wasn't sure how I felt about a sixty-nine-year-old lady joining the tribe. *How would she fit in? Could she handle the heat and the trekking?* Just as the questions swirled about in my head, DeeDee exclaimed in her high-pitched squeaky voice, "Gee whiz, I'm hot. It's time to play in the sprinkler!" She momentarily left the table and skipped over to the sprinkler, where she chased the water and jumped around in the refreshing mist just like a young child on a hot summer day. As I watched DeeDee, with who knows what kinds of stories in her satchel of life skipping through the sprinkler, I hollered out to her, "DeeDee, do you want to join us on the trip to South Africa?" She stopped skipping for a moment as she smiled a smile that extended from ear to ear. "Gee, I thought you'd never ask. Absolutely!"

Wanderlust Diaries: Water is Life

Four girls, four tents, and a big cooler full of food filled the oversized safari van. We set off on the adventure of a lifetime. Zimbabwe was not only struggling economically with hyperinflation and corrupt government, but it was also suffering from a devastating drought. We made our way past three police stops, and I managed to produce enough documentation to keep us moving along. We arrived at our first destination, Hwange National Park Rest Camp. As we set up our tents, I was in absolute heaven as I watched thousands of elephants play in a water hole no more than one hundred feet from our tents. We prepared our staple lunch of bologna and cheese sandwiches as we gazed at these magnificent pachyderms in their element. The way these animals behaved entranced me. I could have watched them for hours. Inside this National Park were over fifty thousand wild elephants roaming free—and fresh behemoth footsteps in the sand informed us that they frequented our bush camp.

One family of elephants would play in the water hole for a few minutes, and then another family would come storming in, and after a few trumpets of their trunks and rough play, the new family would take over the water hole and begin the same routine. We took a safari trek into the park with the ranger taking us to the prime hot spot viewing areas. All life gathered around the watering holes. Giraffes would awkwardly spread their limbs like the off-cambered wheels of an aftermarket Honda and bend their long spotted necks into the pond, skittish and on constant look out for predators. Kudas, which resembled a grand elk, shared the water hole as zebras and impala filtered into the communal oasis. The drought has brought all the animals together—different breeds together as one for survival. The animals all worked together in the circle of life, except for one, the king of the jungle. The ranger radioed another park worker that was out on safari, and we were informed of the hiding spot of this beautiful beast. We took bumpy off roads through the dry savanna as I took my long sarong that I was using to protect my shoulders from the sun and fashioned a sports bra with the material to keep the girls from bouncing all over the place. The ranger stopped and pointed to the bush. Nestled in the shade like a true king was the majestic male lion with his mate pacing nearby. In one day, I had managed to see three of the big five: the elephant, the buffalo, and the mighty lion. I even managed to see giraffes, zebras, impala, kudas, and adorable little warthogs grunting about and sprinting through the arid land with their tails straight up like a bristled flag.

Sadly, I did see my favorite animal, the magnificent elephant, in distress. One of them was alone, trudging along with a broken leg, trying to catch up to its family that was at the nearby water hole. I could see one of its herd members bridging the gap, urging the loved one with a broken leg to hurry along. The pathetic injured elephant could barely move but used its trunk as a crutch to move its massive body mere inches at a time. The determined beast continued its pilgrimage to meet back with its herd, but a new family was charging through the savanna, dislodging the resident family from the pond, and soon, the elephant would become separated. The ranger informed us that the elephant would likely not make it through the night. If it made its way to the water hole, it would probably become stuck in the mud, and its inability to run and isolation from the herd was the perfect target for a pride of lioness that would be on hunt soon and would be a perfect meal.

Life began and ended at the water hole. That night, the girls and I made a campfire and stayed up reflecting on the wonderful day we had. As I sipped my bottle of cider and enjoyed a chicken stew that DeeDee cooked up, I knew a few miles away my spirit animal was likely being ripped to shreds, but that was the way it went—this was the circle of life, and it was a miracle to watch the unfolding of this process happen before me.

Wanderlust Diaries: We All Have a Job

We had joked about the diversity of our group—the nurse, the customer service rep, the homemaker, and the ex-machinist mate nuclear engineer; until today, I never thought my skills would come in handy. As we drove along the desolate highway, miles from any sort of civilization or village, BOOM! Black smoke poured out of the truck and sound of metal scraping sent a chill down my spine. I didn't know what had happened, but this was possibly the worst-case scenario that just occurred.

The girls were scared, but I tried to keep them calm as I crawled under the truck to investigate. As I traced the systems of the vehicle, I diagnosed two problems. The obvious one was that the whole exhaust manifold cracked and the pipe was completely broken into two pieces at a failed weld joint. The intense heat had warped the exhaust piping, and it was deformed, as well as heavily corroded. I shimmied out from under the vehicle and told the girls to dig in our food storage and retrieve the aluminum foil. The girls with a gleam of hope in their eye quickly started to unload our cargo and dug for the requested item. As I returned to my position on the hot pavement in nowhere-land Zimbabwe, I had Mik fold me pieces of foil as I placed the makeshift patches on the broken pipe. As I looked at my handy work, I knew I needed a hose clamp, but without this material, I quickly filtered ideas of what else would snug up the foil wrapping to the severed pipe. As we all dug through our bags on the isolated highway, I had settled on shoelaces, and I began to unlace my sneakers. Just then, Mik informed me that she had a camera strap—*perfect*! The strap was nylon, but I figured it would at least get us down the road until a better repair option was available. I wiggled under the truck again to saddle up the straps and tightly cinched the straps to hold the foil in place. Just like a modern-day MacGyver, I repaired the broken pipe…with aluminum foil and a camera strap.

I noticed some oil that had obviously been leaking for quite a while and was pooled in lumpy globs at the bottom of the oil pan, so I decided to investigate the engine bay. The girls sat on the side of the road in amazement as they watched me calmly go to work. This beast of a safari van had the worst set up—a giant brush guard made it impossible to open the engine bay without removing the beefy metal guard, so I dug around in the included tool kit and prayed that the proper wrenches were included. In the oil-stained bag, I managed to dig up a crescent wrench and a socket set. I knew I could at least make progress with these tools, so I continued on, making jokes along the way to keep the mood light and keep everyone in high spirits. With all hands on deck, the four of us women lifted the massive guard to the grass as I raised the hood. I checked the oil; it was low—very low but still readable. I checked the transmission fluid—still had a tinge of pinkish hue with no obvious metal or gray matter. After a few more diagnostics, I added more oil and cleaned up the leaks I saw with our stash of toilet paper. This would have to do. With anxiety, and some nervous laughter to the girls in the back seat, I said, "Cross your fingers!" as I turned over the engine. She ran! Just a little smoke leaked out of my patch job but enough that I wasn't worried to continue on our journey. I checked the nylon straps periodically, but minus a few melted areas, it held true. Not one car passed us, and we had not a single bar of reception on our foreign cellphones. We were the sole authors of this adventure story, and instead of a drama, we had written an action-packed comedy that none of us would EVER forget.

Throughout the lengthy event of waiting on the highway in the intense heat, Mik's fingers and ankles had started to swell to the point of alarm. I had told her to take those shiny gold rings off her fingers; they attracted unwanted attention in the economically challenged country, but she had refused because they were sentimental gifts from her recently passed husband. Her thumb was as swollen as a link of sausage, and it had gotten to the point where action had to be taken. No amount of dish soap or jellies could escape the golden ring from her sore thumb, but Deborah, the Saudi nurse, developed the treatment plan. Out of her first aid kit, she retrieved some dental floss. I had only seen this on YouTube videos, but with surgical precision, she wrapped Mik's thumb tightly with the floss and wiggled the ring off the engorged thumb. What a group of girls we were! We had so many talents, and working together, we overcame a potential devastating day and emerged like triumphant lioness in nowhere-land Zimbabwe.

Wanderlust Diaries: Currency and Contentment

Most people in Zimbabwe are actually billionaires; unfortunately, due to the crash of the economy and hyperinflation, a billion-dollar note is worth less than one ply of toilet paper. It was not uncommon to see people actually bringing Zimbabwe currency into the restroom to wipe their ass. The currency that was recognized and circulated was the US dollar, but since they could not print it, the only way into the country is via travelers. If you wanted change for your bill, you could expect that they wouldn't have it, so I was always prepared to settle with the cashier by bargaining for some bottled cider to even the tab. Local children would see my white face and come running with fist fills of billion-dollar notes in trade for one US dollar bill.

I never truly understood the extent of the devastation that occurs when an economy falls apart.

We escaped the city, after stocking up on supplies, to a national park that was a rhino sanctuary. Only one kilogram of the rhino horn was worth $100,000, so with insane money like that, poachers were everywhere and even honest men turned corrupt when it came to what would feed their family. There were no fences for the park, only a few armed guards that lived in bush tents and patrolled the land. If a poacher was found, they would be shot on site, so we arranged a foot trek with one of the men to see the rhinos. These men were trusted with the survival of the species. If they decided to take the inviting offers of the poachers, life would be different from toting an AK-47 around through the jungle living in bush tents; they did it for the love of their culture and the endangered animals. Poachers didn't just saw off the horn—they hacked their faces off with axes. On our trek, we saw a couple skulls with obliterated skull fractures from where the poachers would just proceed to mutilate this beautiful creature and leave it to die—all for money.

We hopped in the truck to proceed to the next village and were surprised when a few young school children shuffled onto the streets, waving and smiling at us. Some jumped on the back of the truck and hitched a ride. We proceeded to the village where the economy seemed to be the last thing on their mind. The children danced and laughed and showed me their toys and insisted I play football with them. They brought out an old tennis ball and proceeded to kick it around while chanting, "Football! Football!" I recorded the adorable kids dancing and singing, and afterward, they were in complete delight when I played it back for them. They laughed and pointed at my phone, admiring their moments on the video, leaving little dirty smudge marks on the screen from their fingers. The chief of the village came out adorned in leopard hides, surely for our benefit, and motioned for us to sit, and we grouped together in a small thatch hut. He proceeded to tell us animated stories in his native language, charading the tales with elaborate motions and mimicking the animals of the jungle. As we watched, DeeDee kept laughing and responding to his stories as if she understood what he was saying.

That kooky old bat was hilarious as they seemed to hold a conversation together, and he seemed to be just as amused with her. We spent the evening dancing to bongo drums and playing with the kids. The kids hung all over me like a jungle gym, taking turns taking pictures. They loved my bag that was adorned with patches of the flags of countries around the world, and I was unbelievably impressed as they could even name a few. My favorite little girl that never left my side, wearing a dirty pink polka-dot shirt and an old grass skirt, told me that English was her favorite subject in school. She and her brothers walked seven kilometers every day to the schoolhouse and back, but she was excited to learn. Today was a prime example that you don't need money to be happy. From guardians with AK-47s protecting the rhinos from greedy poachers to a village full of children where their laughter was the sweetest music, money wasn't everything, and life was more than just paying bills.

Wanderlust Diaries: Donkeys and Diamonds

The border crossing from Zimbabwe to Botswana was probably one of the most chaotic and unorganized things I have ever experienced. No lines, just masses of people milling about outside the immigration office. They would let about ten people in at a time, so when the doors would open, people would charge the door like a herd of elephants. The only way to get through was to hold your ground, and similar to battle, when the immigration official gave the signal, the girls and I stormed the gates to get our stamp into Botswana. After we got our visas, the fun didn't end there. Apparently, foot and mouth disease was a real problem in Zimbabwe, so the border patrol insisted that we retrieve all shoes in our packs and sanitize them against the disease. The method of sanitizing was quite appalling and consisted of a small square cofferdam that had a repugnant sponge material on the bottom and some cleaner solution. You would step onto the filthy sponge, allowing the sanitizer to work its way around the soles of your shoes, as the border patrol intently watched to make sure you cooperated—it was gross. This whole chaotic process took four hours, but with fresh stamps in our passports, we were ready to see what this place had to offer.

Botswana differed from Zimbabwe on many fronts. The government ran smoother, and the diamond industry kept the economy strong. There were no checkpoints, and corrupt police officers wanting bribes were pretty much nonexistent. Donkeys grazed the road sides, and life sort of just slowed down in Botswana. Considering the industry that fueled the country, Botswana was anything but diamonds and pearls, but the locals led a simple life in tiny villages. The women strolled the streets in their colorful clothing with bags perfectly balanced on their head; some of them carried babies straddled across their back held in place by a towel. I settled for a nice relaxed evening at the camp, swinging in a hammock. A sweet stray dog kept me company as I enjoyed the slower pace. The donkeys brayed, the wild turkeys gobbled, and I fell peacefully asleep in a new country, Botswana.

Wanderlust Diaries: Diamonds in the Sky

As Botswana faded into the rearview mirror, I wished I had more time in the land of diamonds. We decided to venture the road less traveled, and the village we sought out wasn't even listed in our Lonely Planet guidebooks. Asphalt highways turned to bumpy dirt roads, and rocky pathways proved the grit of our truck. Children would run out waving to the pale-faced travelers. We called home for the night an isolated camp that ran off solar energy in the daylight, but other than that was completely primitive. I opted for a roundavel hut instead of my tent because of the uniqueness of this place. With thatched roofs on top of simplistic reeds and branches, these huts were from another world. Goats with tiny brass bells grazed around the camp, jingling in harmony with one another across the rocky terrain. For a shower, I fetched a pale of water and hoisted it to the pulley that was anchored at a top beam of the roof system, careful not to waste any of the precious commodity. I couldn't help but be thrilled to have the opportunity to live this way, even if only for a night.

There was one man who ran the lonely camp, Camucho, who explained his name meant "comforter." His siblings had tragically died, so he was left to comfort his mother and given this name. Camucho took us on a five-kilometer nature hike that highlighted the diverse terrain of the area; the small village that was nearby was named after the mountain range that we were hiking on. The drought had left a barren stream with occasional cows and goats trodding the ravine in search of water. The view from the top of the massive boulders was beautiful, and a reflection burned into my brain of the real Africa, with the twisted acacia trees and dry red sand. When we returned to camp, Camucho helped us set up our bush TV, which was a blazing fire in a pit. As we all sat around, we would joke about who had to change the channel by adding another piece of wood.

As I looked up, I could see thousands of little diamonds in the sky. It was a perfectly dazzling night. I retired to my roundavel where Camacho had placed an oil lantern at the entrance. As I retired to my bed, I was serenaded to sleep by a pack of wild jackals that seemed to be mere feet from my hut. An occasional bird, sounding like a crying baby, would provide some variety to the songs of the night. Under the tranquil African sky, riddled with stars that shined like diamonds, I closed my eyes and allowed the symphony of the jungle night to whisk me off to sleep.

(This post was dedicated to my sweet fur baby, Kaya, whose name in African actually meant "diamonds in the sky." I missed her sweet little face.)

Wanderlust Diaries: The Village People

If you look on most maps of South Africa, you probably won't find this tiny little village. The roads barely meet any standard for a road because no one has cars—they walked. Camucho, the camp attendant, took us into the village to grab some supplies. We could hear the loud bass of a stereo as we moved closer to the heart of the village. "You want to try local beer?" he asked as we approached the loud music. We accepted the invitation as we pulled into this outdoor gathering spot. Apparently, this was the village bar with plastic chairs grouped together on the dry red dirt, and locals, young and old, dancing to the drum beat. As we sat like zoo animals on display, the local children would run up and take pictures of us. The tables had turned. We were now the attraction instead of vice versa!

Camucho introduced the lady that owned the bar as he brought over a painted bowl and five hollowed-out gourds to drink from. The lady of the bar, in her colorful pink smock and contrasting scarf draped around her head, poured us each a gourd of the ale. It was thick like soup and a milky color. We toasted our gourds as we all had a sip—it tasted like sour snot. I swallowed down the thick ale as I decided to go inside to try a different beverage. The "bar" literally was a counter that had iron bars separating the bartender from the patrons outside. The ambiance was lacking, to say the least, but the life of the village was outside. I ordered a can of cider through the prisonlike beverage station and headed back to the group.

The local girls were all dancing to the loud sounds pouring out of the speakers, shaking and grooving to the music. I joined in as the girls showed me their moves, and we took turns dancing and clapping in a circle, moving to the rhythms of Africa. Camucho offered for us to join him for dinner at his uncle's home, so knowing that eating dinner at a traditional home was a once-in-a-lifetime experience, we all accepted the offer and walked to the house. I can't remember the name of Camucho's uncle, but to me, he will always be the little black Danny DeVito. He was a pint-sized, round little man that rattled on and on throughout dinner. Even though he was speaking English, I still could only make out a couple of words in each sentence. I would follow Camucho's lead, and if he laughed, I would follow suit and giggle along with the family. I was starting to think Camucho's uncle was flirting with me because he was always staring at me with glazed over eyes locked in my direction and a cavalier grin. As the night lingered on, I realized that there was a television directly behind me playing videos of sexy dancing girls, and that was what Danny DeVito was sneaking glimpses of, not me. It was a completely authentic night full of new experiences with a culture unlike any I have ever seen. This is what traveling was all about—dancing to the bongo drums and breaking bread with new people who look at the world through a different lens and in turn change your perspective of life.

Wanderlust Diaries: The Game "Drive"

When in South Africa, a pinnacle destination is Kruger National Park. Kruger Park is actually bigger than Switzerland, so we had a lot of ground to cover in our safari jeep. The girls and I left our remote little village to head for the capital of the big game world, seeking out the big five: the buffalo, the elephant, the leopard, the rhino, and the lion. The park was arid and dry, and it was obvious the ramifications the lack of rain had on the park. We would spot dried-up water holes with only remains of dead hippos on the dry, cracked soil with their skeletal carcass, resembling the framing of a small shipwreck from the rib cage.

Despite the drought, the park was still full of life. We saw herds of rhino and buffalo roaming the plains. Towers of giraffes elegantly nibbled leaves from the tall branches with their long flexible tongues. Majestic elephants paraded about the park like royalty with countless babies at their side. Prides of lions rested in the Savannah, watching the scenery and deciding on their next meal from the bountiful menu. At night, we would book a ride on the park ranger's safari night drives, where we would explore the backroads of the park by spotlight in these lifted off-road vehicles. During the melancholy of the nighttime, we witnessed two lions feasting on a fresh kill of a beautiful zebra. Its delicate black-and-white stripes were bloodstained from where the savage lions removed the guts to tear at the meat and flesh. The lions could not be bothered as they enjoyed their meal as we watched in amazement with our lights piercing into their eyes that were reflecting red under the intense beams. We also came across a pack of hyenas fighting over the carcass of an impala. The lifeless body was dragged by the scavengers through a pond and across the road directly in front of our truck, leaving a blood trail stain on the pavement. We were seeing some of the most beautiful and exotic animals mere feet from the truck, but there was one African creature that I was hopeful to avoid that left its mark on our game drive experience—the day the rain finally came.

The drought-stricken land was badly in need of a drink, and as the clouds rolled in, we were actually not disappointed but thankful that Africa would be getting a little relief. The rain fell lightly onto the land and a slick of water covered the roads, cooling off the sizzling asphalt. Many animals rejoiced and came out of their resting places to enjoy the cooler temperatures. Lions sprawled out on the road to cool themselves, and baboons grouped together like a family picnic on the pavement. I dodged all these magnificent beasts, except one. As I swerved to avoid a leopard turtle that was slowly making its way across the road, there slithered the devil himself, the black mamba. With catlike reflexes, I did my best to avoid the turtle, but the black mamba was hit. We felt a slight thud as I hit the brakes, and we twisted our necks to look out the back window. We intently searched the scene through the rear window obscured by our mound of sleeping bags to check out the carnage, but there was nothing. *Where was the black mamba?* Was the evil reptile hiding in the under carriage? The next fifty kilometers we sat in silence. Any noise could be the slithering of the mamba coming for her vengeance. We even stopped drinking water in hopes of avoiding a pee stop in case she was waiting for us. Finally, we arrived at camp. We looked at one another, and with fear in our eyes, I ordered everyone out on the count of three. One, two, three! We winged open the doors to the safari jeep and ran!

Wanderlust Diaries: You Can Go Your Own Way

Your vibe attracts your tribe—that is for certain. Instead of a solitary journey alone, I was blessed with the company of three beautiful, smart, and funny women. We laughed together, cried together, and made memories that would last a lifetime. As we headed for Johannesburg, we knew our time together was limited, and it was a somber drive to our place where we agreed to part ways. The rain the night before soaked my laundry I had hung to dry, so Mik took the individual pieces and draped them around her arm as she held them out the window to dry while I drove. We motored along the highway, singing Bob Marley on the radio at the top of our lungs with not a care in the world, except knowing we were coming to the end of the road. Deborah, the Saudi nurse, came upon an opportunity in Dubai to continue her contract nursing, so she was anxious to figure out her exit visas and start a new career. DeeDee, the sixty-nine-year-old lady, was quite a handful throughout the trip. The crazy old bird was always getting lost, and I was constantly checking on her like a mother hen. "DeeDee, do you have your passport?" "Where's your camera?" "Do you need some water?" I looked after her because she pulled at my heartstrings. I never got her to fully explain her story to me until the last day. I knew she was divorced with a daughter that didn't speak to her, but I never understood what drove this frail old lady to travel by herself to Africa and join our tribe. The last day, she had said, "I would rather run out of money than time." I stewed on that comment until she expounded to tell us that she had Parkinson's disease (which was obvious by her shaky hand's inability to fill out customs forms; I always did it for her). She was just diagnosed with the beginning stages of dementia, and she wanted a big trip full of adventure that might possibly be the last big adventure of her life. Then there was Mik, my best pal, my Kiwi soul sister that I had grown to love so much it pained me to think of going our separate ways and the possibility of never seeing her again.

As I dropped Deborah and DeeDee off at the airport, Mik and I had one last night with one another. Throughout the trip, Mik had shared some of the most private and emotional stories of her life. Through gallons of tears I learned about the passing of her husband and how she felt her family unit would never be the same. She had struggled with severe depression and was in utter despair when she booked her trip to Africa. We sat in my hotel with bars on the windows in crime-riddled Jo'berg and cracked open some Savannah ciders as the night continued on. Mik then explained to me that because of her husband's death, she was given a hefty sum of money for life insurance. With tears rolling down her face, she opened up her toiletry bag that had a large bottle of pills. Her plan for Africa was to blow the money, and when it was gone, she planned to take the pills and exit the world to be with her husband. We sat on the floor, crying. Looking at the mountain of memories we had made, I could not imagine a world without this beautiful soul.

She explained to me that there was a moment in our trip together when she found her purpose in life. She rattled on about the day when we walked with the rhinos. I remember her talking the ear off the guide (we named him Sexy Kurt. He was an older man with hair growing out of his ears, but he wore little shorty shorts), and I remember seeing her exchange contact details with him later that day. The past few days of full throttle adventure in Africa with me and the girls made her feel alive again, and she knew Africa was not a place where every corner she turned would remind her of her departed loved one. With cider coursing through our veins, she emotionally explained to me what she had decided to do instead of end her life—she was going to start a new one. She was going to go to a job interview that she had previously planned to blow off the next week and save enough money to come back to Africa in the summer to work with rehabilitation of the animals in a volunteer program with Sexy Kurt. When God closes one door, he will always open a window, and Mik found her pathway out of a world of loneliness and feeling inadequate on her own. A life without a purpose was like a bird without wings. Mik found her purpose in Africa, and I was so thrilled at the new chapter for a story that would have had a tragic ending. Mik had imprinted on my soul, and I later reached out to her daughter as a support network to keep her on track. I never expected any of this. I knew this trip would be a big chapter in my life, but I never dreamed that I would have been able to take a leading role in the lives of three strangers. I just booked a trip to Zambia and hoped for the best. I was so thankful I didn't micromanage the trip—life is what happens when you are busy making plans. Wherever you are going, go with your whole heart, and good things will happen. I was so thankful for my tribe. I loved them all, and there wouldn't be a day that went by that I wouldn't think of all the fun we had together in the middle of nowhere Africa.

Wanderlust Diaries: Surfing Nelson Mandela Bay

I found myself in Port Elizabeth South Africa. All my friends I had made were now on planes back to their homelands, and I was saddened to not being woken up by Deborah's god-awful snoring or getting DeeDee's tent packed up or having a laugh and a morning snarky comment with Mik. I traded the party wagon in for something smaller since I was on my own and was handed the keys to a white Kia Picanto—this transport was far from the flare of my rough-rider safari wagon, and the Picanto with its manual transmission was anything but spicy.

I navigated to my hostel and threw my bags on my bunk—off to explore! As I meandered down the summer strand boardwalk of this pleasant town, it reminded me of a Myrtle Beach kind of feeling. I didn't really feel I was in Africa. As I walked the boardwalks, I came across a surf shop. It sounded interesting, so I popped in. A middle-aged Russian lady, with her hair all a mess in a lopsided ponytail, followed me around the store, trying to sell me expensive bathing suits, but that wasn't what I was after. I ended up renting a surfboard for the afternoon, but I was in a bit of a pickle because I didn't bring my bathing suit with me. I refused to spend eighty bucks on a bathing suit, so I decided to just go commando under the wet suit—no one would be the wiser, and at least I wouldn't have to get my nice bra wet and sandy.

I headed to the beach, surfboard cradled under my arm, and paddled out to catch the waves. A young man with golden surfer locks and a charming smile joined me in the fun. As we sat on our boards, waiting for the sets to roll in, I learned that he worked for the surf shop. We spent hours talking about this and that, ranging from travel to the new American president. The waves weren't pipeline quality by any means, but it was a fun way to spend the day. Dan, the blond surfer man, was pleasant company. As the wind kicked up, it was time to call it a day, so we headed back to the surf shop.

The odd-mannered Russian lady followed me through the store on my heels like a terrier dog, barking at me not to stop because if I got her new bathing suits wet, she couldn't sell them. I was corralled to the small wet suit area, where Dan was unzipping his suit. He stripped the neoprene off his tanned and fit body like he was peeling a banana. He was left in swimming trunks to where he then turned on the small shower to rinse off the salt water. Puzzled at my hesitation to jump in on the action, he looked over to me and kindly asked, "Do you need help unzipping your wet suit?" Baffled on what to say, I just stood there with my mouth open like a dope, knowing that there was no good explanation of why I couldn't accept the offer. I was sure naked wet suit wearing was frowned upon, and I didn't know how to explain the situation, and I had nowhere to go! Just as I was about to stammer through whatever ridiculous excuse I could muster up, the eccentric Russian lady opened the sliding door and motioned for Dan's help inside—I was saved!

I quickly ripped off my wet suit and struggled to dress myself, wiggling my dry clothes onto my soggy body. I felt like the blond dummy from *Beavis and Butthead* doing the Cornholio routine. I just could not get the damn clothes on; the more I rushed, the more the garments refused to cooperate. I thrashed around the tiny room maneuvering the clothing onto my wet body. Finally, I was done—no sign of Dan or the Russian lady to have seen my shenanigans. As I opened the screen door and approached the front desk to say goodbye to Dan, I nearly choked. Right behind the register in full view of the whole store was a TV divided into four sections of closed-circuit television—the store, the backdoor, the office, and the wet suit room; they had been watching the whole time. Mortified on the inside but remaining cool as a cucumber, I let out a loud burst of laughter and said, "Have a great day!" as I flashed the *Hang 10* hand sign and walked out the door.

Wanderlust Diaries: Dodging Elephants

I met two lovely and intelligent ladies that asked to join me traveling to Addo Elephant National Park. Staying at hostels, I met all sorts of people, and these girls had previously booked an expensive tour but would rather hitch a ride with me in my Kia. We loaded up in my compact mini rental car and headed into elephant country. As we drove through the front gate, a ranger insisted that we sign into a ledger since we were driving ourselves and not going through a tour group. The man started laughing after he told me that he needed our contact details so they knew who the lions had eaten. With a not-so-impressed look on my face, he didn't even expound on his comment—just continued laughing as he motioned us through the gate in my little clown car. The park was stunning with lush green shrubs and mountain passes that proved challenging for the tiny motor of the Picanto. Thousands of elephants roamed free with the little babies on the heels of their mother. This was my heaven. I would just stall the car and watch them as they walked around to sample the vegetation. The majestic animals walked mere feet from my car as if my little Kia was a part of the herd. What beautiful creatures! I studied them for hours and was in pure elephant bliss.

Clouds rolled in and cast an eerie fog and dark blue hue to the skies. I took the girls to the next town, where they caught a short cab ride back to the hostel. I had booked a night in the only lodge in elephant country that had availability—the Addo Dung Beetle. Since the park gates were closed, I tried to get my navigation system to find me a route that would take me to the far end of the park without taking a huge detour that would add an extra hour to my drive. I could see on the map that there was a small frontage road that bordered the park, but the GPS wouldn't recognize it and recommended the long route. I turned the GPS off and decided to figure it out on my own. I was fighting daylight, and the incoming storm cast a gloomy shadow on the area. Dodging potholes, the road was quite the adventure in itself. I saw a sign that read "Bridge Out, use Alternate Route," but I pressed on hoping the sign didn't apply to me—it did. As I swerved around the chunks of road that was missing, I slammed on the brakes. The bridge was indeed out. In fact, the whole section of road over a rushing stream was completely missing; the road just ended as if someone took a giant cookie-cutter section and forgot about it. I doubled back and searched for another path to lead me through the elephant country without having to go all the way back to the bigger town like my GPS suggested. I found dirt road that headed north in the right direction, so I continued the journey with my trusty Kia that sounded like it was going to rattle apart into a million pieces as I slowly navigated across the washboard road. I realized that this road was a service road for a windmill farm, and as I passed under the giant windmills rotating their massive impellers, it gave me a creepy feeling of utter isolation as I continued on.

I made it to the Dung Beetle Guesthouse, and my jaw dropped as I was handed the keys to my chalet. I was given the most gorgeous cabin I had ever seen. From my deck, I watched elephants drinking from a water hole and listened to a symphony of frogs that was almost deafening. I cracked open a bottle of red wine made in South Africa that had a zebra on the label. Sitting on the porch, watching my beautiful pachyderms, I just breathed it all in. What a day!

Wanderlust Diaries: Point Break My Toe

As I continued the southern route down the eastern cape of South Africa, I transitioned from the "wild" coast to the "sunshine" coast, but the weather was anything but luminous. A storm the night before wreaked havoc on the tiny villages, and the road was scattered with pieces of roof, and the trees were decorated like Christmas, full of rubbish from the heavy winds, decorating them like sullied tinsel. I came across the infamous surfing village, Jeffrey's Bay, and stopped in to check out the vibe. I never thought I would "fit in" in Africa, but with my platinum dreadlocks and cutoff shorts, I was a postcard example of the inhabitants of this surfer's paradise. Jeffrey's Bay was the number two surf zone in the world (behind North Shore Hawaii). Surfers from around the globe come to catch the waves, and the day after the storm left some respectable swells in the Indian Ocean.

I cruised around the town painted with Billabong billboards and surf stores and knew that coming to Jeffrey's Bay and not surfing would be like stopping at New York City and ignoring Times Square—you gotta do it! I picked out one of the many surf shops and was selecting my board when I met Jules. He was a tall lanky Australian with shoulder-length curly blond hair—the exact stereotype of a surfer dude, complete with his Billabong swim trunks and sunglasses. We got to chatting, and next thing I knew, I had the recommended surfboard (not the eleven-foot boat I actually wanted) cradled under my arm, and we were headed to the "Supertube." Apparently, the waves directly in front of town that seemed to be impressive enough were nothing compared to the pipeline that Jules and the surf community flocked to.

I surveyed the scene from the beach, checking out the intimidating waves that crashed onto the shore. I told myself that I only needed to try it once…to say I had the balls to do it, and then I could leave. I heard Jules calling for me out in the ocean and waving his lanky arms from his perched position on his surfboard. It was now or never—I anchored the leash to my ankle and ran into the surf. I paddled through the foam and the fury of the crashing waves to meet Jules. I was already tired from the battle to get into position, so I watched Jules catch a few waves as I stayed back to gain my composure. Jules was a textbook surfer—the way he timed the wave, the thrust he could accomplish from paddling before the wave caught the board, and the perfect smoothness to which he could jump from lying down to the balanced standing position with seemingly little effort; he was unbelievably talented. The perfect wave began to swell. I knew this was my wave, and I heard Jules urging me to paddle. I balanced myself and waited for that pinnacle moment when the wave took the board. I tried to jump up but lost my footing, and the wave won the battle, tossing me like a rag doll into the surf. If I was alone, I probably would have checked the box of surfing Jeffrey's Bay and returned the board, but Jules wouldn't quit chastising me to keep trying.

As we would sit in position on our boards with the hordes of other surfers, I realized that there are good topics for conversation… and bad ones. Good conversation topics include legalized weed in the USA and "sick" surf spots, but the bad conversation topics create quite a stir when I would accidentally broach them. Never say *Point Break* was a great surfer movie. Surfers hated that movie and thought it was bullshit. Also, NEVER say that you are thinking about shark-cage diving. As I casually mentioned this topic, Jules obviously was against the practice and started motioning over to his friend that was surfing a few feet away from us. I came to learn that this friend had a nickname, Sharkbite, for obvious reasons. Along the Cape, many of the cage-diving adventure companies chum the waters to stir up the great white sharks, and the area becomes saturated with them, lurking below the surface, looking for their next meal. Surfers look like a good snack, resembling a porpoise from underneath, and it was far too common that a surfer would get a bite taken out of them while waiting on the waves. As I listened to the story, I tucked my arms and legs onto the board, making it almost impossible to balance but hoping to look less like a tasty snack for any sharks that might be choosing their menu options below us.

The sets started to roll in. Sharkbite took the first one, and Jules took the next one, surfing it perfectly as he yelled in excitement from the wild ride. It was my turn. With all my strength, I paddled hard, and with catlike flexibility that I never knew I had, I sprang up on my board and balanced myself. I was up! I couldn't believe it! After swallowing gallons of seawater and being tossed around the sea, I wasn't sure if I could do it, but I was surfing Jeffrey's Bay! I stayed upright for a little while until the furious wave prevailed and knocked me off my board. I was thrashed around like the inside of a washing machine—I emerged to gasp for air. My tethered board had somehow clashed with my foot and taken a toenail off. I didn't even care. I was on cloud nine that I actually stood up and caught a wave. I forcefully informed Jules that I was done; besides, a bleeding toe was great shark bait, and I wasn't stepping foot in those waters like that. We brought our boards to the beach and retired to a small café to grab some lunch.

I was surrounded by true adrenaline junkies as they obsessed about bungee jumping and something called "highlining," where you zip-lined across a gorge to a net to hang out. It was intoxicating to listen to, and I didn't need to be on drugs to get a high from these guys. Jules tried to recruit me into his pack with offers to join him for some outrageous adventures, but I felt like Icarus. I had already flown too close to the sun, and my wings would soon burn. One step closer into this adrenaline-filled world, I knew I could lose more than a toenail. I gave Jules a hug and returned my board as I rolled on to my next adventure.

Wanderlust Diaries: Enjoy Your Ride

Traveling south on the garden route, every mile brought scenery even more beautiful than the last. The terrain would change from beach sand dunes to craggy mountains with a narrow pass to navigate through. Baboons would play on the roads and refuse to move for me to pass. I found a hostel that was converted railway cars, parked on the railroad tracks. It was quite the novelty, but luxury it was not. The cramped quarters and rock-hard bed reminded me of my Navy days, but the view out of my window to the beautiful Indian Ocean with waves crashing on the beach couldn't be beat.

I took a day trip out to Oudtshoorn, which was a beautiful farming village inland, but the main livestock that was seen running the fence lines were the awkward- and silly-looking ostriches. Pulling the car to the shoulder, I would marvel at these goofy birds. Their eyes were bigger than their brains, so with crackers in my hand, I would move my hand, holding goodies to the beat of the music coming from the radio in my car. The birds would crook and sway their skinny necks to the tunes. I checked out an ostrich farm and realized that you can do anything for five dollars around here, including ride one. The owner joked around, asking if anyone wanted to ride the feathered beast after an exaggerated story about the toenails that could slice you open like a fish. No one volunteered, except me! I saddled up on the strong backed bird, looking for a good spot to hold on to. I wrapped my legs around the bird's torso and found the base of its wings seemed like a good handhold, and I was off! The bird galloped around a pen, with the squealing American holding on tightly, perched on its back. I thought the muscular bird had grown accustomed to his new master, but the fun was just getting started. The cynical bird was smarter than I gave him credit for. He jetted off, and then stopped while lowering his neck, sending me flying over his head and to the ground. Bird = 1, me = 0. What a ride!

Wanderlust Diaries: Chumming for Great Whites

I was so excited for today's adventure that I could barely sleep. I would wake up every hour to check my alarm to make sure I hadn't overslept. I didn't want to miss the boat; I quickly shoveled a little bit of fruit in my mouth as I headed to the pier—it was going to be a great day! Onboard, we motored to the infamous Seal Island that previously I had only seen on National Geographic Shark Week. On the isolated rocky island, thousands of seals lay on the rocks or slid down the chutes like a waterslide into the ocean. We anchored a few feet away as I wiggled into my wet suit and examined the shark-diving cage—the galvanized metal had a few dents and attempts of JB weld, but it seemed sturdy enough.

The bait handler made a concoction of salmon and seawater stew, stirring with a shovel and periodically tossing some of the oily mixture into the ocean, coaxing the sharks to our boat. As I was about to climb in the cage, a mighty shark appeared and breeched for a piece of salmon head that we had tethered to the boat. The beautiful creature was unbelievably impressive. The thrust out of the ocean and the manner he could pull back his jawline to reveal his razor-sharp teeth was enough to send chills down my spine as I watched in reverence to this king of the sea. Inside the cage was a thrilling experience. Sharks do not have hands; the only way for them to explore the cage was to brush against it for sensory notes from their lateral lines. Periodically, the shark would ram the cage, testing the structure with his massive jaws. I kept note to always keep my toes inside the cage even though it was easier to balance with my toes clinging to the outer bars. At one point, five great white sharks circled the cage with the biggest one at about six meters in length. As the sharks would brush against the cage, I could see deep scars and black eyes that seemed to have no soul. These beautiful sharks weren't the vicious creatures that Hollywood created—they were curious, but their jaws were enough to ensure respect when I was in their territory.

Out of the cage, I managed to capture some of the most stunning pictures even though the captain teased me for trying to get selfies with the sharks. When it was time to go, we had trouble pulling the anchor; it was stuck in the rocks at Seal Island. I tried to distract myself from the sway of the boat by watching the seals play on the boulders. I wondered if the innocent seals had any idea that they were the special of the day for the sharks or if they were adrenaline seekers that enjoyed the thrill of taunting the hunters that lurked below. The motion of the ocean was starting to get to me as the crew continued their struggle with pulling the anchor. On the starboard side, a German man started to hurl—I knew it was only a matter of time until I joined him. On the port side of the boat, I unleashed my breakfast overboard. The red watermelon, yellow pineapple, and blueberries created a colorful palette as I puked the rainbow to the sea. As I watched my breakfast linger on the surface of the water, I couldn't help but find satisfaction as a shark emerged and swam through my chumming contribution. Another bucket-list item was checked!

Wanderlust Diaries: Moon over Cape Town

I caught wind of the rumblings of a supermoon…when the moon would be at its fullest and appeared larger than normal. I made plans to have a night alone and hike up Lion's Head, which was a peak in the Table Mountains, overlooking the bay and the lights of the beautiful city of Cape Town. As I made a quick stop to my hostel to grab my sneakers, the owner told me that there was someone hoping to join me if I was all right with having company. I was always willing to make another travel friend, so I waited for Charlie, a fun-loving German guy, to grab his shoes. As I waited, two other German girls asked me if they could join in on the hike as well, which I obviously said yes. Now my night alone turned into a night with three new friends. In my tiny Korean car, three Germans and an American set off in rush-hour traffic to the trailhead.

The hike was anything but a solitary experience. It seemed everyone in Cape Town had the same idea. I was under the impression it was an easy walk, but as we continued the accent, it was actually quite challenging with grappling over rocks and skirting the edge of the cliffside. At the top, we sat among the hordes of locals and travelers, perched on a rock, admiring God's beauty. Photos couldn't pick up the magic that was felt. On the west, the sun retired into the abyss of the horizon, and to the east, the supermoon ascended to the heavens, casting a watchful eye over the city. We cracked open a couple of bottles of wine and sat perched on the boulders, mesmerized by the surroundings. I avoided the pending thoughts of the hike down. I dug in my bag in search of my headlamp; unfortunately, I had staged it in my car, which wasn't going to do me much good as I sat in the darkness on top of the mountain. Guided by the light of the supermoon and the millions of twinkling lights from the city, we started our way down. The hike was actually quite treacherous, so I activated the flashlight function on my Samsung Galaxy and snuggly positioned it in my bra so I could have my hands free to navigate the trail and crawl through the boulders. Looking back on the trail behind me, the masses were making their way down the mountain, leaving a trail of lights contrasting against the night sky—it was magic over Cape Town.

Wanderlust Diaries: Proper Wine and Politics

Stellenbosch was the premier wine region of Africa and one of the highlights to visit in the Western Cape. I did not want to drink and drive, especially while wrangling the right-hand drive Kia, so I booked a trip with a group even though I hated organized tours. I dug through my backpack in search of some attire that would be suitable for a day of wine tasting and slipped on a slightly wrinkled long dress that I was saving for the Muslim destinations of the trip. I even took my dreadlocks out of the ratty travel bun that I had been sporting throughout Africa and let my locks down.

It was on the tour I met Henry after I complimented his huge camera with an impressive zoom lens. He showed me some of the safari pictures he had captured from his travels. I was dazzled by the quality and impeccable timing he had mastered with the photos. Henry was an older gentleman with gray hair, wrinkled eyes, and laugh lines on his face. He lived in Washington, DC, and was the official photographer for Joe Biden, our vice president at the time. Henry scrolled through his phenomenal photos, including some of Joe, but as political conversations crept up, he was excited to show me pictures he had captured of Donald Trump giving him the bird in a press conference a few years prior. Henry was a big Joe Biden supporter, but unbeknownst to me, the VP had recently lost his son to brain cancer, so that was why he didn't pursue the presidential nomination for the upcoming election. I listened to Henry chatter on about Biden as if they were old friends as he passed me his samples of wine he didn't care for.

We continued our pilgrimage across wine country, stopping at some of the cutest farm venues that were excited to showcase the fruits of their labor. Henry snapped candid photos of me, and I felt like I had my own personal photographer. I was his muse, and he found my antics to be perfect material for capturing pictures throughout the day. As I swirled and smelled the wine in my glass, I knew Henry was on the sidelines, and I could hear the rapid clicks of his shutter. As the wine was poured, our conversations continued to flow, and the liberal photographer and conservative cider maker found common ground in Stellenbosch over glasses of proper wine. We had a wonderful evening, drinking the vino and talking about our values and why we thought the way we did. It takes a strong mind to be able to entertain thoughts that go against the grain of your value system but actually hear the speaker, and I was always intrigued to talk to people that saw the world differently than I did. Today wine built friendships instead of walls. Words only attract strong minds or offend weak ones, and Henry's photos were the evidence of a fantastic day.

Wanderlust Diaries: Cape of Good Hope and the Blue Underwear

The sun was shining; the birds were chirping—it was a great day to set off on a drive around the peninsula with my newfound hostel buddies. I sent my laundry out, and the only real clean clothes I had was a nice breezy summer dress. I got ready, and we hit the road. First stop, Boulders Beach, which was home to the jackass penguin colonies. I snapped a few photos of the goofy-looking birds that were looking exceptionally pathetic as they molted their soft feathers for their adult coats. They lay on the giant boulders like tourists on a beach getting a tan. We continued on, stopping at some beautiful beaches and toying with the idea of taking a quick swim in the chilly waters. We approached Cape Point with its rugged, towering cliffs that sank into the sea. We watched the relentless waves crash into the rocky shoreline. Everything was perfect...the scenery, the new friends, the hike out to the lighthouse, except one thing—my dress.

I must have chosen the most inappropriate wardrobe option for the windiest place on earth. Every time I tried to snap a picture, my dress would blow over my head, revealing my color-coordinated blue undies to the unsuspecting tourists. I was helpless against nature's fury, and despite my best efforts, I could not keep that dress down, but I refused to let it inhibit my urge to take a million photos. With my scarf blowing in a frenzy like the Red Baron and my hair swooping into the air like Donald Trump on a bad hair day, I savored every minute of this beautiful place. We stood on the top of the cliff, mesmerized by it all—the blue sky, the blue sea, and even my blue undies.

Wanderlust Diaries: Sand

When I first arrived in Cape Town with my backpack cinched on my hips, the front desk attendant at my hostel asked me what I had wanted to do while I was in town. I remember a flurry of adventures flying through my head as I rambled off plans to hike up Table

Mountain, swim in the sea, play with the penguins, shop at the market on Long Street, and sip wine in Stellenbosch. As she searched through her brochures of possible tours, I knew that this regimented form of travel made me feel like I would be missing out, so I made my own journey, meeting some of the most fun-loving people and seeing amazing things. Looking back on my relatively short time in Cape Town, I accomplished EVERYTHING on my bucket list for this great city and even squeezed in a few more shenanigans that were unexpected.

On my last night in Cape Town, the hostel held a braai, which was an African term for a barbecue. We feasted on the different African game meats and staple dishes while toasting our ciders. It was a perfect last night in the cosmopolitan city that still maintained a relaxed vibe and stunning scenery. The next day, I struggled with the thoughts of what to do on my last day in South Africa. I just wanted to breathe in the sea air and be at peace, so I loaded my backpack into my tiny car and said my goodbyes with big American hugs to my hostel buddies and headed for the beach. I laid out my airplane blanket on the milky-white sand and nestled into the softest beach I had ever felt…until the wind kicked up. The blissful paradise was turned into a consuming sandstorm with the once-enticing sand particles piercing my bare legs and assaulting my face. I tried to wrap a scarf around my head to keep the grit from clogging my ears, and even though I looked ridiculous, I still tried to enjoy the moment.

I drifted off into a half slumber until I was awoken by loads of debris being dumped on my head. As I unwrapped my headdress to investigate, I realized that I had a visitor—a sweet long white-haired dog had assumed his rightful beach position beside me and was digging the sand up to make himself a nest to relax in, sending the rejected material in my direction. The dog was almost completely camouflaged against the pearly white sand that matched his coat, and we sat together enjoying the sunshine. I noticed a surfer coming out of the ocean with his long board, and as he made his way to the beach, he started waving at me. After a nice chat, I learned his name was Arturo, and my new furry friend was his dog, Bruno, that hung out while he surfed. Arturo laughed at my attempts to shield myself from the penetrating sand and offered me a new refuge from the winds. I followed him along the beach and to a small pathway forged by the mighty waves eroding the boulders. As I navigated through the path, on the other side was another world.

The cliffside isolated the beach into a private oasis, shielding the white sand from the intense wind. I laid out my blanket on the silky sand and enjoyed watching Arturo surf the waves while I relaxed on the beach with my book and my furry companion. It was a perfect ending to a perfect place, but time refused to stand still, and I knew I had to leave. As I packed up my beach bag, I made my way across the giant boulders, taking in one last look to my private wonderland. Bruno was already just a blur in the white sand, and I had lost sight of Arturo in the crashing waves. My oasis disappeared behind the boulders and few palm trees as I made my way back to the car, shaking off the sand like a wet dog.

Wanderlust Diaries: The Museum Hustle

I arrived at my hostel in Cairo on my red-eye flight from South Africa, where I met the other travelers that were just waking for breakfast. I quickly made friends and set up plans for a Nile River dinner cruise. To fill the day, I headed to the Egyptian Museum that was near the hostel. The hustle and bustle to get in was like a circus with lines forming that seemed to go to nowhere and Egyptian men yelling in Arabic. *Just blend in… Go with the flow* was my motto as I pulled my scarf over my blond dreadlocks and hid my bewildered gaze with my heart-shaped sunglasses.

As I entered into the museum that was a world-renowned historical sight, I honestly was a little disappointed at the utter chaos inside. It was a representation of the great city, so many ancient antiquities, but you had the search to find the meaning and deal with the disorganization. As I wondered around reading the tattered literature posted on random walls, I was approached by a man with a kind face that spoke good English. His name was Moses, and he asked if I wanted a guide through the museum. I normally would say no, but with the lack of information I was gathering on my own, I accepted the offer, and we wove through the massive complex while he explained the history and answered my questions. The history lessons of mummies and Canopic jars were brought back to life as I toured the exhibits and tried to put myself back in the days of grandeur. I imagined the belief systems these mummified people possessed as I observed the tombs staged with treasures, food, and carriages in hopes of needing them upon returning from the afterlife. The dirty relics that were barely more than dust proved my beliefs—*you can't take it with you when you're gone.*

As we finished up, I made a mistake. I should have known better, but my sleep-deprived self said yes to an offer to see a papyrus and oil shop "nearby." Almost as quickly as my head nodded, Moses grabbed my hand and held on tightly as he dragged me through the crowds and gates of the museum, shouting in Arabic to the touts that were scavenging the perimeter, looking for fresh meat tourists to scam. He interlinked his fingers between mine, which made it impossible for me to escape his firm grasp. We crossed a five-lane highway adjacent to the museum as if we were in a real-life *Frogger* game, dodging cars and buses that were speeding down the motorway and maintained forward progress across the road. I played out the scenarios in my head of deciding if it was better to kick and violently escape in the middle of the highway or possibly be run over by a speeding car. Was I being *Taken*? Where was Liam Neeson when I needed him?

We entered a small storefront, and I completely understood the hustle. The storekeeper started his story, talking about the craftsman-ship of the papyrus making as he shaved some branches that were soaking in water and began to pound them with a mallet and lattice the strips together. Seeing my lack of interest and reading my every facial expression, he changed directions by pulling out dusty apothe-cary jars of essential oils and dabbing samples on my arm. As I began to smell like an Arab hooker from all the exotic scents, I calmed the fears of the peddler that was obviously hungry for a sale by buying a small jar of Nefertiti's Essence—the least offensive scent that was sweet and actually quite intoxicating. With my wits on high alert, I made my way back to the hostel where I quickly took a shower to remove the South African sand and Egyptian essential oils off my tired body.

With clean clothes and a couple cups of coffee, I was ready for the Nile. My newfound friends and I piled into a cab and headed for the river. We spent the evening watching belly dancers as we cruised the life vein of Cairo. Wow, Egypt. The country seemed not to sleep, and neither did I. The country assaulted my senses with the tenacity of the people and the repugnant stench of garbage in the streets. The country was trying to scare me away from exploration of its hidden gems but had only piqued my interest more.

Wanderlust Diaries: The Once-Great City

The day's plan was to take on Alexandria, which was once the most thriving and scholarly city in Egypt. Looking at the history of this coastal hot spot, it seemed it was conquered by almost every major key player of the old world—the Romans, Arabs, French, Persians… the list goes on. We hired a cab to take us out of the smog-filled Cairo and headed north toward the Mediterranean Sea. To pass the time, I made us an Egypt bingo game on some paper with things to spot: camels, Muslims wearing abayas, mosques—it was actually hilarious as we engaged in our surroundings to win the game.

When we arrived in the city, the first impression was appalling—rubbish filled the streets. I am not talking about an occasional wrapper and Coke can, but piles upon piles of garbage heaps littered the roads and sidewalks forming mountains that competed with the historical buildings. The street vendors barely even had room to set up shop with the trash requiring so much real estate. Oddly enough, Alexandria was not set up as a tourist town. One of the blocks on our bingo game was a postcard; scouring the city, we couldn't find one postcard or souvenir magnet. The souks weren't filled with knockoff tourist items, but the everyday needs of the Egyptians ranging from car repair parts to laundry soap. You could even hire a little boy to sew a custom set of underwear from his small table with an antique sewing machine if you wanted to. The roads through the old town seemed to have no logic or rules. Swarms of motorbikes and cars with dents and no side view mirrors crashed into the narrow asphalt, honking incessantly but somehow managing to zipper in while yelling at each other through the windows in their Arabic tongue. If someone cut me off in traffic, I would be enraged, but it was the norm in Egypt, and the driver would loudly yell, "Habibe," which is "friend" in Arabic, which kept the camaraderie between the drivers and pedestrians.

We started in the ancient catacombs, where we unleashed our inner child while we ran through the darkness and hid from one another to give a good scare. It felt like it was the beginning of a horror movie with three tourists captured in this ancient ruin, but it was a surreal place; the cavernous trails went on and on, leading us deeper and deeper into the belly of this burial ground. We then headed to Pompeii's pillar, which was the largest monolithic freestanding pillar in Egypt and was guarded by ancient sphynx statues. It signified the Roman victory over an Alexandrian revolt, but to me, it was a premier area for a photo shoot. Void of any tourists, we had the place to ourselves. My new friends learned about my off-humor regarding bazaar photo poses. I used perspective and lighting to unleash creative Photoshop genius on this amazing location of ancient times that was surrounded by shanty villages.

We toured the town, enamored by it all, and found treasures beneath the rubble. This once-great city was still captivating. The modern world of consumerism had taken its toll, but it was still there under the surface, begging for acknowledgment of the history and culture that remained. With no tourist magnets or postcards as proof of my journey, I would always have the memories and photos of this once-great city. Like the Persians, Romans, and French before me, we conquered the town and left only footprints to remember this marvelous day.

Wanderlust Diaries: Giza

The day started with a text from my friend I met in Japan that ran the taco stand in Yokosuka. Kalid was a native Egyptian, and I was lucky that he saw my Facebook posts in his homeland and gave me a call. He picked me up at my hostel and gave me the best tour of the town. All the hagglers and touts paid me no mind as Kalid shouted in Arabic, pointing to his ring finger, asserting that I was his wife and to leave me alone—it was perfect. Kalid even threw the keys at me and let me drive down the chaotic Egyptian roads. By all traffic laws, there should be a million accidents, but the cars flowed like a river through the decrepit streets with no regard to lanes or pedestrians, honking and weaving to their destinations.

We explored the pyramids and tombs while I played on the massive boulders like Indiana Jones. We hiked into the belly of the greatest pyramid and touched the tomb. It was humid and sweltering inside, but that added to the surreal feeling of being present in the very moment—the moment I had dreamed of since I was a little girl reading *Return of the Mummy* book by R. L. Stine. I was here! Kalid worked out a deal with a local Egyptian for me and my friends to ride a camel across the desert to get some photos. My camel's name was Whitney Houston, and as I saddled on her lumpy back, we made our way across the cream-colored sand to the most panoramic spot I could have ever asked for. I grew accustomed to the awkward gate of Whitney's steps and crooked my leg over her neck to balance on top while I was in photo heaven. I would force myself to put my camera away and just enjoy the view, but it was too spectacular. I would quickly dig through my purse to find my camera again as another gorgeous view would come into sight, beckoning me to capture the moment.

There were so many things in this world that I yearned to see and knew that I would not feel complete without stepping foot on them. I had always known one day I would be in Egypt at the Great Pyramids of Giza; I was not sure how or when, but I always felt it when I would see the wonders in movies. It was the textbook definition of my wanderlust—to long for places I had only been to in my dreams. That day, my dreams came true.

Wanderlust Diaries: The Middle of the Middle East

If I had to describe Jordan, I would use the following words: madness, chaotic, friendly, and beautiful. The friendliness of the Jordanians was unlike any I had ever met. The scenery was beyond stunning. I had moments where I couldn't even talk because it was unimaginable. It was a whole new world and I was ready for my magic carpet ride. At the airport, I was checked by security three separate times before I could retrieve my bags at the baggage claim. Police had officers in civilian clothes with gun holsters on their hips that kept watchful eyes on the crowds, and uniformed officers marched the streets with AK-47s, wearing masks to hide their faces.

On the bus ride to Petra, a village was blocked by police vehicles where I watched and videotaped the most bizarre episode take place. Civilians stretched the outskirts of the road, held back by armed guards as a SWAT team of uniformed men with assault weapons scurried around our bus, and kicked in a door to a building directly in front of us. After a couple of minutes, the officers dragged out a man wearing a brown robe with only small slits in his headdress to see through. After some yelling in the Arabic tongue, the man was loaded up into a van, and the streets cleared as we continued our journey. Despite this craziness, the people were intriguing and kind beyond words.

At my camp, the civil unrest felt a million miles away as I sat on the cushioned floor of a bedouin camp, drinking tea. The men smeared thick eyeliner on their eyelids to protect their skin from the sun; their dark hair was dreaded, framing their dark faces. The bedouin lifestyle was nothing less than entrancing. It was bizarre to think as I sipped sage tea on a cushioned mat in a tent made of goat hides that I was surrounded by countries all at war. I would enjoy my safe haven with the bedouins and relish in the sanctuary of this beautiful place.

Wanderlust Diaries: Petra, the Lost City

I had never watched the Indiana Jones movie that made Petra so famous, so you can imagine my surprise when I laid eyes on this magnificent place that had been lost in time. I made friends with Noah, a Boston boy I had met in South Africa, again in Cairo, and as we became fond of one another, he joined me in my travels to Petra (small world for such a big place!). We had already had some misadventures trying to navigate to this great city. We accidentally got out of a bus way too early and ended up stranded on a road called the Lost Desert Highway until a cab picked us up, and we haggled for a ridiculous fare to take us to Amman, the capital city. As two Yanks in a foreign world, we must have hiked all over the medina, looking for a bottle of wine to calm our nerves, but it was almost impossible as we enjoyed the wild around us, and we became good friends.

As soon as we got to Petra, we stormed the gates and made it only a few feet before haggling for a horseback ride through the Indiana Jones trail into the heart of the great ancient city. Saddled on my horse overlooking the most jaw-dropping landscape I have ever seen was epic. The terrain was wild, and the guide would have to walk the horses as we navigated through giant boulders. We were on top of the world, and every minute was another scene that would take my breath away. The hike down was interesting; I wasn't prepared with the right attire, but I maneuvered through the insane cliffs and rocks, slinking my way down the mountainside like a billy goat to enter the village. The giant facades that were carved into the rose-colored cliffs were nothing less than glorious. The jagged cliffs and caves that encompassed the city were magical. The aura of the place made me feel like I was in another world and in another time period. I have never felt this unattached from the real world, and it was truly transcendent.

After the amazing hike and photo opportunities, we cruised around the city to find a celebratory drink, which was not an easy thing to find in a Muslim country. After a few odd looks and the call to prayer blasting on the town's loudspeaker, we settled for tea back at the campsite. We followed the glow of the candles on the mountainside to the secluded camp, consisting of canvas tents and a large communal area with a toasty fire. The bedouins poured tea and enamored us with their genuine personalities. Finding the Lost City was one of the greatest things I would ever treasure in my memory book.

Wanderlust Diaries: Alone in the Desert

In my minimal research for what to do in Jordan, I came across Wadi Rum, a protected area that was a stone's throw away from Israel. I heard it was away from everything and a beautiful place, so I shared a taxi with a girl that was headed the same direction. The misadventure started there, as we approached the gates to Wadi Rum, where she was whisked away with another driver to her "luxury camp" she had booked. I, on the other hand, was not so lucky. I had booked the basic "Bedouin camel ride and sleep under the stars," which was exactly what I got. At the entry port to this vast desert land, the small town was in poor shape with barefoot children running around to greet the pale-faced stranger. I found the man I made a booking with, and through a lot of confusion to work out the details, he introduced me to Hassim. Hassim spoke zero English but stood there in his Arabic robe and turban, smoking a cigarette with one hand and holding the leash of two camels with the other.

Hassim and I headed out into the middle of nowhere, stopping periodically so I could snap some photos and climb the mountains to check out the view. I became really good at charades with Hassim, trying to act out conversation, but I could tell he was growing weary of my antics as he chain-smoked his cigarettes while I enjoyed the scenery. That night, we made our way into the heart of the desert. The tents were completely basic and just a small block for the torrid desert wind. Nighttime was cold—bitter cold—as we made a fire to keep warm. The night sky was the most spectacular I had ever seen; hundreds of shooting stars blasted across the heavens as the rest twinkled like diamonds. The Milky Way galaxy seemed superimposed on this textbook night sky. As I lay there, with my turban wrapped around my head and four camel blankets piled on top of me for warmth, I was in disbelief of where I was. When you are alone with your thoughts, the thoughts can be deafening. I actually started to wonder if I was crazy for being here. My lips were chapped, I was covered in bruises from the insane hikes, and now I was lying under the stars with my only company being Hassim and our two camels.

Finally, my thoughts subsided, and I allowed a peaceful slumber to take over.

The next morning, I didn't want to even get out of my cave of blankets because it was so freezing cold. My bones ached from the chill of the desert night, but I knew we had to get moving. We loaded up the camels and were on our way. I knew Hassim was bored, but I never thought he would leave me. As we meandered along, following Jeep tire tracks in this isolated wonderland, Hassim hissed and snarled at his camel to get it to kneel down. (This was how you did it—it sounds ridiculous, but the camels understood the noises.) Hassim then knelt to take a piss by a bush and then stood in the sand, waving down a Jeep that was in the far distance. Hassim slapped my camel's ass, as he jumped into the Jeep, disappearing into the horizon. A feeling of fear and complete isolation took over my body as I continued my trek with Sasha, the camel, and Hassim's camel that walked along beside us. I was in disbelief. *How did I get myself in these positions?* I knew that it had taken at least six hours to get to the village the day before, so I hoped that I was headed in the right direction. Fear and adventure cannot live in the same body, so I swallowed down my angst and tried to let the thrill of riding across a desert on a camel completely alone take over.

Sasha, the camel, was actually quite moody. As I balanced on top of her, making videos to document the absurdity of the situation, she would swing her neck back to bite me. She actually took a chunk out of my hand as I made a block maneuver to keep her from biting my leg. As I continued on the pilgrimage, I actually thought my mind played tricks on me. The pink sand in the distance would sometimes appear to have a sheen of water. I would follow the mirage, just to realize it was nothing, just all in my head. Finally, I could make out a distant resemblance of a village coming into view. After hours of being perched on top of moody Sasha, I prayed my mind wasn't playing tricks on me again. A hopeful sign of life appeared as a Jeep motored toward me. As the Jeep approached, I recognized the man in the back—Hassim. With no words, he hissed at his camel as it knelt for him to mount it. I guess my "guide" was back.

As he led the way, I glared at him in disgust. I was sure his boss had no idea the manner in which he conducted his "guided camel tours." We reached the village as I hissed at Sasha to get her to kneel. It was a happy moment as I dismounted from the bitchy camel and waved goodbye to Hassim as I collected my bags. He looked at me with his hand out for a tip as I scoffed at his audacity. The owner greeted me to ask how the camel tour was. I kindly smiled but I was ready to escape the madness I had just experienced and wanted to return to the beauty of Petra. I decided not to endure any more haggling and thumbed a ride with two fellas that were headed the direction I needed to go. I have never been so alone but alive, but I was glad to be leaving. I pushed my limits those past couple of days—physically, emotionally, and psychologically. I was leaving the desert bruised, chapped, and bitten, but it was a hell of a ride.

Wanderlust Diaries: The People You Meet

The world is full of interesting people. You never know who is sitting next to you, drinking their coffee or reading their newspaper. Traveling solo had afforded me the ability to open doors into the lives of people I never would have met otherwise. As I left Wadi Rum, I was thrilled to hitch a ride with Kaan, a Turkish guy who was involved in biodefense. We shared travel stories, and I was thankful for a glimpse of decent conversation after a couple of days of isolation. When I returned to Petra, I had no intention of listening to the hagglers inside the gates of the park, asking me to take a donkey ride, so I roamed the streets where I met Ali. His demeanor was different from the other street vendors, and when he offered me a seat at his curbside store, I accepted. I spent the next few hours getting to know him better. The tables turned when instead of him trying to sell me stuff, he dressed me up in all his silly scarfs and turbans, and I helped him sell his handicrafts to the tourists exiting the gates of Petra. He taught me how to make the sand art, and I would beckon the tourists into "my" store while he sat back laughing at my sales gimmicks.

The next day at camp, I sat next to a gentleman, who introduced himself as the "Dark Lord," at breakfast. He had an eccentric sense of humor, but I found him to be quite interesting as he gave me a nickname of *Mutant Melissa* with the green eyes. After some hilarious conversation, I discovered this man was a famous author of a series of children's books, the *Dark Lord*. We spent a few hours hiking Petra together as his wild imagination would narrate the landscape and warn me of the trolls that were hiding under the giant boulders. We laughed as he promised to send me some signed books when I returned to the States.

The next day, Ali, my new store friend, had arranged a special ride for me with his uncle that wouldn't charge the arm and a leg tourist price I had been quoted to take me to the Dead Sea. His uncle was willing to drive me and only charge for gas as a favor. As I met his uncle, Basaam, we spent the day learning about each other. I picked his brain about the geography and history of the area, and as the hours passed, these benign topics morphed into very personal and deep value-driven conversation. He explained Islam and what it meant to him and his opinion on the radicalized Muslims. He spoke of his fear with anti-Muslim sentiment in America, and he discussed the challenges of living in Jordan. I learned more about Israel and Palestine as we viewed their coastline from the Dead Sea, sharing a plate of hummus. It seemed there was so much more to reality here than what the media fed the world. Even though he was a Muslim, he happily drove me to landmarks of Christianity, such as the spot where John the Baptist baptized Jesus, Mt. Nebo where Moses lived out his last days, and we even drank a coffee at the location of Sodom and Gomorrah. He told me the Muslim rules of divorce, and holding back tears, he explained how his wife had just left him, and he missed her dearly. The kicker of the conversation occurred when we started to discuss family. This was a hard topic for me. I didn't want to be a downer and tell a new acquaintance when they ask me about my parents that they were both dead, but after the hours of honest conversation, I felt I had to reveal some of my skeletons.

I talked about the day in my life that time stood still; it was June 3, 2005. I remember what I was wearing, what I was doing, the way I had my hair in a long ponytail as the police officer pulled into my driveway to tell me my mother had died in a small hotel in Port Townsend. I remember the details of the police officer's face, and I remember the feeling of emptiness as I fell to the hard-gravel driveway, sobbing; that day would live in infamy for me. Basaam had one of those days too, March 26, 2003. Basaam's dad was living in Iraq and working in a government facility as a chef, trying to make enough money to send Basaam to a private school as a boy. As Operation Iraqi Freedom gained momentum, Basaam's father was taking refuge in a building in Baghdad. It was bombed, and his father died as a civilian casualty of the war. As I listened, I couldn't help but feel sick inside as I knew that the day that would haunt Basaam for the rest of his life was a day that I was serving on an aircraft carrier in the Pacific Fleet, deployed to the Persian Gulf. I remember hearing the song "Bombs over Baghdad" play on the 1MC of the ship as I went about my daily routine, oblivious to what was really happening in the world outside my steel hull.

Basaam dropped me off, and as his car pulled away, our paths were now split again into our separate worlds. It was crazy to imagine how the billions of people that walk this earth are interconnected. My stories were not isolated but one page in a chapter of humanity in the greater book of history. I was happy to be able to see the energy in the empty space between me and the stranger next to me. It had enlightened me beyond measure.

Wanderlust Diaries: Here's to Looking at You, Kid...Twice

As I boarded my discount flight on Egypt Air bound for Morocco, I tried not to think about the airline's reputation and curled up in my economy seat with my eye mask on to catch some sleep. Just as I drifted off to catch some much-needed ZZZs after the whirlwind of Jordan, I was awoken by the flight attendant barking at me with an offer of coffee. It startled me, and I let out a loud shriek as my imagination initially assumed Egypt Air flight 702 was in trouble. When I arrived in Morocco, I had been toying with the idea of whether or not to tour around Casablanca before making my way to Marrakesh. A quick look in the mirror at my disheveled dreadlocks and bags under my eyes gave me the validation I needed to skip Casablanca and head out on the next train. As I loaded up my heavy pack full of handicrafts from Africa, I grabbed a seat on the next train inland. I knew I needed to transfer trains, but the stations didn't really advertise where they were going. I knew I was on the right platform, but as I boarded and watched my train pull away from the station, I instantly knew I made a mistake; I was headed back to Casablanca. I took the opportunity to check out my guidebook on the things to do and considered this an omen that I needed to see this city. As it turns out, Casablanca was pretty boring, boasting the financial hub and business districts of the country. I couldn't find the romantic landscapes from the movie, so I considered the town a bust and headed back to Marrakesh for the second time.

I had lost daylight and knew I would be navigating to my hostel at night, which was not preferred. My hostel was right in the middle if the famous D'Jamaa el Fna Square, which had been victim to a bombing a few years back, but the city had revived vibrant as ever. As I meandered through the crazed alleyways, I was in the midst of the great old-time caravansery; this grand place was the new age trading post connecting the spice route across the Sahara. The directions to my hostel had me turning left at the snake charmers, navigating through the myriad of food vendors, where I circumnavigated the touts with their monkeys and then turned right at the street performers, and finally, after a slew of carpet peddlers, I arrived at my tiny hostel.

I was staying at a riad, which was basically a traditional Moroccan house with multiple rooms and a courtyard. It was painted vibrant colors with old mosaics and a plethora of colorful plush couches hosting a rugby team cheering for a live game on the TV. The other travelers were boasting good spirits, and I knew I found my new home for the next few days. Morocco went from pretty mild to pretty wild, and I was excited for what adventures this country had to offer.

Wanderlust Diaries: Funky Cold Medina

Marrakesh was a riot. Walking through the main square, I was either dodging a cobra lying on the ground staged by a snake charmer, dodging a man trying to throw a monkey on my shoulder, or dodging the fortune-tellers rattling their jars of teeth at me wanting to predict my future—it was madness! A woman grabbed my arm and, within one minute, had clumsily drawn a henna design that I would now remember for at least a couple of weeks. I didn't even fight the hustle but played along with it; it was all a part of the game. "*Best price for you... I like Rasta... Where you from... Come into my shop...,*" the same old line from different faces all looking to earn a buck. I didn't do what many tourists did and completely ignore the vendors or refuse to engage in any conversation. I joked back at them and gave them high fives as I walked through the medina. As I was haggling for a tea set with a local shop owner, I actually got a lot more than I bargained for.

I could tell Abdou, the young store owner, had taken a fancy to me, but I wheeled and dealt with him until we settled on a fair price for the tea set. Abdou joked that I should come work for him as he insisted I stay for tea. He ran to the adjacent storefront, grabbing various fresh ingredients in exchange for cavalier smiles from the other shop keeps as he returned with a basket full of goodies. He pinched various spices and flowers into the teapot as he placed it over a flame. As we waited for the tea to boil, Abdou took advantage of my captivity by asking, "Tagine?" This was a traditional dish of Morocco. I had entertained taking a cooking class while I was there, but this was so much better. Sitting on the tiniest stool in the middle of his open-air storefront, I peeled the potatoes and sliced the onions. Abdou meticulously arranged the layered vegetables, meats, and spices into the tagine cooker and placed it over a propane stove. The other storefront workers would make comments to Abdou, and knowing I didn't speak Arabic, I was sure it was along the lines of a good-hearted teasing for Abdou going through so much trouble to impress me with his cooking skills in the middle of the market. The smells were divine coming from the ceramic cooker and permeated the streets. When it was finally done, Abdou, his two brothers, and I gathered around a small table while we ate the delicious dish Moroccan style with no forks, just bread and our hands. I could tell Abdou was becoming overly flirtatious, so when he asked to meet for dinner, I kindly declined as I took my bargain goods and tagine techniques with me.

The next bucket-list item for Morocco was to visit a hammam (a sort of traditional bathhouse). I wasn't quite sure exactly what it was, but in Morocco, it was quite the rave, and I was up for just about anything. My awful henna job was already a wreck from a man that tried to toss a monkey on my arm while the henna was wet. My artwork was a blurred mess, so a trip to the bathhouse couldn't make it any worse. The hammam was perfect solace away from the chaos outside. The sweet-tempered ladies directed me to undress and enter a steamy cave full of other naked ladies perched on marble slabs. The steam was so thick it was nearly impossible to make out anything. Every few minutes a figure would emerge into our eerie den, and I could make out the outline of a finger pointing to one of us and curling it in a "come hither" manner—beckoning the chosen to exit to cave. When it was my turn, the next station was where we would be washed from head to toe and scrubbed. The attendants would pour pitchers of rose water over us like goddesses and then escort us to the next area, where they massaged exotic oils on our bodies. It was quite the experience. I wasn't quite expecting group naked bath time, but regardless, it was lovely.

I continued the night getting lost in the funky cold medina, haggling for swag. This was life—breaking bread, breaking boundaries, and embracing all the detours!

Wanderlust Diaries: Swept Away in Taghazout

I needed a break from the crazy Marrakesh medina. With just a small-day pack, I headed to the coast. At the bus station, I was torn between bus to the tiny fishing village of Essaouira or else a surf mecca, Taghazout. I surrendered to the will of wanting to catch a famous wave from another renowned surf spot, so I bought the ticket and waited for the bus. I believe in serendipity—of being in a place at the precise right moment and being open to allow new people and experiences to come into my circle. While waiting for the bus, I met Mohammed or "Moe" for short. Moe, his brother, and friend were from the United Kingdom, and every year, they came to Taghazout to relax. I spent the three-hour bus ride in seamless conversation with Moe. We arrived in Agadir and all joined in a taxi to Taghazout. Yakuv, Moe's friend, was a brilliant haggler. The years of coming to Morocco had made him an exceptional bargainer; in fact, he enjoyed it. We sat back and watched Yakuv work his magic with the taxi driver…with the initial price, the passionate yelling, and then the pretend walk away; he was like the Godfather of this place and had it nailed down to a science to get the right price. When we arrived in Taghazout, it was one of the mellowest and chill places on earth. I had to go my separate way to check into my hostel while Yakuv made some deals to get them an apartment on the beach.

I arrived at my hostel which was piled high with surfboards and the floor covered in sand. The hostel travelers were the epitome of washouts in a surf town with dreadlocks and neon sunglasses perched on their tan sun-kissed faces. I joined the tribe for lunch and smoothies at a chill café they had become addicted to and downshifted life into a slower gear to just unwind and take in the intrepid scenery. The waves crashed into the beach with the perfect roll, hosting a myriad of surfers enjoying the ride. With lots of daylight left, I declined the offer to watch movies in the hostel and set out to the beach. Nipping at my heels as I left the hostel was the cutest little puppy that seemed hell-bent on following me to the ocean. I picked up the little scamp and gave her kisses on her sweet puppy face. In the distance, I could hear a voice coming from down the street. "Bunny… Bunny!" From down the alley, I watched a young Moroccan guy come trotting over to me in his flip-flops and wild curly hair. It was his puppy that had taken a liking to me, and after a few quick conversational exchanges and many puppy kisses, Amir joined me for a walk down to Anchor Point—a picturesque point to the famed Taghazout Beach.

Amir, Bunny, and I strolled the beautiful shoreline, navigating across boulders and a few trails to enjoy this beautiful place. Amir was a surf instructor, and as we passed his shop, I quickly replied with a predetermined "Yes!" as he offered for us to take a board out to catch a wave at the Hashpipe beach. We surfed and laughed as Bunny scampered about on the beach, watching us and greeted us when we made it back to the sand. As I dried off, I heard some commotion coming from one of the villas overlooking the beach. "Melissa! Melissa!" I scoured the balconies in this prime location to see Moe waving his arms at me with a giant smile on his face. Yakuv had negotiated for likely the best villa on all Taghazout—and for pennies! Moe met me on the beach as I hugged Amir and Bunny goodbye. I followed Moe up through the white-and-blue-painted villa that was three stories high with an open-air roof at the top. This was paradise. There was likely not another place in this world that could have beheld so much beauty.

Yakuv, being a perfect planner, had bought an assortment of liquors from the Duty Free market in the airport. Without this type of planning, the only beverage you would get in a Muslim country was tea, juice, or coffee. I had hit the jackpot with my new friends. We toasted the night away until the sun faded into the abyss of the dark blue Atlantic, casting wild and vivid colors over the horizon. We kept ourselves entertained with a pizza run and a night of playing charades while singing along to the fantastic playlist of the phone of Moe's brother. The night was nothing less than perfect. I crashed at their villa, on top of the rooftop terrace, watching the stars dance in the night sky and listening to the thunder of the waves crashing under the villa.

I thought about what had transpired in the past twenty-four hours…with meeting Moe and his friends, then the tribe of travelers from the hostel, Amir and Bunny, and now being with Moe and the group again. I was like the waves that were singing me to sleep, being washed away to a new place and grouping together with like people. When the moment would lose its energy, I would follow the tide and be swept away with the next wave of friends, enjoying the thrill of the ride and allowing any rigidity to be lost at sea. When you don't know where you are going, any road can take you there; if you are lucky, that path is exactly where you need to be.

Wanderlust Diaries: Tapas for Breakfast

There was heavy fog in Portugal that delayed my connecting flight to Barcelona. Finally, we were cleared to board the plane, but I had a sinking feeling that my checked bag full of African handicrafts was not going to make it. I was giddy when I saw my turquoise travel companion, looking about as dirty and disheveled as I was, fall down the baggage chute. All loaded up like a pack mule, I navigated the new waters with ease, making my way to the bus, then the metro, and then a short walk to my hostel. I was pleasantly surprised when as soon as I entered into was greeted with a welcome beer and a heaping plate of pasta from a communal dinner they had just prepared.

I could feel the life in the city, even without even seeing a single sight yet. The energy was palpable, so I grabbed a quick shower and joined some new friends for a night out on the town. My sidekick for the night was an American named Brad. He was a bass guitar player for a band that had been opening for Evanescence. They had been touring around the United States, and his band had a gig in Europe, so he took a quick jaunt out to Barcelona. It was very interesting that Brad didn't drink, especially being in a rock band. I kept teasing him about when he was going to bust out the hard stuff, but with a charming confidence, he just enjoyed the nightlife without having to give himself any liquid courage. Brad would hold my drink and be my roofie patrol when I would head to the ladies' room and was the perfect partner to hang with while we absorbed the scene.

It had been a long time since I had been subjected to the club atmosphere, and I know why I didn't usually partake. The club was three stories of pulsating music and filled with an assortment of tourists and locals that stood together in the crowded dance floor, not even able to move more than a slight bounce of the feet. The only real movement in the club was when a group of girls decked out in their tight mini dresses and bright red lipstick would hold hands to slither through the crowds like a glitter snake, making pathways to the different quadrants of the club. As I looked at my watch, seeing it was 4:00 a.m., I was proud that I was still upright, but this wasn't my scene anymore. The clubs didn't even open until two in the morning, so these partygoers weren't turning in any time soon and would be dancing into the wee hours of the morning. Brad caught me checking the time, and with a knowing smile, we wiggled our way out of the packed club to catch a cab back to the hostel. It was a great first night in Barcelona, but there was a world outside my bunk bed ready to be explored. After the alarm chimed only a couple of hours after my head hit the pillow, I was off to work off the hangover from one too many mojitos. As I walked down the famous Los Rambles Street, an open-air café was serving tapas and coffee, it was like it was meant to be!

Wanderlust Diaries: Paella and Football

Today could not have been ANY more saturated in España! From a breakfast of tapas to drinking my weight in sangria, I was completely immersed in everything that was Spain. I walked around the Gothic Quarter, admiring the beautiful architecture—it was stunning. For lunch, I hung out with a new acquaintance I met through the hostel. Jose made a huge smorgasbord of paella that he shared with all the travelers at the hostel. Then it was off to the Magic Fountain, an impromptu Flamenco dance, watching the Barcelona versus Madrid football game, and then indulging in many tapas and pinchos I washed down with liters of sangria.

The city was so easy to flow with—the clean streets welcomed pedestrian and bicycle traffic, and besides the occasional dodgy pick-pocket that might be lurking, the city felt so safe. Children and dogs ran free in the street to all hours of the night while the parents enjoyed vino in the open-air cafés. I realized that I did not need to continue to charade my way through life because I did not speak Swahili, Zulu, Afrikaans, Arabic, French, or Berber, but I could actually speak the language and order a café con leche without getting confused looks from the street vendors. Even though Barcelona tied with Madrid in the big game, Barcelona had won me over! Viva la España!

Wanderlust Diaries: ART-Chitecture

Barcelona was home to some of the most beautiful buildings in the world. Famous architect, Antoni Gaudi, was the mastermind behind many of the iconic buildings, including the Sagrada Familia Basilica. This stunning tribute to God and nature left me breathless as I crooked my neck toward the heavens, mesmerized by the ornate sculptures and stained glass that all told a story of the Passion of Christ. The symbolism was inspiring as the architect mimicked a forest made of stone pillars inside the basilica and included nature and man in a cohesive montage that left spectators in complete reverence at the abstract beauty. The weather turned to rain, but that caused me no bother as I took refuge in the Picasso museum and was lucky to be given free admission. As I strolled the galleries of the works of the great Picasso, I found it interesting the drastic progression of his work—from realistic portraits and nudes to the modern renowned abstracts and cubism that he was famous for. The right side of my brain hurt from the acute dose of art in one day.

I took a break lying on the beach, watching the progression of the waves that never grew weary and steadily thrashed from the dark blue Mediterranean onto the sand. I reflected on what all I had seen in a day—the amazing works of two eccentric individuals that chose not to color inside the lines. The rules of art were mere guidelines that these masters exploited and found their own identity. I found it inspiring what they had accomplished and realized that, in one way or another, we are all artists.

We come into this world with a blank canvas—an empty foundation. Through life, we learn things and grow from experiences that cast an array of colors on our palette. It is up to us how we paint the picture. You can be subtle, bold, blue, vibrant, void—the choices are endless. Some people go their entire lives looking at the empty slate, afraid to commit the brush to canvas...afraid of letting others know what compels their spirit and their vulnerability. Some people slice open the vein of creativity and bleed all over white space with heartfelt expressions of their emotions and tribulations. Art was about leaving your mark on this world, showing that you did more than merely exist, but you lived—you were happy, sad, in love, hopeful, and you had a purpose. As I sat on the beach, listening to the symphony of waves, I counted my blessings for the life I have made for myself and the characters that were illustrated in my mural. The art

I was creating was a work in progress and free from any heaviness of disapproval from others. Life was about painting your own picture, not criticizing the work of others. It was my journey, my experiences, my art—my masterpiece.

Wanderlust Diaries: Falling Down the Rabbit Hole

I followed the white rabbit to a town close to the French border, Figueres. The town wasn't a usual tourist spot and was mainly normal, everyday Spanish life, but it was home to the Salvador Dali Museum. I loved Dali...more than any other artist. His skill was not only his paintbrush but his mind. Every piece was something that I could interpret a thousand different ways, but he had a way of connecting with my soul. He told a story with his art and wasn't afraid of whom it offended. The biggest theme in Dali's work was the personification of inanimate objects and also the use clocks that reminded the viewer that time was a precious gift and should not be squandered. The museum was more like a trip into Wonderland with its whimsical decor, and I was Alice. The clocks would chime, and all around me were paintings that most people would consider nonsense, but I understood them.

As I looked deep into the paintings, I reflected on my trip. I had explored a world that most people only saw in their dreams—only I had just been dreaming with my eyes open. I had tea parties with the Mad Hatter in England, ran along the beaches with the Dodo bird in Dubai, been the wildflower in the jungles of Africa, puffed hookah with the caterpillar in Egypt, found adventures with the curious oysters in the desert of Jordan, lost my way with the Cheshire Cat in Morocco, and now I had painted the roses red in the gardens of Spain. My time as Alice had taught me many things as I had navigated through my personal Wonderland.

Life lessons I pondered started with the fact life can and should be "Much More Muchier." As we get older, sometimes we seem to lose our "muchness," so as long as we have a pulse, we should live life to the fullest. Second, it is okay to dream impossible things; no one in life should be able to define what is possible for you. Third, my reality may be different from yours, and that's okay; *normal* is a relative term. And lastly, it is okay to follow the white rabbit, and not all who wander are lost; blessed are the curious because they will find adventures. As I stood in the museum, the clocks continued their relentless ticking; the sideshow-like mirrors throughout the space reflected the image of a blond-haired girl that appeared to be admiring an abstract painting, but in reality, her head was in the clouds. The fairy tale would be ending soon. I would have to wake up.

> The girl could not sleep, because her thoughts were too deep… Her mind had taken a stroll and fallen down the rabbit hole.
> —Lewis Caroll, *Alice and Wonderland*

PROLOGUE

SOUTH AMERICA

With so many bucket-list items hidden in the bowels of South America, I couldn't pick just one. The continent was vast, and I had no idea how I was going to cover so much ground, but I was willing to give it a shot. I was excited…there were no other words to describe the feeling. My friend, Canela, decided to join me for the first leg through Peru, and I was giddy to have the company of such a free-spirited girl; I knew we would have a blast. We had only had adventures together in Washington, but each of them always ended up with a crazy story told in the midst of friends of the shenanigans we got into, so I knew we were in for a good time. Looking at flights, I noticed that South America was unlike other travel locations because there were not any budget airlines servicing the continent. If I was going to do my normal backpacking gig with cheap accommodation and travel, I was going to have to get creative.

The shipyard job was going good, and I had saved up enough vacation days to spend almost two months on the road, but I had to be in Texas by a certain date for my cousin's wedding, which provided the only bookend to my travels. With only a roundtrip ticket out of Peru, I set my sails south and was ready for the next chapter in my Wanderlust Adventures.

Wanderlust Diaries: Trip to the Moon

As the plane circled the capital city of Lima, I was surprised at the arid and dry landscape. Tiny ramshackle pueblo houses made up the majority of the vista, and it didn't seem like much to look at. My friend, Canela, was joining me on the first leg of the trip, and despite the lack of character in our initial impression of the country, we looked with eager travel-hungry eyes out the window of our taxi as we made our way through the slums of Lima and further south to the Bohemian seaside village of Barranco. As we checked into our scuzzy hostel, we weren't the only ones on a trip. The hostel was in the beginning stages of a full moon party, and many of the residents were enjoying their own "trip to the moon" via little lines of powder. The lack of tourism in Lima left travelers to their own devices, and our hostel seemed to attract vagabonds that cared less about the cultural side of Peru and more about exploring the depth of their own consciousness while dancing and smearing body paint on each other. Everyone was on their own ride, whether it was from catching a wave off the coast or riding the effects of the ivory dust left behind on the dirty hostel bathroom sink.

Canela and I chose to explore the city and found a cozy restaurant that overlooked the ocean. We sipped our pisco sours over a goblet of ceviche as the sun retired over the smoggy horizon. Street performers clogged the road with no regard to the concept of pedestrian traffic areas as the musicians entertained the masses. The Latin rhythms seemed to beckon our hips to sway and feet to tiptoe to the beat. We made our way back to our hostel through the cobblestone streets to see that the rest of the residents were still in full orbit and boisterously celebrating the night of the full moon.

Locals took refuge in the few hammocks that were decorating the rafters of the communal area and unfortunately right outside our room. I had sensed that this crowd would be rowdy and locked our windows and doors after we headed for bed, which proved to be a very smart move. The locals that were smashed out of their minds must have been entranced by the exotic foreign girls as they bellowed songs of Peruvian amor outside our door with no regard for keeping the peace. I had even brazenly tipped one drunken fool out of his hammock that hung two feet from our door as he sang and called to us after my patience had worn thin, but this seemed to only increase his desire to swoon us out of our safe haven. Sleep we would have none as the drunken idiots paced outside and their silhouettes danced in the moonlight that cast shadows on our curtains.

When we awoke after a less-than-peaceful sleep, it was like a disaster had occurred outside our room. The trip to the moon must have had quite the crash landing as bodies hung lifeless in hammocks or littered on the ground. As I brushed my teeth, one young man I met from Venezuela entered the bathroom wearing nothing but a dirty hostel blanket and his money belt draped across his neck. His cheeks and forehead were covered in hot pink body paint as he washed his glasses in the sink. As I continued to wash my face, a young man sprinted to the toilet to spew an offering to the Porcelain God. His retching noises were enough to make me thankful that Canela and I had settled on pisco sours. I'm sure the moon is great, but la luna was not why I flew nine hours and worked so hard to take time off from the shipyard. I came to explore Latin America and all it had to offer. Trips like these were once in a lifetime, and I would rather remember it. Canela and I left the white cloud that loomed over the hostel and fogged the minds of the many travelers. We were here for epic exploits and left to see what Peru had to offer two girls with an adventurous spirit.

Wanderlust Diaries: Peruvian Amazon

We flew into Iquitos, the largest city in the world that was not reach-able by road. I had booked a place that prior to this had only resided in my Pinterest dream board, an Amazon Treehouse Lodge, but I didn't realize this paradise was not reached by the faint of heart. After already traveling to Iquitos that didn't even warrant a page in my Lonely Planet guidebook, we were off in a wooden boat, headed down the mighty Amazon. On our three-hour journey to the abso-lute middle of nowhere, I sat back and enjoyed the ride as the legendary pink dolphins swam next to our boat. Finally, we arrived. Words could not express how amazing and inspiring this place was.

The owner had a vision to create a lodge with the most beautiful tree houses in the world in this jungle oasis. The lodge had boardwalks on stilts that allowed for the rainy season and a master lodge with hammocks, but this wasn't the real treasure. I had booked the tallest tree house, Alta Vista. After a long walk deep into the jungle, about twenty ridiculously steep flights of stairs built around the tall ficus trees, two wobbly canopy bridges that looked like something out of Indiana Jones, we had made it to our home. Alta Vista was a magnificent pillar of strength in the rain forest and a place of peace and solitude that overlooked the entire canopy into the wild, untouched Amazon. The engineering marvel of how this beautiful tree house was even possible was mind-boggling. After a long day of travel, there couldn't have been a better ending than the symphony of frogs and crickets that serenaded us into slumber as I watched countless fireflies flicker against the midnight sky. It was hard to believe that places like this really existed. I needed to pinch myself to make sure I was not dreaming.

Wanderlust Diaries: Mas Machete and the Creatures of the Amazon

The Amazon wasn't quite what I had imagined, but then again, I was pretty much going off Hollywood movies. We headed out in our little boat with a Yamaha 15HP outboard to see what sorts of adventure was lurking in the quagmires and bends along the mighty river. At the helm was our guide, Willy, who fearlessly led us to all the best-kept secrets of the Amazon wildlife. We spotted monkeys, sloths, macaws, herons, and so much more. Willy had thrown us some bamboo rods in the boat, and as we took a break from weaving in and out of the small "backroads" of the Amazon, we tried our luck at piranha fishing. As soon as our hooks hit the black waters, the simplistic pole would tug and twitch as the carnivorous beast hit up the bait of some chicken skin. It was almost too easy. Within seconds, it was "Fish On!" But the real trick was to marry the excitement of pulling up a fish with the reality that the little devil on the end had razor-sharp teeth, so good luck on getting your hook back without losing a finger. Willy showed me the scars on his hand where the fish got the better of him as he tried to recall the stories in his broken English.

I gave a sincere effort to brush up on my Spanish before this trip but found that in the real world outside my Duolingo app, I could understand what Spanish people were saying, but the reciprocation of anything intelligent was escaping me as I would embarrassingly mutter a couple of words at a time in my Spanglish. I had mentioned that I would like to see the giant lily pads, and after the linguistic exchange, I could tell Willy was determined. As we wove through the different nooks and crannies of the river, we took a route that I had wondered would possibly be our last. The thing about the Amazon was that the whole area had water but changed every day. An area that was a lake one day could have so much plant life grow rapidly; it would be almost impassable the next week. As Willy revved through the water jungle, the hyacinth lilies had trailed through all the narrow passageways and continually clogged the motor of our old decrepit boat. As the motor proved useless in the boggy wonderland, Willy busted out an old machete that he kept razor sharp. Willy whacked his way through the bush, and we inched our way through the marshes. It was hard to know what to think. I tried to help, but there wasn't much I could do with one machete, a bogged motor in piranha-infested waters and no clue where the hell I was. I would grab trees as we inched by and pull us along the marshy bogs, hoping that my helpfulness would negate any intentions to hack Canela and I up with a machete if he ended up being a weirdo. After hours of fighting the vines and undergrowth of the jungle, our boat finally was freed from the unyielding heaps of the backroads of the Amazon, and we motored freely along the wide-open murky waterway.

Once the sun went to bed, a whole new set of creatures came out to play. The pink dolphins eventually stopped their barrel rolls on the crest of the water, and the many songbirds began to rest, but nighttime on the Amazon was anything but peaceful. The nocturnal noises were almost deafening as we putted along, only guided by Willy's super strength headlamp and the moonlight that highlighted the details of the river. We were looking for caiman, which was basically a slightly smaller crocodile and only detectable by red eyes beaming from just above the water's surface reflected from our headlamps. Just being out in the wild was thrilling enough, but as Willy ran from stern to bow with no warning, throwing his body halfway over the side and arms into a bog of grass, it was quite the surprise, especially when he came back with a tiny baby caiman!

The diversity of this place was beyond words. Over the next couple of days, we explored hidden lagoons that were home to the river otters, spent the afternoons watching the sunset from the boat as the dolphins circled around us, and my favorite (NOT Canela's favorite) was when we took a kayak out on the river and came across a tree that hosted a family of wooley monkeys. I sat in the back of the kayak and would paddle in to be closer as she tried her hardest to back paddle against me to avoid the monkeys deciding to jump in our kayak with us. They were so curious and seemed to be putting on a show, but I will agree that the big one did seem a little put out and maybe was a little threatening to Canela as it charged down the limbs to within inches of our plastic kayak that offered zero protection, but regardless, no one got rabies, and it was funny as hell.

At night, we would retire to the heights of Alta Vista in our beautiful treehouse. Canela would pass out from a healthy dose of Benadryl to soothe her many mosquito bites while I lay in my bunk, writing. The clicking noises in the rafters of the tree house were a dead giveaway of my little bat friend that dive-bombed his way into our refuge, and I knew Canela would not be impressed by our guest when she woke in the morning. The little bat skirted the mosquito nets and the perimeter of the tree house like a fighter pilot with his keen radar, allowing him the ability to explore our little piece of the world. This place was absolutely beyond words. I was enchanted by the life in this refuge. For a magical sanctuary so remote, there was nothing but vitality emerging in every form. Trees beside the running water bear more fruit, and I was so thankful to have chosen such a miraculous place for an adventure. The fruit from my memory tree are the stories I will tell of dreams that actually came true—in that tree house along the banks of the mighty Amazon.

Wanderlust Diaries: the Jibaroo Village Visit

After spending our Amazon time by day in a boat and by night in a tree, it was good to put our feet on solid ground. The jungle heat was intense, made worse by the relentless mosquitoes that seemed to care less about my attempts to deter them with repellent. I had put on enough DEET insect repellent that my necklace had lost all varnish and the dyes in my clothes started to fade, but the mosquitos persevered. We hiked through the jungle pouring sweat but still enjoyed the diversity of our surroundings. The leaf-cutter ants carried foliage on their backs in a perfect line and seemed to be making the pilgrimage alongside us.

The village we were trekking to was rare, and the tribal members had dwindled to a mere ten people. They lived in a completely remote site isolated from the outside world, but Willy had arranged a visit for us. Not many ever see these people or care to learn about their customs, so I felt honored for the privilege to spend a day with them. After hiking for hours through the mud and thick jungle forest that we cleared with machetes, we finally arrived. It was a simple tribal community, and we were greeted with warm smiles and painted faces. Willy was our translator to a tribal member that spoke Spanish, who then translated to the rest of the tribe into their native tongue. It was like playing the telephone game, where it went from me saying something to down the line, and finally a reaction, and a reply to make its way back up to me. I had asked about their bright orange face paint and what it represented, and I think something was lost in translation as the chief came to me with some sort of exotic fruit that he chopped open and dipped a twig into the juice to reveal a bright orange liquid. Without hesitation, he drew a design on my face that resembled a cat as the rest of the tribe clapped and smiled.

They offered us a shell of a coconut that was filled with some sort of drink. It had constituents of palm tree and maybe some banana, but it honestly had the consistency of snot, but it was rude not to drink it. Putting off the offering any longer wouldn't help matters as the juice heated under the blazing sun. The women squatted on the ground and began to take plump, wriggling grubworms and squeeze them to release a fat, but it somewhat just looked like guts to me. The ladies then skewered them on some sticks like an Amazonian shish kebab. The chubby little worms wiggled for their life, but after they were placed over a fire of burning palm tree trunks, one by one, the worms gave in and wiggled no more. Canela and I looked at each other, knowing that they were going to want us to eat them. They spent all afternoon preparing for our visit and probably picked these worms from the trees of the jungle; for us gringo girls to decline was not an option. The time had come, after a couple of hours of slightly awkward conversation and polite smiles, the worms were done; it was time to eat. We squatted down where they had prepared the feast displayed over some oversized banana tree leaves. They had salt (thank God!), so I rubbed a little between my index finger and thumb webbing and took the worm like a tequila shot; I tossed the grub in my mouth and licked the salt from my hand, then lifted my arms in victory as if I had just won a marathon. I hollered at Canela as I saw she hadn't reciprocated the action, but she was too busy laughing. It wasn't bad, but the next one I placed between two slabs of yucca plant and just told myself that it was like a Peruvian tapa. We picked at the meal for long enough that we weren't rude and started to plan our departure technique as I managed to gulp down the last little bit of snot juice in my coconut bowl. I was not forewarned of the hospitality custom that if you do not immediately return the bowl upside down that they will refill it, and that's exactly what happened. I was mortified as the tribal hostess scurried up to my bowl and filled it to the brim. After another bowl of whatever gooey juice that was, we finally said our goodbyes and headed back.

It was a long hike through a tiny jungle footpath. We learned later from Willy that the juice they had served was not juice, but their version of beer, so it was no wonder that after two heaping helpings of this fermented craft brew, we were quite giggly and wobbly on our way back. This was our last day on the river, and I gained a new respect for the mighty Amazon. The biodiversity and the way all the living creatures worked together to live in harmony was insightful. The dangers were almost insurmountable, but the way the locals allowed nature to take its course and work with their surroundings instead of against, it was inspiring and something to learn from. I had enjoyed our time on the Amazon, and leaving our beautiful tree house, we would have a constant reminder of our stay—in the form of a million mosquito bites, but the itch would eventually fade, and the memories could never be diminished.

Wanderlust Diaries: The Sacred Valley Peru

Flying into Cusco, it felt my head was still in the clouds from the extreme altitude. Canela and I loaded bits of coca leaves under our lower lips like a heap of snuff to help remedy the light-headedness. The city was truly amazing. We did the normal tourist "must-dos" of walking the streets of Plaza de Armas and hiking around the Jesus Blanco while admiring the towering statue that looked over the city like a shield of protection. We bought the fun street vendor items and alpaca wool sweaters and danced to the salsa rhythms at the disco, but all this was biding time until the ultimate adventure of Peru—the one that needed no introduction, Machu Picchu.

I did not want the typical gringo trail or day trip from Cusco packed with hordes of tourists, so we took our time meandering through the outlying villages and eventually dead-ended at the final stop, Aguas Calientes. This small village was the choke point to one of the greatest wonders of the world. The train and buses all ended here, and Canela and I walked about the town and enjoyed what it had to offer, including ponds of natural hot springs. I would love to say it was surreal, but the reality was that this tourist trap smelled like pee and looked like broccoli soup, so after trying to rinse off this failed relaxation stop, we checked into our hostel. It was quite the Bohemian paradise with bright murals decorating every wall like a hippie canvas. The vibe was almost too chill as we hung out on the rooftop bar, where the bartender could not be bothered to get us a couple pisco sours because he was getting a freebie tattoo on the couch. But none of these things really mattered—what mattered was that the mountain was calling, and I heard my name.

The next morning, we woke at three in the morning to catch the first bus up to the sacred site. Words cannot express the beauty and was one of the most photogenic places I had ever been so blessed to lay my eyes upon. We were one of the first visitors, and the ruins were peaceful without the disturbance of tourists with selfie sticks. We took in every square inch of the place, including our prebooked hike up the tallest summit, Machu Picchu Montaña. The hike was strenuous. The elevation gain was unreal with over two thousand feet of accent up the unrelenting boulders that snaked its way up the mountain. At the top, we rejoiced because we both knew there were quite a few times we wondered if we would be victorious to the climb, though both of us were too proud to actually verbalize what was going through our heads and the pain in our knees. We conquered the day—it was truly a carpe diem kind of adventure.

As we boarded the train with our sweat-stained clothes and muddy shoes, it did not matter the disheveled hot messes we appeared to the outside world—to us, we were Inca goddesses who conquered the mountain, and we had the aching bones and photos to prove it. My head was still in the clouds, but it wasn't due to dizziness—it was because literally we were in the whimsical clouds that danced over this Incan paradise. This was one of the most spectacular places on earth, and it's a bucket-list item completed!

Wanderlust Diaries: Higher than I've Ever Been

A shuttle bus picked us up at the hostel at 3:30 a.m. for the day's adventure, the Rainbow Mountain. Vinicunca, also called Montaña de Siete Colores, was a mountain in the Andes of Peru with an altitude of over seventeen thousand feet at the summit. To put that into context, Mt. Rainier is a little over fourteen thousand feet, so I knew this was going to be difficult. The bus ride was nerve-racking as the driver hugged the turns on the narrow switchback, leaving mere inches between the tires and a giant cliff. I tried to just pass out to avoid thinking about how outrageous the driving was, but as the driver throttled through the washboard dirt roads, I knew sleep was unlikely, and I would just have to deal with the anxiety of this scary ride. Ironically, the driver had a Bob Marley CD playing on repeat for the five-hour journey; even though I wasn't convinced this bus was going to get us to the entry of the hike, I trusted Bob with his mellow Rasta vibes telling me, *"Don't worry, every ting gonna be all right."*

When we finally arrived after a bus ride from hell, round Peruvian ladies tried to sell coca leaves and coca candies to the foreigners to help them acclimatize to this extreme altitude. I already had my stash, but it honestly felt like my eyeballs were going to pop out of their sockets from the extreme headache I was suffering from. Canela had researched that Viagra has some inconclusive studies that suggested it helped with altitude sickness, and she had bought some just in case. After it seemed our coca leaves weren't alleviating our ailments, we popped a couple of little blue pills in hopes that it might take the edge off.

The hike was beautiful beyond words. We hiked through green pastures filled with alpacas grazing and drinking from the babbling brooks, and then the landscape changed to glacial snowy peaks. But despite the beauty, this wasn't what we came for, so we continued on. Six people that were on our bus had to stop for medical attention as trail rangers rushed emergency oxygen to them. I found myself completely light-headed and dizzy, but I had come too far to turn back. I think my body must have had a coping mechanism to deal with these extreme conditions because my brain was shutting down certain parts to help me continue. To keep my feet moving, my brain sacrificed certain things, such as my cognitive functions, sense of humor, and even my desire to take photos. To people who know me well, my camera is a part of me, and I was quite the shutterbug; to choose not to take a photo to conserve energy was a sure sign I wasn't myself. The trek looked more like a pilgrimage of zombies with the many tourists unhurriedly taking each step in a sluggish and methodical manner. I had never walked so slowly, but this was the only way it seemed possible to keep my heart from exploding out of my chest. There were a few medics that made their rounds on the trail, and when they would do a check, I would reply, "Mi Corazon es bien" even though Canela and I were averaging 170–180 bpm on our fitness watches. We could see the top of the arid colorful mountain, and we were such a short distance from our goal, but then it started to snow and sleet; the little ice chunks pelted our faces. Going only about fifteen feet at a time between breaks, we finally made it.

The hills were like a watercolor painting from God with bright reds, greens, and yellows blending the earth together. I sat for a while, just enjoying the views, and finally got the gumption to snap some photos once the sun peaked from behind the clouds. My sunglasses hid the weariness in my tired eyes from the trek and were my only disguise to try to get a good photo of myself in this surreal place. You don't need drugs to get high in Peru, only a crazy bus ride, six-mile hike, seventeen thousand feet in elevation, and an adventurous spirit will do—and a wonderful friend that I love dearly!

This post is dedicated to a fiery, hilarious, free-spirited goofball that I am proud to call my friend—that "may or may not have" wore a fake llama head with a formal sequin gown for a photoshoot, had to deploy a rape whistle first night ever backpacking, and shit on an Incan ruin. I love ya, girl!

Wanderlust Diaries: Uros, the Floating Islands of Lake Titicaca

After saying goodbye to Canela early in the morning from her hostel bunk, it was time for me to head south and Canela to head back to Washington. As she rubbed her eyes in a half sleep and gave me a hug goodbye, I was very thankful for having her as my sidekick through so many adventures in Peru. I found my way to the bus station and loaded up for the next leg of the journey solo. The bus ride was very scenic, but it was hard to stay awake, considering the past week I hadn't been sleeping much. We stopped at the archeological site of Andahuayillas to see San Pedro's church, and Raqchi, which is an archeological site with ruins from the Incas. The narrow road led me between where the Andes split and through La Reya pass with stunning vistas. I was excited to get to my next destination, but as the bus finally made its way to my planned stop, I was a little concerned. Puno was a town that sat on Lake Titicaca on the Peruvian side. I was not sure what I expected, but ramshackle adobe brick buildings and garbage all over the street made the place seem a bit dodgy. I was lucky to have Wi-Fi on the bus, so I quickly searched for a hostel to plant roots in for a couple of days. In my query, one stood out among the other seedy-looking hostels—one that was located on a floating island made completely of reeds. Compared to the other choices, this was the obvious one, but now I was faced with the excitement of figuring out how to get myself and backpack to this seemingly mystical place. As the bus parked and we unloaded our bags, I took refuge in the tiny office of the bus station to collect my thoughts and plan my next move. Hordes of taxi drivers stood outside the door as if a riot was to ensue, beckoning for me to take their taxi. It was quite overwhelming, so I took a few moments to practice some Spanish words that would hopefully get me to a boat dock that would lead me to Uros floating islands. As I took a deep breath, I exited the door and picked my driver, hoping he could understand my broken Spanglish.

I was a little nervous as the place he brought me to was nothing more than a rocky beach with a narrow dirt pathway leading to the water. I had no idea what was going on, but through my little understanding of some key words from the taxi driver, the boats from the port had stopped running an hour ago, and he wanted me to wait. To wait for what, I was unsure, but I didn't have many options. A few minutes later, a small boat with a family pulled up to the beach and motioned for me to come aboard. They had been fishing, but I was in luck that they were headed in my direction and, unbeknownst to me, were the owners of the place I was going to stay at. I loaded my bags onto the tiny boat, and we were off. The sun was setting over the Andes that surrounded this grand lake and cast beautiful pastel colors over the sky. I was in complete heaven as I snapped photos of the islands. As we pulled up to where I would call home for a couple of days, I knew I had made the right choice.

This island was made completely of reeds, and as I stepped foot in the island, my foot squished into the soggy pseudo land. Little huts built of reeds and grass peppered the property, and as I walked about exploring the tiny island, it was the most bizarre feeling as my shoes squished through the boggy surface. I felt completely at home as Mama Elsa offered me tea, accompanied with a delicious dinner of maize sopa and fresh trout from the lake. This place emanated complete tranquility from the outside world. The warmth from the family welcomed me into their simple life on Lake Titicaca. The air was still thin, but my heart and stomach were full from such a great start to a new place.

Wanderlust Diaries: Mi Familia on Uros Island

I do not think I have ever slept better than my night on the Floating Islands of Uros on Lake Titicaca. The gentle waves rocked the anchored reeds and made slumber inside my thatch hut a dream. Mama Elsa had given me a rubber hot water bottle to warm my bed and a heap of alpaca wool blankets to bear the cold night. I met two girls that made for good company on this isolated island. Ella was a sweet girl from the countryside of England and had been traveling and doing some freelance English teaching along the way. Madison was a very driven Polish lady who had a strong entrepreneur spirit and was currently living in Southern Spain. I had so much in common with these girls, and we spent the morning atop the tiny lookout mirador post that overlooked the lake. We watched a spectacular sunrise, and the girls wanted to start the day with meditation. I wish I could be skilled in slowing down my mind in such a tranquil place, but I used the time to listen to the birds and the soft rolling waves. The occasional boat would be a slight distraction, but it was a special moment with two wonderful ladies in a beautiful place.

Ella and I took a ride on a reed boat with the husband of the homestay, Juan. He didn't speak any English, but I was lucky to have Ella translate how the reed islands were made and the day-to-day things that were a part of his life. He showed me the way the islands were anchored with their root system and how weekly they must cut fresh reeds and dry them and add them to the top layer. Eventually, time would take its toll, and the rotting reeds would sink the island. This happened about every twenty years, and they would just start over. Lake Titicaca was considered ancestral land, so if the locals belonged to the right lineage, they could make their own floating island for free. It sounded almost too good to be true, but Juan told me that this way of life was fading out as the children grew up and decided to move to the city or go to the university instead of keeping up with life on the Floating Islands. He suspected that within his lifetime or the next generation, the people of Uros Floating Islands would be no more. This saddened me but made me feel quite honored to have been a part of this and seen how special it was. Juan grabbed a fishing net as he spoke and untangled the mess of nylon and eventually cast the net into the water. This was going to be our dinner, so we were hopeful to catch a few trout.

We visited the school of his daughter, Sara-ee, the little girl I had grown fond of that picked me up in the boat. This little sassy girl was quite a lot to handle as she competed for my attention while I chatted with my new friends. I had taken the time to read her a story from this tiny book of Disney fairy tales she carried with her, trying to translate the stories in the pictures to the Spanish words I knew. She was patient as I narrated, as she smiled and corrected me with the proper Spanish words. I had drawn a fairy on some drawing paper, and as I helped her color it in, she became so upset that I colored the fairy's skin brown and hair black. It hurt my heart when she told me I had ruined the picture and the "hada es fea!" which meant the fairy was ugly. I insisted that brown skin was beautiful just like her as she settled for me drawing another fairy beside it with blond dreadlocked hair like me.

I had been blessed to spend so much time with this family and see how their life was interwoven in the reeds. I would miss their smiling faces as I traveled to Puno in preps for the next leg of my journey. My new hostel didn't have a sweet family that fed me fresh trout and maize sopa, but it did have Wi-Fi to help me organize my next route, and it was time to move on. Mama Elsa, Juan, and sweet Sara-ee and the stories of fairies and life on the reeds will forever be woven into my heart.

Wanderlust Diaries: Barefoot Bolivia Border Crossings

Rec-i-proc-i-ty (noun): the practice of exchanging things with others for mutual benefit, especially privileges granted by one country or organization to another. I had researched that Bolivia had a reciprocity rule to US citizens. Apparently, Uncle Sam liked to meddle in Bolivian affairs and had been overstepping his ground with the coca farmers and bribing them to destroy their plantations to aid in alleviating some of the US drug problem. The Bolivian government has had a hard time stopping Big Brother, but what they could do was make it extremely difficult for Americans to enter their country. By difficult, I mean most tourists from other countries just step right in and get their passport stamped free of charge, but not Americans. Besides the $160 visa fee (which was outrageous—I had never paid even half that!), I also had to supply passport photocopies, passport pictures, lodging confirmation, transportation confirmation out of Bolivia and proof of return to USA, yellow fever vaccination certificate, and even a copy of my bank statements. I had researched to some extent into these ludicrous requirements and was somewhat prepared, but it was hard for a backpacker with no real agenda to produce all this paperwork.

In Puno, I had booked a bus ticket with a reputable company that would allow me to hop on and off different locations throughout Peru and Bolivia, but there was a requirement in BOLD RED letters that stated I needed to confirm pickup twelve hours before departure. Just like in most sleazy South American hostels, Wi-Fi was quite spotty, and I had a hard time getting the website to confirm pickup at my hostel. As the clock was ticking, I finally got connectivity to book the bus, but it was not within the twelve-hour rule. I had asked the hostel clerk to call the bus company just to make sure I was good to go, but whoever said, "Si', Ella es bien," was a big fat liar. As I waited in the hostel lobby the next morning, I watched the clock tick past the scheduled pickup time. Anxious, I had another coca tea and tried to have faith that the big bus would come rolling my way any minute, but unfortunately, that never happened. After a grumpy phone call with my broken Spanish to the bus company, I learned my bus was on its way to Bolivia without me. I had two options: to take a local bus to the border and meet my bus in Copacabana or wait until tomorrow. I didn't want to wait, so I found the nearest local bus station that would take me south. These buses, or collectivos, were smaller but packed as many people as possible; when people wanted to get off, most of the time the driver didn't even stop, he just slowed down, and people jumped. With my big backpack and nerves on high alert, this was not the way I wanted to make my way to the border, knowing I already had another stressful situation ahead of me with the visa. The bus was jam-packed, and at one time, I had an elderly plump Peruvian lady with long black braids basically sitting on my lap; it was awful. The collectivo stopped one village short of the border where I found a taxi that would take me the rest of the way.

An English man, John, was somewhat ill prepared like me. We shared a ride with Hector, our eccentric cabbie, in his white taxi decorated with rainbow stripes and a hula Jesus on the dash. Things were looking up, and I was ready to get this border crossing over and done with. As Hector pulled to the curb at the border, I prepared my things. I decided I wanted to switch back into my tennis shoes from my flip-flops. I shuffled through my bag to make the switch, and as I was preoccupied, all of a sudden, I heard a loud "thud," and men screaming and cursing. Alarmed, I jumped out of the taxi, where John pulled me onto the sidewalk. Luckily, he had grabbed my bag from the trunk of the cab before all hell broke loose. Hector apparently was not well-liked in this border town, and when his taxi rolled up, his enemy happened to be there at a roadside shop, watching. He confronted Hector by throwing him against the cab, and when Hector escaped the angry grasps of his foe, he peeled out, leaving nothing but skid marks but taking something very important to me—my only pairs of shoes!

So there I was, barefoot at the Bolivian border. With no other options, I confidently retrieved my Peru exit stamp and marched onward to the next post. The Bolivian entry post was about a quarter mile down rocky pavement with the street lined with guards and a few locals still trying to sell their wares and Peru souvenirs. I kept walking like there was nothing to see, ignoring all remarks and keeping my eyes to the border. When I finally arrived with my documents in order, and after sliding the customs agents eight crisp twenty-dollar bills, I was in Bolivia, barefoot, but I made it. John and I had stopped for coffee and were planning the logistics on how to make it to Copacabana. I could not believe my eyes when a rainbow-striped taxi with a hula Jesus dash mount pulled up to the curb in front of the coffee shop. MY SHOES!

Hector had noticed that my shoes were left in the seat after the hustle at the border and had taken the time to cross the checkpoint with his cab to return them to me. Hector pulled up a chair, and we traded our coffees for three cervezas as he explained the drama in his personal life that led to the encounter. Hector even took us to Copacabana where I met my bus. In the end, everything that goes around comes around. Bolivia might be pissed that their coca farms are being destroyed, but they have my $160 and the joy of tormenting American tourists. Hector may have gotten roughed up for diddling the shopkeeper's wife, but he has his cab fare and good karma for helping a stranger. And then there's me. I may sometimes bend the rules and not follow instructions that led me to a Peruvian lady sitting on my lap, but at the end of the day, I have my Bolivian visa, my shoes, and a whole new country to explore. Reciprocity, it can be a real bitch, but it makes one hell of a story.

Wanderlust Diaries: Mi Gusta La Paz!

My bus dropped me off at the Wild Rover Hostel, which unbeknownst to me was the party capital. In La Paz, the city was full of color, life, and contradictions. I instantly fell in love with this wild and crazy place. Not minutes after dropping my bag into my dorm, I was caught in a whirlwind fiesta, which led to a few late nights partying with my new travel friends and some local Bolivians who showed us authentic La Paz. The bars served the local Pequeña cerveza as we became part of the crowd. With the good times rolling, three in the morning would come sooner than expected as I enjoyed being swept up in the frenzy that was Bolivia.

During the day, my two new Canadian friends and I would explore the town and put miles on the cobblestone streets exploring. Funicular cable cars dotted the skyline as a major transportation source to get the poor working class from the mountaintop vista of the city outskirts to the belly of the town. The plump Bolivian women with their vibrant clothes and rigid top hats would sell their wares on the sidewalks. Full streets would become host to local markets, selling anything from normal housewares to black market goods from the surrounding countries. The offensive smells from the witch market would permeate our nostrils as we walked past the countless booths selling llama fetuses and other oddities that would be used by the locals as an offering to Pachamama to ensure health and good fortune. Cholita lady wrestlers offered quite the show as they sported ringside events with WWE flare with the goal of bringing awareness to domestic violence as they pummeled each other and grabbed each other's long black braids.

After a long day exploring the nooks and crannies of this great city, it was assured a good time would be brewing at my hostel, where the cheap drinks and good times were always flowing. One night got the best of me with this intoxicating city as I stayed out much too late with my new Bolivian buddies. I had made it back to my hostel and set my alarm for the adventure the next day, Yungus Road. The road had quite the reputation due to its abnormally high death rate from thrill seekers wanting to conquer this feat. I had planned on mountain biking this dangerous road with a group from the hostel, but I awoke not to an alarm but to a hostel staff worker knocking on my dorm room. "Melissa, Death Road time. You're late!" Not the best way to wake up, but adventure awaits, and life begins at the end of your comfort zone.

Wanderlust Diaries: Israel versus USA on the Death Road

I woke to a knock on the door. "Melissa, wake up, you are late for Death Road!" Not the best wake-up call as I scrambled to throw on my shoes and throw a jacket over my nightshirt and shorty shorts. Grabbing my toiletry bag as I ran out of my dorm, I realized that my late-night party in La Paz with my new hostel homies and local Bolivians might not have been the best idea. I looked like a true American shit show as I tried to brush my teeth in the bus and remove the last night's makeup off my tired face as we headed out for the notorious Yungas Road.

We picked up a few Israelis from another hostel and set out for a once-in-a-lifetime adventure mountain biking down the "Death Road." I tried to grab a quick catnap on the bus, but the boisterous Israelis speaking in their Hebrew tongue was loud enough to wake the dead and did nothing to help my hangover or need for sleep. When we arrived at the top of the mountain, I was very thankful for the provided jumpsuit that covered my nightclothes so my shameful beginning to the trip was less apparent. Even with a headache, I was not even half the ass as the Israelis who completely disregarded every safety rule and request given to us by our patient guides. The Israelis acted like buffoons and were given the pet name "Jardi'n Infantils" (the kindergarteners) by my new Austrian friend who provided comic relief throughout the day. The group naturally split into two. Myself and four guys were in the lead, but the Israelis were hours behind us from crashes and damaged bikes. Some were too scared to finish the course and rode the shuttle bus.

The Yungas Road was the connecting road from La Paz over the mountains to the Bolivian Amazon, and the waterfalls, rivers, and hairpin turns on the rocky dirt road made for quite the treacherous path for all who dared to take it. It was given the nickname "Death Road" due to the abnormally high death rate from the many thrill seekers who biked the road or motorists who failed to successfully make the pass. White crosses lined the road as a remembrance of the ones who were left behind and sent chills down my spine as I did my best to hold on to the handlebars as I navigated down the steep slope that was full of boulders and cracks in the earth. The hangover was long gone as I turned my brain over one hundred percent to focus on safely making it off the mountain. I finished fourth out of eighteen people, which was not bad, especially considering the group of Israelis was over an hour behind us.

Me and my new adrenaline junkie friends, who were coined the names Austria, Columbia, Chile, and Australia, celebrated our ride with some beers while we waited for the "Jardi'n Infantils" to make it down the mountain. It was a great time, and my new friends and I continued the party on our long drive home on the bus. "Columbia" was a boisterous fifty-two-year-old police officer that was in better shape than all of us, and his loud laughter and charades to get his point across was not taken kindly to by the Israelis who slumped in their seats, battered and bruised by the ride. We all sang to the music on the radio in high spirits that was dampened by the uncalled for remarks from the pouting Israelis. One girl piped up in her phlegmy Hebrew voice and started rattling something at us, and then finished her sentence with "Shut the f—— up" directed to my Columbian friend. Maybe politically the USA and Israel were friends, but not that day on the bus—that day, Columbia was my Allied Force, and I didn't take lightly to disrespectful behavior, especially after the antics the Israelis projected all day with no respect for the group, the guides, or even their own life. I hurled back some remarks to put them in their place as the levity of the bus ride turned sour. We continued our merriment but had to make a bathroom stop once our cervezas kicked in. As I progressed through the narrow aisle of the bus, the mouthy Israeli girl pulled my dreadlock braid as I passed her. Without a moment to think, I quickly karate chopped her throat and grabbed her nappy hair and bashed her face into the seat in front of her. As I saw nothing but red from the audacity she had to touch me, she had her fair share of red as her nose poured blood down her shocked face. My buddies in the back began to chant, "USA! USA!" I just glared at her with my vehement green laser eyes and slowly exited the bus as her friends tended to her nose.

In Israel, the men were forced to do a three-year stint in the military, but apparently, that wasn't enough to teach them discipline, or even manners for that matter. So if the military can't teach them, and the Death Road couldn't humble them, then by God an American blond deadlock woman was glad to put them in their place. Don't fuck with USA. (PS: I'm really not crazy. She had it coming.)

Wanderlust Diaries: Chasing Butch Cassidy into the White Oblivion

Starting from the small desert town if Uyuni, with not much more than tumbleweeds and packs of stray dogs, I joined a group of travelers on an intrepid adventure. We had multiple Toyota 4Runners with our dirty backpacks strapped to the roof rack as we set out to one of the most beautiful and fairy-tale places I had ever seen. The landscape was vast and for the most part untouched by tourism. Our local drivers raced through the dunes and salt flats as if we were in the Dakar, leaving nothing but tire tracks and a whirlwind of dust. The next few days would be very rough on the body but great for the soul.

The ivory salt flats extended beyond where the eye could see, and we played like children in this magical place, taking hundreds of photos with fun perspectives. We hiked islands within the flats that were oddly populated by cactus and surrounded by mountains. We enjoyed a spectacular sunset, drinking a few Bolivian Pequeña cervezas to celebrate the day. We slept in run-down shacks, shivering, but knowing the price was worth the reward of this virgin landscape we were a part of. The next day, we would climb to the higher altitudes that took its toll on many with some needing oxygen to handle the perilous atmosphere. I chewed on coca leaves and drank my weight in water, but it was difficult to adjust. I tried to just ignore the draining feeling on my body and focus on the beauty I was surrounded by.

We traveled past lagoons filled with vibrant flamingos and the warm nothingness of the Salvador Dali desert. We took our trusty Toyota trucks into the belly of a massive caldera, using the bowl of the volcano as a berm for out 4WD as we passed by the spewing geysers. One night, we found a hot spring, and despite the frigid cold outside, we lounged our aching bodies in the warm water while the night sky danced before us. Shooting stars and the galaxy seemed to be superimposed over the millions of twinkling stars that were not polluted from the lights of civilization. There wasn't a moment that my heart and soul were not captivated by God's creation. I experienced the lifestyle of an intrepid traveler over those past few days. A part of me knew that this wild and raw manner of travel wouldn't last once the country became more developed and the tourism industry had actual infrastructure. I knew how lucky I was to experience unadulterated Bolivia.

Wanderlust Diaries: San "Perro" de Acetama, Chile

I wasn't sure about the dusty town as I walked from the bus station loaded down with my pack accompanied by my other travel buddies I befriended in Bolivia. This town was pretty much one street that consisted of a few shops and a couple of restaurants, but by the end of my time in San Pedro, this adobe ramshackle desert village would dazzle me beyond belief and leave a luminous glow on my trip, not only from the billions of twinkling stars in the desert sky but from my friendships created in this little oasis.

Lucas and Mia were Aussies, and almost instantly from our meeting in Bolivia, we became friends. We made meals of local avocado and mango in our chill hostel hosted by the beautiful Alejandra, whose smile resonated from the walls of the bohemian refuge. A highlight of exploring this place was when we rented mountain bikes and rode twenty kilometers out of the village to the Valle de la Luna (Valley of the Moon). The desert sand dunes mixed with the geometric rock formations and moonscapes made this place unbelievably surreal. The terrain was tough, even causing Lucas and Mia to take a tumble, but we found something very special at the top of the trek.

As we took a break for lunch, a lone stray dog came up to us and plopped at my feet. She stole my heart as I offered her water to satiate her thirst from the desert heat. She ended up following us the entire way home over the rugged terrain and acting as our tour guide as we explored caves and caverns of this magical place. I worried about her little paws as she trotted along back to the village on the hot asphalt. I named her Luna, and this sweet creature would not leave my side for the next couple of days. The hostel eventually gave up on making her go outside, for every time the door opened, she would dart in to find her new companion (me!). I even gave her my tie-dyed bandana to set her apart from the numerous other strays that wandered the streets of San "Perro." The mini market must have wondered why in the world a crazy blond girl had bought packs of hot dogs every day, but Luna loved the special attention, and I loved her.

When the sun went to bed, the village truly glowed from the lights of the universe blessing us with the majesty of the night's sky.

Since it was so spectacular, I decided to go on a group outing for an astronomy tour to see the constellations and galaxies in their full glory even further away from the village with zero light pollution. The small village had a myriad of options, despite the tiny town. The constellation tours were just as important to the lifeblood of the town as the markets. I decided to go with an economical option half the price of some I had seen advertised, and the owner said I could bring my sidekick, Luna, along for the adventure. Little did I know, the budget tour was no more than a local man that escorted us to his backyard in the countryside, but I enjoyed it regardless. The local man's name was Jose, and when we wiggled out of his Astro Van that also doubled as his family car, he showed us a silly science video in Spanish on their living room TV. Our "tour" group then was escorted to the backyard where we hung out drinking wine while Jose showed us things on his fancy telescope and pointed out the different constellations with a high-powered laser. It was actually pretty chill as I sipped my vino and petted Luna, watching meteors zip overhead and bedazzled by the abundance of stars that glittered the sky.

Unfortunately, I knew I had to leave this desert paradise, but I would be leaving something very special behind—I left a giant bag of dog food and a Facebook friend request with Alejandra, who promised to take care of sweet little Luna and send me pictures, and I left my new friends Lucas and Mia that I shared so many experiences with. I knew I would be seeing them again one day. Some people imprint on your soul, and you know it is never really goodbye. Adios, San "Perro" de Acetama. You treated me well!

Wanderlust Diaries: Bright Lights, Bear City

Checking into my new hostel in the Bellevista district of Santiago, I could not have felt more at home as a gaggle of Brazilian rugby players cooking meat on the grill insisted I take some. A Chilean boy, Vincent, poured me his concoction of pisco and Mountain Dew. It was quite the welcome wagon as we sat on our hostel rooftop balcony, overlooking San Cristobal and the beautiful city, except I didn't speak Portuguese, and the Brazilians didn't speak a lick of English as they persistently queried me about American football (soccer). Vincent was different from the rest of the guys and patiently translated and became my amigo for the night. As we chatted, I absolutely loved this guy and his flamboyant mannerisms. He had the ability to have an in-depth conversations with me after we had just met hours ago. I felt comfortable with him, and after he had dropped a few clues of his alternative sexual orientation, I felt even more at ease with our newfound friendship.

Santiago nightlife didn't even think about starting until after midnight, so after a quick bite to eat and some more piscos on our roof, it was time to hit the town. Vincent cracked me up when I asked if my jeans with holes was okay to wear, but he abhorrently objected to my flip-flops and insisted I changed. In tow alongside us was Gabriella, a gorgeous Brazilian chica, whose afro and leg warmers reminded me of something Cher would wear. As we paroozed the endless venues of nightclubs in our barrio, Vincent was set on a certain one that promised a good time. But as the line to get in seemed so long, my patience grew short, and I asked him why we couldn't just go in the one next door with no line. He blushed as he responded to me that it was a "gay bear" place. Assuming it was just a language barrier and he meant gay bar, I assured him I didn't mind, and it would be fun, but he kept telling me I didn't know what I was asking for and that he was correct in the wording with gay bear. Finally, after getting nowhere with our disagreement in lingo, he typed into his phone what a gay bear was, and I saw that this was ACTUALLY a thing. A Gay "Bear" was a way to identify the masculine types of the LGBT community. The men dressed up in manly costumes sporting their well-groomed beards and rugged outfits. This sealed the deal for me as I insisted we give it a go.

As we entered the club, hordes of men wearing anything from a sexy grizzly bear thong to a tailored lumberjack getup populated the dance floor. And if one floor of dancing bears wasn't enough, this club had three floors that alternated music between electronica, pop, and disco beats. I ping-ponged my way through the dance floor as I was requested by many of the bears for selfies as they probably wondered what the hell I was doing there. Vincent kept close, as if I was his party favor that he didn't want to share, and we danced the night away. I was worried that my Fitbit had malfunctioned as it started to buzz and chime at 1:30 a.m., but it was actually because I had already gotten my steps for the next day in. Moreover, the night was still young! I moved and swayed to the Latin rhythms and was very thankful to recognize some of the songs from my Zumba classes, where the exaggerated moves not only fit in here, but we're encouraged. When an American song would come on, you would have thought I was a Beyoncé backup dancer from my excitement in understanding the words to what I was dancing to.

The night was a blast, and there was no better start to my time in Santiago. My travel day went from the empty deserts of San Pedro de Acetama to an underground discotek full of sweaty dancing bears and a new friend. As we stumbled our fabulous asses back to the hostel, barely missing sunrise, Vincent confided that he has never met an American girl like me, who would have hung out in the bear den all night and felt so comfortable. Even though part of the night was fuzzy, I knew I would not be soon forgetting the friendship I had with Vincent and our escapades of the night. I barely beat the sun from beaming into my hostel dorm, and I slept well, knowing I put a good mark on Santiago and my night as the den mother to my Latino sleuth of dancing bears.

Wanderlust Diaries: Central Chile and the Cool Shit I Did

As the days passed, I had pondered how to clump all my exploits into a cohesive story, but I was at a loss. But a quick recap could include dancing, human rights museum culture shock, a hike up to San Cristobal, and driving a shitty manual rental car to Valparaiso that put the hills of San Francisco to shame. I climbed and jumped over a ten-foot-tall castle wall, met the beautiful and smart sister to my Chilean Zumba instructor, and met up with my travel buddies from Bolivia. Whew, a mouthful! So now to put some detail, because I love to overshare, here is how much I loved Central Chile.

I already shared my first night of dancing the night away in the gay bear den—it set the bar high, but the rest did not disappoint. I took a walking tour where I met "no-Facebook Celia," an Aussie that I knew was a kindred spirit. Chats never skipped a beat, and before I knew it, I had invited her to join me in my rental car to the coast, which she agreed, but first, we took a moment for some history as we visited the human rights museum. I want to preface that I felt like a complete moron for not knowing what all had recently happened in Chile, but to my defense, these things were not published in US history books, or at least not the whole story. If you have an inter-est for history, look into the Pinochet dictatorship and the torture, mass killings, and even the part the US played, but this is too deep for my diary post. It made me think of how history repeats itself and some parallels with where we stand as a country now. The next day, Cecelia and I were off in my hooptie rental car that didn't even have an RPM gage and barely made it up the mini hills of the Andes Mountains that encompassed Santiago. We stopped at a few wineries before entering the madness of Valparaiso. The bohemian sector I was drawn to was a small segment of the bustling port town, and just as Celia complemented my driving among the craziness, a taxi came alongside me and took off my driver side mirror. We weren't hurt, so I laughed it off like a mad woman as I assured my reluctant passenger that I was getting my money's worth from maxing out the insurance on this POS car. We explored the city, but as the night dragged on, she returned to Santiago on a bus as I headed north to the scenic beach town of Viña del Mar.

I checked into my hostel, which was actually a remarkable old castle with tall fortress walls. It was really thrilling as the owner gave me two skeleton keys and showed me to my chambers for the night. It was only me and two Argentinians that were traveling the country on their motorcycles. The castle innkeeper instructed that he would be leaving for the night but showed me around the premises. It was really fantastic staying in a castle, but the next morning, I might have reconsidered. I had plans to meet my Zumba friend's sister that lived in town, and I needed to leave early, but no one was on site to let me off the grounds. I used my set of the skeleton keys to open the grand wooden entry door and laid my set of brass keys on the front desk as I made my way outside into the courtyard, followed by a loud clunk as the oversized door shut behind me. I walked through the gardens where I was stopped by the castle wall. *SHIT!* The gate was locked, and I had already surrendered my set of keys. I was locked out of my castle like a reverse story of Rapunzel. The ideas of my next move rolled through my blond head as I settled for a strategic plan to stack the lawn furniture into some staging to take me to the top of the brick castle wall fortress. This was not as simple I had hoped because to cross the ten-foot-tall wall, I first had to plant the cushions from the patio furniture outside the wall to make a landing pad. I was not built like a puma, and jumping was not my forté. I wanted a soft landing when I screwed it up. But alas, after much to-do, I jumped over the castle wall with my pack and was off to start the day.

I headed north to have breakfast with my Chilean Zumba instructor's lovely sister, Elizabeth, but I hit another snag. My offline maps do well 90 percent of the time, but the other 10 percent when it decides not to cooperate was usually when I needed it the most. My frantic morning jumping castle walls had put me behind schedule with my planned rendezvous with Elizabeth. I had no way of contacting her, and the address we had planned to meet at appeared to be a bar that was closed until a more appropriate hour for drinking. There was an employee that was inside sweeping the floors and organizing the books, and he reluctantly unlocked the entry door to hear me out as I tried to ask for help navigating to the intended coffee shop. My Spanish was obviously terrible as I could assume he thought I was desperate for a date and wanted his phone number when all I was really wanting was to borrow his telephone to call Elizabeth. After the employee slipped me his phone number and tried to shoo me out so he could finish his morning routine, I started roaming the streets, and luck would have it that I found the coffeehouse, and inside, it was patient and beautiful Elizabeth with silky brown hair and a genuine smile that matched her sister. For a blind date, so to speak, it was absolutely wonderful as we sipped our coffee and had a gigantic piece of cake for breakfast. After parting a great visit, I met my Aussie friends from Bolivia back in Valparaiso and eventually took my ragged rental car home to Santiago.

This was why traveling solo was so amazing. If you had no plans, it didn't matter which path you took, and I was lucky that mine led me to meeting new wonderful friends, great Chilean wine, beautiful sunsets, bohemian street art, and even jumping castle walls. You need no skeleton keys, only tenacity to unlock any adventure.

Wanderlust Diaries: Patagonia, the Blushing Bride

After I woke up from another crummy night's sleep in my hostel in Puerta Natales, I anxiously tapped my fingernails on my coffee cup, waiting for an acceptable hour to head to the Great Torres del Paine. Even though I was up early for the day, the Southern Hemisphere was slow to rise and took a while for the darkness of the early morning to disappear and dawn to take its place. I topped off my gas tank in my rental car, grabbed a few snacks, and hit the winding road that would lead me to my next adventure.

It was autumn in Patagonia, and a clear day was considered a blessing, but I crossed my fingers that I would get lucky. The long drive gave me time to address all the many thoughts that had been swirling through my head that I had compartmentalized until I had time to give them. It was radio silence as I hugged the turns and made my way through the eerie fog. Unfortunately, I was suffering from acute barotrauma in my ears, and I was dealing with only the sound similar to pop rocks inside my ear canal every time I swallowed. The altitude had taken a toll on my body, and even though I made it through the perilous heights in Peru and Bolivia, it was my left ear that was going to pay the price. My ear still refused to clear, and the sounds of every fluid in my head trying to escape was my only distraction to the long drive since I had failed to upload any songs to my phone. It was quite a melancholy morning with the mist, fog, and the deafening silence of my thoughts and rattling of my left eardrum. I anxiously waited for the Great Torres del Paine to present itself, but she stayed hidden behind the clouds and fog as if veiled from her impatient onlooker.

I admired all that was her beauty, despite not being able to see her striking countenance. Her body was the rolling foothills comprised of the plentiful colors of trees and grasses that displayed a rainbow of color. Her bosom was the rugged cliffs that were colossal, curvy, and harrowing to behold. Just as I began to lose hope of seeing the great tower and the face of my beautiful mountain, the clouds gave way. It was as if my beautiful bride had lifted her veil, knowing how patiently I had waited for this moment. Her wrinkles and laugh lines were the deep crevices that showed the stories of where she had been and the toll time had taken on her, and they were beautiful all the same. Her white hair was long and draped down over her body with the silky snow that covered the top. But the greatest beauty of all was her eyes—an artic blue that left me speechless as I returned the gaze into the stunning glaciers that capped these mesmerizing mountains. My mountain had reveled herself and now had offered herself openly to me like a blushing bride.

Adventure awaits, and despite the relentless snow and sleet pelting my face, I summited some of the most beautiful peaks I have ever seen, dipped my toes in the frigid glacier ponds that were hidden from the eye of the simple traveler and slept in a hobbit dome and refugios to shelter me from the chilly nights. Every moment that led me to exploring this fantastic place was worth the wait to spend time in solitude with my mountain. I only saw a handful of people during my time in the Chilean Patagonia, and even though sometimes loneliness would start to settle in, I assured my jealous mountain bride that my place was alone with her. I had been so lucky with many new friends along the way, and this was my time to reflect on the blessings I had been given and focus on the beauty around me—and to just BE for once. This time in utter solitude had been a time to understand what grit and gumption I had within me and how far I could push myself, knowing that at the end of the day, I had no one to lean on, and I had to figure things out alone. This feeling was not something I could obtain anywhere, and it has the ability to make me fold…or focus.

I would later learn that the following week, the park would be closed for the season. I was very fortunate to spend a few wonderful days exploring the beautiful trails and the towering heights of this spectacular place. Soon, my mountain would go to sleep for the season and awake to a new set of suitors, but now she was all mine without the hindrance of any crowds—it was beautiful. Patagonia, the place with zero Wi-Fi but the greatest connection with the nature around me.

Wanderlust Diaries: Fin del Mundo with Sully and the Shit Tanks

Leaving Torres del Paine, I prayed the few liters of gas left in the tank would get me back to civilization from the boonies. One last bucket-list stop was to see the penguins in the Straits of Magellan and to hit the "Fin del Mundo" (End of the World). As I ran for the pier, I was very disappointed as I just missed the boat, and away drifted my chances of seeing the silly little creatures in their Antarctic playland. Bummed, I took a load off at the adjacent pub and rested with a cerveza.

Sitting at the bar was a silver-haired Rasta man with dreadlocks as long as my own and a cavalier Sam Elliot sort of smile that looked at my pack and me and said, "You missed your penguin boat, didn't ya?" I replied back in Spanish, to which he put his hands over his ears and announced "I speak English" in a joking manner, teasing me about my broken Spanglish. After days of solitude and no human interaction, I thoroughly enjoyed the banter to which I insisted on speaking Spanish just to mess with him. My one beer turned into a few more as Sully, his fisherman buddies, and I all joked around the table. Sully was something else, and his uniqueness made me comfortable. He was always insisting that I could be his daughter from how alike we were. I asked him where he was from, as he was obviously not Chilean. His true hippie emerged as he told me it wasn't important where he was from—what was important is where he had been as he sank into deep nostalgia from his past decades of nomadic travels and crazy stories. Sully now ran a small fishing operation for sardines and various other fish in the Straits of Magellan, and I begged him to take me to see the penguins. He laughed off my request and teased me for being the silly gringo girl who wanted to pay money to go on a crowded boat to see penguins. We ended up with a bet where Sully said he would take me if I won. The bet was on who had had the dirtiest name for a boat they owned. I thought I had this bet in the bag with my previous sailboat, *the Bearded Clam*, but sure as hell, Sully had me beat with *Between Her Legs*, as we all laughed and livened up the dank bar that smelled of fisherman boots.

As we parted ways, Sully took me aside and said if I was a good cook and would be at the dock bright and early at 4:30 a.m. that I could join his crew for the day; in return, I only needed to prepare lunch for the boys. You could bet that the next morning, I was there on the pier with a sack of groceries, ready and willing to take on the Straits of Magellan with my new fishing buddies.

The day in the straits was more than I bargained for—instead of a crowded tourist boat with a mass of penguin lovers, I had my crusty old fishing boat, *Between Her Legs*, which smelled of sardines and the salty sea air. The decrepit boat had the essence of adventure and good company. I saw more than my fair share of penguins, so I kept my end of the bargain and started a giant kettle of clam chowder in the mess decks. As my clam chowder simmered with some of the freshest seafood possible, I couldn't help but notice and off smell coming from somewhere nearby. I was horrified that one of the guys would come down and think it was my cooking, so I started to investigate the rancid aroma. With my nose as my guide, I found the offender—the sanitary tanks (a.k.a. shit tanks). The top of the tank was massively corroded and had an area that was completely disintegrated, leaving the foul smells to permeate the people space. I asked Sully what the deal was, and he told me that they had a backer plate to weld on top but hadn't had the time or patience to deal with their welder that came with English instructions. He knew the tank wasn't pressure tight, but as long as his nets were full of fish and the boat still floated, he was completely content and couldn't be bothered with small details like an open shit tank.

This was one of those uncanny moments where I felt I could offer more than just a tasty clam chowder and funny gringo comedic antidotes. I knew how to weld, and I knew I could interpret the manual to Luis, who seemed to acquire all the side jobs on the boat that involved maintenance. Within a few hours, we had the weld prepped and grinded, and a new backer plate installed on the tank, and it was time for lunch. I spent the rest of the afternoon helping with the catch and enjoying being on the water with my new friends. I listened to Sully go on with his existential beliefs and tried to see the world through the eyes of a salty dreadlocked sailor. Sully (*a.k.a.*

Bunny Eye) even gave me my own Rasta name, *Little Bird*, and told me to use it and think of my day as a sardine fisherman on the edge of Antarctica. I proved to be more than a silly blond gringo with my skills in the kitchen and with my handy welding abilities. Sully offered me a job on his rusted-out boat, but I declined the offer. The world was big, and I still had a lot to see. It was memorable day at the Fin del Mundo with my salty seamen on the *Between Her Legs*, and I thought I was only going to see some penguins!

Wanderlust Diaries: Ice Ice Baby and Mas Montañas!

After my hikes in Torres del Paine, my body was pretty wrecked, and upon arriving in laid-back El Calafate Argentina, I kind of just wanted to relax. That was hard to do when I had so little time and so much to see—and the mountains were calling my name. The Argentinian Patagonia was much different from the fierce and brutal Torres del Paine in Chile. The Andes Mountains deflected the storms from crossing over into Argentina, so while I had been fighting the insane winds, sleet, and snow in Chile, over in Argentina, there was not a cloud in the sky over the snowcapped mountains. It was complete winter bliss, and I knew I couldn't just let a day slip by without exploring this Patagonian wonderland.

I started with a trek to the Perito Moreno Glacier, which was one of the biggest attractions in the area. This glacier was a part of third largest ice field in the world, topped only by Antarctica and Greenland, but what made it very special was that it was not receding like other glaciers but advancing. I could not settle for just seeing this spectacle but rented some crampons and proceeded with a specialized guide to navigate a trek on top of the glacier. The feeling of digging my spikes into the ice and hearing the crunch with each footstep was thrilling, and the view from the top was even more magnificent and worth the adrenaline rush of hoping I didn't slip and slide down the treacherous path. I was the Ice Queen on the glacier, and I made this magical place my kingdom as I explored the deep crevices and ice-blue caves. I was even treated with a whiskey at the end of the trek, that was topped off with a hunk of ice I chiseled from the beautiful glacier.

The next day, I refused to sit idle as I traveled to En Chaltén; this oasis was known for some of the best hikes and picturesque landscapes. The mountain hosted quaint villages nestled into the hillsides that served as a refuge for the most spectacular treks imaginable for an adventurous spirit and shutterbug like myself. The reputation did not disappoint, as I set out to the iconic hike of Laguna de los Tres, or Fitz Roy. Every kilometer was another postcard-worthy moment with the fall colors decorating the hillside, but the paramount focus could not be stolen from the diva in the background that demanded all my attention, Fitz Roy. There she stood, center stage with the blue-sky backdrop, and the sun as her spotlight, shining on her perfect image that was my ultimate goal for the ascent. To get close to her was quite the challenge as all the mud and rain created an icy path, but it was worth it as I slowly made my way to see her up close and personal. The ice and snow managed to completely rip my shoe in half, removing the sole from my boot, but I managed to fix it with a hair tie—nothing was going to stop me from my backstage pass with the mountain. It was as if I was the mountain's biggest groupie for the day's concert, and I was hell-bent on crowd-surfing my way through the hillsides to get to the front, despite any bruises that might come my way.

I eventually boulder climbed to the beautiful lagoon that she kept special for only the most determined hikers, considering it was over ten kilometers one way to her grand vista. When I arrived to the summit, it was worth every slip and fall I took along the way as I sat on the icy earth, admiring her beauty. Like a siren, she beckoned me to take a dip in her frigid glacier waters, but I settled for dipping a toe in to avoid becoming a permanent ice sculpture to the landscape. This would be the last mountain I would climb on my Patagonian adventure, and it ended on quite the high note.

Wanderlust Diaries: Buenos Aires and a Tango through Time

I usually do not like the big cities; as a traveler, they served their purpose as hubs to get where I needed to go. I always tried to pick up the city vibe, but there was something very special about this place. My first day started with a check in at my hostel which was almost impossible to find. Once checked in, the gracious innkeeper kept telling me I was just in time for "Asada" and had to join in with the other travelers. My tired ears kept hearing "Sodomy" with his thick Argentinian accent, and I wondered what kind of place I was in for, noticing all the boisterous youth surrounding the communal table. After the confusion cleared and we laughed off my misunderstanding, I was just in time for dinner, which included all-you-can-eat carne and wine until the wee hours of the night. At one point, I looked at my watch, and it was after one in the morning, and the grill was still smoking and our glasses were full. Buenos Aires had a reputation for parties that lasted all night, and then the partygoers slept all day. I settled for half of that plan with enjoying the festivities and waking with only a couple of hours of sleep so I could explore the city. I learned so much about the history, and this was where my love affair with this place began.

Just like the iconic tango, my day of exploring began with mixed emotions, but by the end, I was fully captivated in the embrace of this city. The ease of walking the boulevards made me comfortable with the surroundings as I was drawn in closer and started to want to know more about my mysterious dance partner. I was educated in the history of past conflicts, revolutions, and victories. I learned of the stories of the people and how demonstrations in the plazas where I was standing were monumental in shaping this country. The silent memoirs played in my head of Evita singing in Plaza de Mayo and gave me reverence to seeing how one person could change the world and the face of a nation. The echoes of her voice rang in my head as I continued my dance through the decorated streets. The intensity of being drawn in so close made me see hidden symbolisms with this multicultural place. The breath of my partner was the salty sea air from Puerta Madras, which was the gateway to millions of immigrants that arrived at the port with hopes of a new beginning and shaped the essence of the city. The city has had many partners that have all left their mark on this place, from the obvious Spanish influence, the French city design and architecture, and the quaintness of Italy with the food and cafés. I reciprocated the sensuality of the dance with this city by exploring every inch of its body, and no parts were off-limits. I explored the poor areas of La Boca that were the foundation of the working class and the opulent parks and houses of Recoleta that was home to the most affluent that made their fortunes from trade and meat commodities. I headed south to San Telmo to the old cobbled streets and found myself in the heartbeat of Palermo, watching the dancers and listening to the Latin music pulse the night air.

Buenos Aires became more than just a big city to me that day. It was my dance partner that I learned from and gained a better understanding of the culture. I may have been wearing tattered jeans, flip-flops, and my messy hair held up in a bandana, but in my mind, I was adorned in a red dress with a slit up to my hip and heels as I allowed the city to captivate my heart and set my soul on fire. Once the dance was finished, I yearned for more, but the song was over, and it was time to go. But the tango never dies—it lives in your heart forever, and I know this will not be the last dance for me. I will return when I have more time. But until then, Buenos Aires, thanks for the dance and my tango through time.

Wanderlust Diaries: My Life as a Traveling Buscar

Yes, you read the title right, but first, let me explain the *WHY*, and then I will explain the *HOW*. I woke up early for my flight from Buenos Aires. Travel days, I had my routine of nicely packing up my pack and separating the liquids and getting all my documents in order. I was all set to go, but I checked my e-mail one final time before leaving for the airport, and the subject line from Aerolineas Argentinas read, "Your flight has been canceled." This did not bode well for my travel plans. As I prayed this was a mistake and tried calling the help call centers, I realized that I was out of luck and that there would be no flight no. 3088, and I would not be arriving in Rio de Janeiro that day. I was appalled. I searched other airlines for flights, but their fares were outrageous, and I refused to spend that sort of money for a flight.

As I steamed in the hostel common room, chance would have it that when one door closes, another one opens. This is when Paulo, a handsome Argentinian fellow, walked into my life. He didn't speak much English, but his kind smile and bright eyes were just the antidote to this frustrating start of the day. Over some tea, I explained the audacity of how the airline would cancel my flight mere hours before I was scheduled to leave, and even though he probably only understood a fraction of my rant, he patiently offered me comfort with his sincere kindness. He was in a travel dilemma himself, needing to get to Rio de Janeiro as well, but he could not afford the expensive flights and was worried he was going to miss his brother's wedding that was upcoming. This was when I knew my unfortunate situation might have happened for a reason. It appeared to be two paths of complete strangers were cosmically connected and merging into one.

I quickly did a search on the web to price out a rental car. I checked to see if the price for dropping off the car in a different country would be astronomical, but to my surprise, there happened to be a company that offered a reasonable rate. Looking at the drive time, it was quite a haul, but I knew this was my only good option for getting to Rio in a time frame that could get me to my connecting flight back to the States. With hopes Paulo would be onboard, I pitched my harebrained idea of renting a car and splitting the costs. I could tell he was interested, and after calculating out his finances, he agreed, and we were off to pick up our car for what would end up being one of the most comical and ridiculous two days of my life.

I was intrigued with Paulo's traveling style. He carried a small backpack, but his main luggage was an old-time-looking suitcase that seemed to be an antique with wooden handles and a woven design over the aged framing. I had never seen a traveler use a suitcase such as this, and I found it quite interesting. The drive was fun at first with unexpected stops in Uruguay and the colonial towns, but as the sun went down and the journey became miles of highway, we grew quite weary. Conversation had dwindled past the fun topics, and I was forcing myself to find new things to learn about each other that were easy to interpret with our language barrier. We stopped for coffee in a bustling town north of Montevideo, and I found us a small bistro table outside as I waited for Paulo. As I sipped my coffee, I watched Paulo open the trunk and grab his tattered suitcase. I gazed with curious eyes as he opened it to reveal a small accordion instrument. He traded his beanie for a straw hat, and he made his way to an adjacent street corner, where he placed his open suitcase on the sidewalk and began to play music for the pedestrians and onlookers from the nearby street corner.

I watched in complete bewilderment as my roadie that I had been getting to know for hours just unveiled such a huge part of who he was. I sat there with my jaw wide open. I was intoxicated with the cheery melodies coming from my friend. After a couple of songs, he packed up his gear and headed over my way with a fist full of crumpled bills that he handed to me and said, "For gas." It all made sense to me now. Paulo didn't have a lot to offer monetarily for our trip, but he wanted to make sure his share was covered, which was why he had planned on earning a little extra along the way. The next leg of the trip, I was so excited about this side of Paulo. Conversations never went idle as we blared the radio to his playlists and made plans for the next coffee stop. His solo act had now doubled as I insisted to be a part of the action as lead vocals and tambourine. We used the drive time that previously was pretty monotonous as our practice sessions for the next "gig" to earn some gas money. From his playlists, the only songs I knew were Bob Marley and the one Blondie song "One Way or Another," which became our closing act because of how badass it sounded on an accordion and my dreadhead belting the lyrics on the South American street corners.

I was sure our drive took almost twice as long as it should have, but traveling through three countries with Paulo, an accordion, and a tambourine were some of the most ridiculous and epic days of my life. As we parted ways, I was so sad to say goodbye to my Argentinian vagabond. Our merged path diverged into two again as he waved adios. When I arrived to my hostel in Rio, I checked my e-mail—there in bold on a subject line from my favorite airline was the subject: *Flight status confirmed, new booking.* Apparently, my hostile e-mails to the customer service of Aerolineas Argentinas had not gone unnoticed, and they had rebooked me a different flight into a nearby airport and even upgraded me with a complimentary snack pack of roasted peanuts and a beverage of choice. *HA!* Thanks, but no thanks. I wouldn't trade my days as a traveling buscar for anything, and you can keep your peanuts.

Wanderlust Diaries: Rio, Favelas, and Friends

Wow, upon arriving in Rio de Janeiro, I had never seen so many tanned and beautiful people congregated in one spot. It would seem that all these sculpted bodies would somehow create a black hole in the universe from the unfairness of this many Adonis bodies in one location. The only unfortunate part of being surrounded by all these beautiful people was that the common language was Portuguese, of which I spoke none. My hostel roommates would use Google translate every morning to wish me a good day and tell me I had pretty eyes and hair; it was absolutely adorable. I was pretty stoked about soaking up some sun on the sandy beach of Ipanema, which was only one block from my hostel.

As I prepared my little piece of heaven on the sugary sand, I realized that I was in the midst of a fashion faux pas. My tasteful one-piece bathing suit had no place on this beach, and seeing how I was the only person not wearing a bikini with the bottoms riding up my butt crack, I feared being not only ridiculed but possibly extradited out of Brazil for such an egregious error on my part. I honestly would have been more comfortable sporting dental floss than what I was wearing. I quickly addressed the situation with using some scissors to cut out the middle section of my suit, but while the top seemed to look quite nice, the bottoms looked dreadful, and every time I would run from the surf, I was like the blond dreadlocked version of the Coppertone Girl, trying to hold up my saggy makeshift bikini bottoms. While the Brazilian men seemed to be carved from obsidian, the women, on the other hand, came in all shapes and sizes, so my few extra curves weren't noticed.

While I sat on the beach, a young fellow, Joao (the Portuguese version of John) asked if he could sit with me, and I was pleased to meet my first Brazilian friend. We talked for hours under the hot sun about everything, and he educated me about the current realities facing Brazil. I didn't ask his age, but he couldn't have been over twenty-four, but this didn't keep him from many life experiences. On his dark skin were cuts from a few weeks ago when some bad guys of a favela robbed him, and after taking his money, they jammed a broken beer bottle into his skin. Apparently, Rio was in the midst of a pseudo civil war that started from the police integrating into the crime-riddled favelas, which was not taken to lightly. Gunshots in the streets were common, and the corruption in the city armed criminals with M16s. After weeks of traveling, dodging metaphoric bullets with the shenanigans I frequently found myself in, I had to be extra cautious in Rio. There wasn't one local I had spoken to that didn't have their own story about the notorious favelas and how it wasn't a joke. Some tourists were known to roam a favela to see the way of life, but I couldn't bring myself to do that. The gringos taking photos of the poor like they were animals in a zoo didn't sit right with me, and I refused to take part in exploiting the less fortunate. I found my peace on the beaches of Ipanema, where there were no traces of war, only ice-cold caipirinhas on the sun-kissed playa with my new friend.

Wanderlust Diaries: The Redeemer, Redemption, and Reflections

Rio was full of iconic things to see—from Sugarloaf Mountain, the famous mosaic steps, the favela of Santa Theresa, and of course, the epic guardian on top of Corcovado Mountain, the Christ the Redeemer statue. I hit all my bucket-list stops, so of course, it would only be prudent to celebrate the evenings in the samba capital of world by keeping hydrated with sweet and tangy Brazilian caipirinhas.

I met a few guys from Turkey and was flattered when they offered a night out on their massive yacht moored in the prestigious Gloria Bay. I was just excited to meet someone who spoke English, but the offer to hang out on a yacht seemed like something from a Hollywood movie. I was given permission to extend the yacht invite to some of my hostel homies. My hostel had a routine of free caipirinhas cocktail hour, and it was there that I was going to see who wanted to join me. My Brazilian dorm mates were a given, as I tried to communicate the invite over Google Translate, in the same manner in which we had frequently had to converse with one another with casual conversation throughout the day. I was sure I had a taker from my bunkmate, Antonio, who was a handsome boy in the prime of his youth with tan skin and muscles that showed what a prime specimen of Brazilian genetics he was. A perfect smile caught between his cute dimples was all the translation I needed that Antonio wanted to join me for the night as he continued his translations on his smartphone. As I sipped my free cocktail, Antonio motioned for one last Google translation before he headed upstairs to get ready. "You ready to go" the translation read, as I told him to give me fifteen minutes more minutes to finish my socializing. Antonio headed up to the dorm to get ready as I organized the last few friends that were to join me on the yacht. After fifteen minutes passed, I did not see Antonio, but I needed to grab my purse from my locked bunk bed storage. My new friends joined me to my dorm room for the last errand, and as I turned on the light, I was shocked to what I saw on my bunk bed.

Apparently, the Google translation that Antonio had meant of "are you ready to go" had nothing to do with going anywhere as he was under the impression that I wanted a "go" at him and his Adonis Brazilian body, as he lay naked in my bunk bed, covered by my white sheet. My other friends laughed as I stood paralyzed in the doorway, not knowing how to handle the translation faux pas. I still needed my purse, so I motioned for Antonio to get up as he used the sheet as a robe to cover his sculpted body while I rummaged through my bunk and retrieved my purse. I waived adios to Antonio as I headed out with my friends who had no idea what had just happened in my bunk.

It was quite the get-together as we boarded the massive yacht in Gloria Bay, just me and my crew, and about one hundred of the Turkish gentleman's other intimate friends. I was excited nonetheless, despite the outing being more of a boat party than a sophisticated night on the bay. We finally returned to the port at five in the morning with a boatload of crazy memories to remember the night. From gazing at the massive Redeeming Cristo that protectively loomed over this intoxicating city to probably needing redemption from a night of wild and crazy debauchery, it was a full day that couldn't have been filled with more life.

Blame it on Rio, but this was a wonderful stop full of nights I probably wouldn't remember with friends I would never forget. As I headed to the airport, I looked up to see that beautiful statue perched on the hillside, and it made me think of many profound things. I knew wholeheartedly how lucky I was for a safe journey, especially with the manner in which I traveled. I thought of the many friends I made along the way. No matter where we all washed up in life, we had some very special moments together. Though I might not see many of them again, except for on Facebook, we would always have some spectacular memories. I was forever grateful to have met them—each played a significant role in making this a fantastic adventure. I saw some pretty amazing things. Whether sleeping in a tree house in the Amazon, ripping through the desert of the Bolivian Salt Flats, or hiking to the towering mountains of Patagonia…the real adventure was just enjoying the journey and allowing myself the ability to let life happen and not be inhibited by too many plans. I didn't pack a guidebook on this trip—only relied on intuition and banking that good people and good times would come my way, which they assuredly did, in abundance. The lesson in these past few weeks was to know things can go from ordinary to extraordinary at a moment's notice, but I had to have my eyes open. Life moved pretty fast—if I blinked, I might miss an opportunity for greatness. As I gave one last look to the Cristo, his open arms cast over the city made me think that he was not only the Redeemer, but a REMINDER that this world was full of adventure and to take advantage of the time we had and tackle each and every day with gusto. You never know what life has in store.

I conclude with this, there are many reasons out there why people don't seem to follow their dreams, but I had been blessed to make magic with travelers who were older, poorer, busier, and much less fortunate. Don't consider your situation any different or something that holds you back. Never let excuses or other people's influence on what they think you should be doing dampen your spirits because, in the end, we only have one life to live, and there are many roads untraveled and friends you haven't met yet. If I listened to the voices of others, I wouldn't have half the stories in my memory bank account. Whenever I leave this world—whether it is on an Argentinian sardine fishing boat off the coast of Antarctica, or lying in my bed at eighty years old, I was guaranteed I would be rich with experiences from things I have seen while surrounded by amazing people from around the globe. Also, don't be fearful of living outside your comfort zone—a comfort zone is actually the most dangerous place of all, and my metaphor to the high altitude deserts of Bolivia. While I enjoyed it thoroughly, the reality was it is hard to breath, and nothing grew there.

Even if you tiptoe, take that one step forward every day that scares you, and do not settle for a life that is less than the one you are capable of living. This trip, I suffered injuries, canceled plane flights, damaged rental cars, and half of the time, I barely understood what people were saying, but there was no misunderstanding the universal language of friendship, kindness, and the thrill of doing something you've never done before. I wouldn't have traded one moment of it, and I chose to redirect difficult circumstances into new opportunities for adventure. Like the Cristo watching me from that beautiful hill as I finished my journey—live your life with open eyes, an open heart, and open arms, and good things will happen…or at least be one hell of a story.

CIDER COUNTRY ENGLAND, EASTERN BLOC EUROPE, AND A LITTLE MIDDLE EAST AND AFRICA

It was time for another session of cider school. A trip across the Atlantic was a perfect excuse to pack my bags for another epic adventure. I had over a month of vacation days, and I was up for anything. I had traveled to a few European destinations, but there was something about the Eastern Bloc countries that seemed a little more "rough around the edges" and piqued my interest. I wasn't quite sure where this trip was going to take me, but I had started to get a crazy high from flying by the seat of my pants with no agenda, so the fact that I was too busy to plan and make an itinerary didn't matter... I didn't want one anyway. I spent the free time I had before my trip to produce a healthy cider stash of kegs for my cidery accounts and was excited about another chance to see the world.

Wanderlust Diaries: My "Ticket" to Ciderland

After my Boeing 777 touched down in London, I beelined to the rental car counter. An older man with gray hair and pink pants was having a meltdown with the clerk, arguing over a few quid for his rental while flamboyantly waving his hands about like the inflatable swinging arm man at the local tire shop. He warned me to be prepared to be ripped off, but when it was finally my turn, the sweet young clerk that was interested in my trip to cider country upgraded me to a Mercedes sports car with a built-in navigation system. As he tossed the keys in my hands, Mr. Pink Pants had returned and paced frantically behind me to complain about something else. After I tossed my bags in my shiny new Mercedes, I attempted to personalize my ride by getting the radio and navigation set up to take me to the heart of England.

Changing the radio from the stodgy BBC proved simple, but the car seemed to be from the future with buttons, dials, and joysticks. I couldn't figure it out and even had to ask the rental car clerk to help me. Once on the road with my right-hand drive beauty, I found how agile and fast she was. As I cruised down the motorway, blaring London's Top 40, I found myself behind a Porsche that I deemed my pace car. We sliced through traffic like a bat out of hell. I felt like Charlize Theron in the *Italian Job*, but the euphoric feeling quickly diminished when I passed a police car. What made me feel sheepish was that the patrol cars weren't undercover like in the United States. They resembled more of a circus rig with bright blue, orange, and neon yellow graphics, warning motorist not to speed. As I zipped past him and looked in the rearview mirror, it was no surprise when he pulled off the shoulder and lit me up with his lights like a Christmas tree. I had already made it past London, Windsor, and Reading, so I didn't have a proper shoulder to pull off on. I frantically looked for my hazard lights to acknowledge that I knew I was busted, but with all the bells and whistles on the car, it took me awhile to find the button. Once on the shoulder, with the officer tapping at my door, I continued the struggle of trying to find the damn button that opened my driver window. You would think it would be obvious, but the button was among the many options on the steering wheel. As the officer peered in at me, struggling with his request to open my window, I found the button for the windshield wiper sprayer, sending a healthy dose of soapy water directly into his face. I wanted to laugh out of the absurdity of what just happened as

I giggled inside at the dripping wet policeman, but as I finally got my window down, the only words I could muster was, "Sorry, Officer, you looked hot."

The officer in his nicely pressed uniform with new water splotches and brimmed hat tilted his head to give me a devilish look from over the top of his aviator sunglasses. I realized how my greeting must have sounded, so in my sleep-deprived state of mind, I quickly retorted with "I meant temperature hot, not sexy hot." His glare deepened at my ramblings, but I kept digging a hole. "Not that you are not sexy hot… I'm sure you are that too under your uniform, but you're probably married. Are you married?" *What the fuck, Melissa! Shut up!* I just kept talking, but to my bizarre luck, my nervous chatter entertained the officer who finally broke the awkward monologue with questions on where I was headed. I told him of my quest to Cider Country in the Midlands, and he seemed quite interested as he removed his aviators, showing me his placid blue eyes, stating how I was a long way from home. I followed suit by propping my sunglasses onto my head in front of my messy pile of dreadlocks and countered his stare, hoping that my slight suntan would hide the bags under my eyes from traveling all day. We chatted for a moment about cider, and the tension between us relaxed. The officer wrote down some things while managing to still hold a light conversation, and I wondered if I was going to get a ticket. It turns out, he did hand me a paper, but it was a recommendation of a pub he liked to visit with great cider in an adjacent town in Cotswold. As the cute officer walked away, my stomach settled out of my throat, and I reflected on what a dipshit I was, but it all worked out.

As I made my way to cider country, the long stretches of motorway turned into rolling hills full of orchards and grazing sheep. Hedges and quaint farmhouses dotted the countryside, and I knew I was almost there. This was my Disneyland, but instead of princesses and roller coasters, I was greeted with the Polish immigrants working the orchards with their mismatched flannels and sweats as they ran the machines. I didn't need the animatronics of a theme park to make me giddy, just miles of hedged carriageways and local taverns with half pints of cider the owners brewed in the back room. My accent and upbeat personality gave me an edge, and the locals loved to strike up a conversation with the transient blond Yankee that loved her cider. There was no better place than the heart of England during harvest season, and I had made it to Ciderland…and without a ticket!

Wanderlust Diaries: Life Lessons from Polish Tom

I was enjoying the cider school and learning many new things about sensory analysis and the complexities of fermentation, but there was one thing about the United Kingdom that had always befuddled me—the showers. If I could learn the way certain yeast strains can strip away amino acids and the chemistry behind it all for making cider, I didn't understand why the showers in England were so bizarre. There was a box in the shower that should have explained the power and temperature control, but as I stood in the shower, struggling to get the water to flow, it became increasingly frustrating. *Why have an on-and-off button that did nothing? Was this some sort of joke?* I scanned all the options at the mystery shower, but to no avail. I was staying with a friend, Jack, that I had met couchsurfing a couple of years ago. He lived in a village adjacent to my school, so I opted to stay with him again. This time, I got my own room, which was nice, but there were frequent transitory immigrant workers that crashed there who worked on Jack's family farm. It was "Polish Tom" as we called him, who came to my shower rescue to explain that this random string across the bathroom—nowhere near the shower—was the magical switch to turn on the water.

Polish Tom could barely speak English but knew the value of a hard day's work as he woke before the sun, milked cows all day, and returned home after the sun had set over the green pastoral hills. I frequently met him in the kitchen for coffee, and after our shower experience, we always found ways to communicate our plans and start the day off with a friendly smile. Every morning, I left Jack's early to catch a sunrise over a different little village and then make my way to school where I listened to my stodgy professor lecture. Even though he wasn't much for people skills, he was the best in the industry, so I bit my tongue as he seemed to demean the class with his rude commentary at questions he felt was beneath him.

At night, I would join my new friends to pub-crawl different English taverns, hoping for a pint of gnarly cider that I could bring back to class in a sample bottle that was secretly stored in my purse. The smellier or more rancid the cider, the better, and I hoped for cider faults that would allow me to explore the inner workings of lactic acid bacteria and the other problematic cider traits in the lab the next morning. The pursuit of learning more in my industry was unbelievably satisfying. As we get older and caught in routines, it seemed to be more difficult to teach an old dog new tricks. It was more important than ever to strive to better myself and open my brain to new ideas and learn from others. Whether it was something as benign as my lesson on English showers from Polish Tom or the complexities of advanced cider-making techniques from the balding professor in his tweed jacket, the act of learning kept me alive and from finding myself in a rut. The value of knowledge was priceless.

Live as if you were going to die tomorrow. LEARN
as if you were to live forever.
—Mahatma Gandhi

Wanderlust Diaries: Chance Encounters

I graduated my advanced course at the cider academy! I celebrated with a few of my peers by heading to a nearby town, Cheltenham. I hadn't planned on leaving Ledbury, where I was couchsurfing with my friend, Jack, but he fell ill, and it seemed like the stars were aligning for me to leave my quaint little village I had called home and celebrate with my new friends. We had some cider at a fun little pub, and everyone started to part ways, returning to their normal lives from around the world. I did not have a plan on where I was to stay for the night, but the new town seemed lively, and I was excited to explore.

My new Russian friend, Ivan, was staying in this town, and I knew there was the possibility of catching up with him, but as he needed time to pack his belongings for the next day, I grew bored of waiting on him and decided to tackle the town solo. I knew I needed a place to sleep, so I decided to try a Holiday Inn that was near where I parked my car. As I held open the door for a sweet elderly couple, I thought to myself that this wasn't really my style of lodging, but after couchsurfing for a week, it was acceptable to splurge on a hotel. When I got to the check-in desk, the lady behind the counter informed me that the couple right in front of me got the last room. Slightly disappointed, I cruised the Wi-Fi on Booking.com and found a hostel in the city center with availability—*perfect*!

As I meandered my way through the old town, I admired the architecture and took in the vibe of the city. Walking along a narrow cobbled street, I was startled when a young man with frizzy, curly blond hair that resembled a tan surfer came running out of a pub, yelling, "Melissa!" It took me a second, but on this random cobbled street, in a random town I decided to stop in, was my friend Tom that I had met in Buenos Aires a few months ago. Tom worked in the hostel I stayed at in Argentina, and we spent a few nights in South America laughing the night away, forgetting to sleep, with some of the coolest people from around the globe. I remembered the last time I saw him he was making out with a girl on the couch, and we laughed as we recollected the foggy memories with our current seren-dipitous chance encounter in England. He was home from Argentina and had just started working at the bar I was walking past that night. He recognized my blond dreadlocks and stopped everything to run out to greet me. I bellied up the bar and made conversation with Tom between his services to patrons. I noticed that many beautiful ladies were all dressed up in Halloween costumes and were taking their drinks outside and through an unmarked side door with only a small paper sign that said, "Feathers."

Curious, I followed them and made friends with a group of four that were all dressed up. We became instant friends as they found random bar items to fashion me a costume. Lucy was a fun-loving artist that was dressed as Maleficent with her curvy black horns fram-ing her delicate face. There was something about her with her sweet British accent escaping her crimson lips. I thoroughly enjoyed the company of her and my new group. It didn't take too long until I realized that this back door had led me to an underground LGBT party with costumes and karaoke! The night seemed to never end as we danced, and I took a turn at singing. I chose a song that always seemed to be a crowd pleaser with "What's Up" by 4 Non Blondes, and my alternative crowd made me feel like a rock star as they sang along, and I took turns passing the microphone to my groupies in the front, adorned in their creative attire. I was a hit after I belted out the melodies, and people requested me to sing their favorites from Lady Gaga, Queen, and even Whitney Houston. It was an epic night dancing with my tribe of ladies and random partygoers.

As time passed, as if our dancing bodies were standing still, I knew I had to go. After all, it was three in the morning, and I still hadn't checked into my hostel. I gave my girls giant hugs as I opened up my map on my phone to navigate to the place I had booked. The streets were quiet by now with just the rustling of animals of the night in the bushes lining the narrow streets. When I arrived, the door was locked, but there was a few people hanging out in the lobby area. A sweet young girl opened the door wrapped in a tattered gray blanket. As she let me in, I asked where the check in was, and her confused look on her plain face instantly told me something was off. She explained to me that this was not a hotel or hostel but, in fact, a homeless shelter for people with nowhere to live. I was flabbergasted because I knew I had the right address. As I told her that this place was on Booking.com, I instantly could feel myself listen to what I had just said, as if I floated out of my body and watched myself try to explain to the homeless girl wrapped in a dirty blanket that there must be some mistake because I booked this on the internet. After chatting for a couple of minutes, weighing my options, I learned her name was Eliza. She must have come from Liverpool or some-where up north because her accent was different from what I was used to. Eliza and a couple of others from the shelter did not have beds but were allowed to crash in the lobby. Eliza gave me a blanket and an offer to join her and her friends outside in an adjacent park. Apparently, a shelter regular, Peter, scored a pack of sausages, and they were going to have a small fire and enjoy the late-night snack in hopes of staying up all night and being first in line for a bed at the shelter the next day. I accepted the offer of the blanket and company, partly due to the chill in the late-night air but also to cover up my proper clothing that was a dead giveaway that I didn't belong.

I learned a lot from Eliza and her friends who joyously sat around a small metal trash can fire that Peter started, feeding the flames with litter from the street. Eliza was a real human interest story—nothing spectacular or bizarre that led her here, with no home and only the clothes on her back, eating a sausage next to a trash fire. She seemed relatively normal with only a story of a semibad upbringing, but she earned a scholarship to the local university where she met a boy. This boy ended up being her demise, she explained, as she suffered through domestic violence that caused her to quit her scholastic endeavors and lose everything to flee from him and his abuse. It was a sad story that oddly enough seemed so believable and real, making me thankful that I never had fallen in those same footsteps.

Quietly in my head, I diagnosed at least five mental illnesses in the group as I learned about them and listened to their stories, but what was lacking in the brain was made up for in the heart as they took comfort in one another's company. I desperately wanted a photo of Eliza to remember her, but showcasing my brand-new Samsung Galaxy S9 would have been poor form with the current circumstance, so I just told myself that her face would always be in the back of my mind. I felt guilt festering inside as I clutched my loaner blanket that smelled similar to a rodent cage. These people were not the druggies or crazies I would have passed them off to be—just people with a few bad strokes of luck. I left sweet Eliza with my blanket as I excused myself. With nowhere to stay, I found my car and leaned the seat back. I had a lot to think about as I faded off to sleep in my loaner Mercedes Benz.

It got me thinking about how random this world was. This day was a roller coaster that started with graduating my course, seeing my friend Tom, whom I had met on an entirely different continent, meeting my troop of beautiful ladies, and then sitting in a park, wrapped in a borrowed blanket with Eliza and her homeless homies. What if Jack would not have gotten sick and I stayed in Ledbury?

What if my cider friends chose a different pub to grab a drink and I never came to Cheltenham? What if I didn't hold the door for that elderly couple who got the last room at the Holiday Inn, and what if I wore a hat that night that covered my dreadlocks, would Tom have ever spotted me? Would I have never entered the bar where I met the girls that kept me up all night, failing to secure proper lodging, which is how I met sweet Eliza? My mind swirled trying to comprehend the randomness of this world. As daylight beamed through the tinted windows of my luxury rental, I looked over to where the shelter was—it was a YMCA shelter for the homeless, but the next building over was the hostel that was also a part of the YMCA that held my booking. I must have missed the sign in the darkness of night, but reflecting on what had transpired, I did not really "miss" anything but gained insight to a world I never would have known.

As I left Cheltenham, I reflected on how so many things happen by chance. Whether by fate or dumb luck, I had a great day. Life could be considered 90 percent planning and hard work, but there was that random 10 percent that you have no control over—the slice in life that can lead you to an all-night LGBT disco with beautiful ladies in the underground clubs of rural England or can leave you homeless eating sausages by a trash fire. That random 10 percent of chance can be everything or nothing at all. It is hard to believe in pure coincidence but even harder to believe it could be anything else.

Wanderlust Diaries: The Backroads to London

It was time to move on, but I was still enamored by the small time life in the quaint villages and hamlets of rural England. I opted to take the backroads all the way into the big city, which were mainly teeny tiny carriage roads barely suitable for one car, never mind the occasional oncoming vehicle. It was surreal, like something Thomas Kincade would paint, and you hang in your living room, imagining what it would be like to live inside the acrylic masterpiece. Each village had its own character, whether it be an abbey, thatch roof houses, or just miles and miles of green pasture with grazing sheep.

The shutterbug inside me had to be bridled when I noticed the clock ticking away. I had booked a cheap flight on Easy Jet for just twenty quid (twenty-five dollars), and this gave me a time limit to finish my Old World explorations.

So many people never see the side of England outside the normal London tourist Instagram posts. I felt obliged to capture them, if not only for my Facebook, but as a way to stop time just for that moment. After all, that's what photography was about—it was the only way we can momentarily stop time and give physical evidence of when at one time everything seemed to be perfect. The backroads were the way to go, especially considering my track record with speeding down the M5 and narrowly avoiding a ticket my first day in England. The backroads had wild hares playing chicken with my Mercedes as they sprinted across the road and a random collection of equestrians all dressed up in their riding boots, jackets, and hats headed out for a ride. I had recently learned from Ancestry.com that the tale of me being mainly Cherokee Indian and Irish was bullshit, and my roots were from England and Scandinavia. As I meandered down the country roads, I would secretly claim a farmhouse that in my imagination was my family homestead and build a connection with the beauty around me while thinking of how there was the possibility my ancestors plowed these fields and lit fires in the hearth of these homes.

I arrived at the airport hassle-free and boarded my plane to my next destination. The next airport was small and deboarded the tiny jet on the tarmac. It was nighttime when I arrived, but stepping off the plane, the humid air surrounded me like a sous vide cooker. I quickly was off in my new rental car and found lodging for the night. It was too late to find a place in the city center, so I opted for a small villa that was snuggled along the coastline with a handwritten vacancy sign. I finally got a decent night's sleep; knowing that a whole new place would be unfolded at daybreak made me anxiously await the morning. I awoke to the crashing of waves mere feet outside the villa. I draped myself in a white robe as I stepped onto the small balcony outside my room that was decorated with vibrant purple bougainvillea shrubs climbing the trellises. The mist from the

Adriatic Sea kissed my face as the sun glistened off the sand and terra-cotta roof tiles from across the bay. I had arrived in Croatia. Let the adventure begin!

Wanderlust Diaries: Shelter from the Storm

The off-season in Croatia had the perks of not being surrounded by hordes of tourists, but I gambled with the chance of bad weather. Leaving the seaside villa in Split, I was lucky enough to not have rain on my travels up the seaside route of the Dalmatian Coast, but the wind was engulfing and relentless! It was unbelievably blustery, and there were times I thought I might just blow away into the choppy Adriatic Sea. I had set my sights on the Plitvice Lakes that lie in the Balkan mountain region, neighboring Bosnia. The road changed from the beautiful curving coastal views to the inland mountainous region that was exploding with vivid fall colors. The road would burrow through tunnels, and I would play a game to see if I could keep up the melody of the song on the radio as the music faded out. I would consider myself victorious if I could keep the rhythm of the song all the way through the tunnel until the radio received signal and could play again on the other side.

Once in rural Croatia, I found it utterly charming that every couple of kilometers, a farmer had a stand on the side of the road to sell their honey and homemade cheese. It was bizarre because there was nothing around, but you could depend on seeing a honey stand every so often. I stopped for some cheese and even splurged on some honey, not sure what I was going to do with it in my backpacker life, but I appreciated the entrepreneurship from the remote farmers. I would pass through ghost towns with the remains of old building and churches, and the deeper I got into the countryside, I wondered, *Where is everybody?* A random car would at least put my mind at ease, but the scenery almost seemed postapocalyptic. I had doddled too long on the coastal road, so by the time I had gotten to the lakes, it would soon be dark. I decided to tackle the hikes the next day. There were no hostels I could find near the lakes, so I opted for a small rustic guesthouse. I again questioned where all the people were as I was unsuccessful at finding any sort of pub or even a marketplace to pack a lunch for the next day. Alone in my adorable little cabin nestled deep in the Balkans, I enjoyed the solitude while I nibbled on my newly acquired cheese like a mouse and decided to check my phone to see what the weather had in store the next day. I was alarmed to learn that AccuWeather had red alerts for tornado warnings in my area! The news had barely settled in as the lights in my cabin went out, and I was in complete darkness, deep in the Balkan Mountains, a stone's throw from the Bosnian border. There was nothing else to do but to force myself to sleep.

I woke up early to find that the storm had pushed the nasty clouds away, or at least momentarily, and this was my chance to explore the lakes. The tornado scare mixed with the off-season and my ridiculous morning wake-up time allowed me to have the park to myself. In my minimal research about the place, the only complaint from TripAdvisor was the sheer number of other people that clogged the boardwalks and made a photos seem less majestic with other tourists shoulder to shoulder, competing with the waterfalls for focus, but I would not have this problem. The place was absolutely enchanting. There were no other word to describe. The autumn colors were luminous, and a small gust of wind would send the bright orange leaves dancing over the trail like fall confetti. The waterfalls cascaded over the jagged rocks and complimented the lush green landscapes—it was pure magic.

Just as I was finishing the full trek around the entire park, a bus full of Chinese tourists emerged. They were loud and ruined my complete silence that was only interrupted by the rustling of the falling leaves and an occasional duck splashing in the water. I looked at the group from a distance and noticed how they reminded me of a Chinese army, armored with their selfie sticks and umbrellas as they poured onto the trails in an unorganized mess. The clouds grew thick, and despite the cackles from the new visitors, I could hear thunder in the distance. It was time to go, and I realized how lucky I was. It was as if God himself opened a small window over Plitvice Jerserka just for me and allowed me to explore his playland. Once I was done, the window closed, and the floodgates opened again, sending rain and flooding the trail with tourists.

I white-knuckled my way on the highway back to Split, where the unforgiving winds felt like it actually lifted my car up from time to time. I checked into my hostel where I met a sweet young man, Adam, who was a computer guy from Texas. He joined me for a walk through the old town exploring Diocletian's Palace and climbing to the top of the bell tower in the cathedral. As the wind whipped through the structure, I held on tightly to everything I owned and gripped the omnipotent structure with all the strength I could muster as the ferocious winds tore through the tower. We walked along Riva Harbor, watching the sailboats twist and turn in the angry sea. The sounds of the wind whistling through the numerous masts of the tossing sailboats in the marina was an eerie noise and was a physical testament to the power of Mother Nature. As I was admiring the swirling of the waves and the white caps off the boardwalk, a rogue wave crashed and completely drenched Adam and I from head to toe. We could do nothing but laugh as he cleaned off his glasses, and I squeezed out the salty seawater from my spongelike dreadlocks. It was no laughing matter when I returned to the hostel to see that my phone would not charge due to water in the charging port, but my hostel mates were like dear friends as they offered ideas on how to help. We sat in our tiny ramshackle hostel as the thunderstorm crashed around us, telling our travel stories as I performed surgery on my phone. It was the perfect shelter from the storm.

Wanderlust Diaries: All Aboard to Dubrovnik

There were a couple of travelers I met in the hostel in Split that wanted to head south to Dubrovnik. The sun was shining, and it was a beautiful day outside, and it would be a shame to waste it on the bus. I offered the thrifty travelers a ride, which they happily accepted. There was Mark, an Australian guy with beach-bum dirty-blond hair and a genuine smile that had been doing a workaway on a farm, and there was Victor, a petite Lithuanian with glasses and mismatched clothing. Victor didn't speak much but was very thankful for the ride; in fact, I think the only English he knew was "thank you," which would come out as "hank-yoo." Victor climbed in the front seat, sitting as erect as a pencil, holding his one backpack in his lap while Mark chatted with me about his workaway experiences from the back seat.

My GPS insisted that I hop on the A1 motorway instead of the coastal road, so I turned it off and let nature be my guide. With the Adriatic Sea on my right and the rugged mountains on my left, that was all the navigation assistance I needed as we meandered down the road, taking in the breathtaking views. I warned the guys that if they wanted a ride from me, they were going to have to deal with frequent photo stops, which they didn't seem to mind. Mark would get out and stretch his long legs. He was probably around six feet, four inches tall, and it would have made more sense if Victor sat in the back, but Victor kept his place in the front, hugging his back-pack with wide eyes. After a few stops at the jagged cliff top photo opportunities, I decided to have a little fun with the quiet Victor. As I pulled into a market, there was an obvious sex shop next door with neon phallic lights and pictures of sexy girls in the window that appeared to be faded porn ads from the eighties. Instead of pull-ing into the market parking, I pulled right in front of the sex shop and shut off the engine. I lifted my sunglasses to top of my head as I turned to Victor, still clutching his bag. "So...do you need any-thing?" I devilishly asked as I ignored Mark's cackling in the back seat and lewd funny comments. Victor just kept his eyes forward, as he replied, "No hank-yoo."

The road trip down the Dalmatian Coast was beautiful. There was a side shoot through the agricultural area in the mountains that seemed road trip worthy. We took a couple of backroad detours through the citrus orchards. We found many farmers with roadside stands, boasting beautiful vivid oranges for sale in bags and also com-plementing products, such as sun-dried tomatoes, olive oils, liqueurs, and grappa. I bought a few goods as I chatted to the lady who ran the stand as she explained why her sun-dried tomatoes were the best and how people came from all around to buy her tomatoes. Whether it was a sales gimmick or not, they were delicious, and I was happy to take some off her hands.

Back on the road, I was a little startled when I saw an official booth. I couldn't tell if it was possibly a tollbooth or some sort of police checkpoint, but as I drove up, a butch lady with short auburn hair requested our passports. I got them sorted and handed them to her as she solemnly stared at me and then began to inspect them and then applied a stamp. I sheepishly asked her, "We are still in Croatia, right?" as I hoped she would give me insight to why she was stamping our passports. She looked at me as she roughly handed them back, and with a gruff Eastern European accent, she shortly replied, "No!" I was in utter disbelief as she handed them back, and I drove away. *What the hell just happened? What country was I in? I know I took a little bit of a backroad, but did this road take me to Serbia, Kosovo, or Bosnia?* We all laughed as I motored along, and Mark sifted through his passport Visa pages to clue us in. About a mile later, we passed a billboard. *Welcome to Bosnia and Herzegovina.* In my lack of planning for this trip, I failed to realize that Bosnia had a small strip of coastal land that broke up Croatia, giving Bosnia access to the sea. Shortly after, we were back in Croatia, but it was worth the stomach flip to refuse GPS and see where we ended up.

I parted ways with my backpacker friends as Mark gave me a big hug, and Victor gave me a very awkward handshake and said his parting line of "hank-yoo" for one last time. The best part of road trips was not the destination but all the wacky stuff that happened along the way between the stamps in our passports. Some of the most beautiful things and people can't be discovered without getting just a little lost.

Wanderlust Diaries: Goldilocks and the Three Croats

As I arrived at Dubrovnik to my hostel perched on a hill overlooking the city, I was greeted by a nice man that saw me struggling to parallel park on a hill with my stick shift car on an adjacent driveway. The man was David, the son of the owner of the hostel, and his kind smile and attentiveness was very welcoming for the new city. I was the last guest for the season, and they were expecting me, but as I brought my bags up to check in, this was not like any hostel I had ever been to. As I opened the door, I was greeted by a happy black Labrador named JoJo and welcome hellos from an elderly man sitting at a dining table, enjoying some cheese and prosciutto. I was sure I must be in the wrong place, but as a short little woman scurried out of the kitchen, she welcomed me to Dubrovnik Backpacker Hostel.

That answered my question that I was in the proper place, but this was indeed someone's house, and this was indeed the family dog, and the man was indeed having lunch. The older man insisted I have a welcome drink as he offered me three choices of homemade brandy that they had made with various flavors. I enjoyed the sweet mixture of brandy and walnut flavors as the mother pulled out a map of Dubrovnik and showed me the attractions on their kitchen table. The attractions seemed interesting, but what was even more appealing to me is that I had seemed to be welcomed into her home. She explained to me that the downstairs to the apartment was the normal hostel during the high season, but they would soon be closed and were retrofitting the dorm rooms, so I would be staying in one of their bedrooms with the family on the top floor with a beautiful panorama view of the city. I could use the common room below if I liked, but I would be the only guest. Even though this seemed a bit bizarre, I thought of it as a cool experience to live with a family instead of a group of backpackers for a couple of nights, so I followed David for a tour of the house.

I learned there were six children in the family, three boys and three girls. All the girls had gotten married and moved away, but the boys all lived within the building complex. David was the only one who did not work for the hostel as he told me about his job as a teacher. He seemed to fit the bill with his pressed pants and nice sweater with a collar sticking out of the neck, but he was very kind and thoughtful as he offered to take me to a low-key brewery in the harbor. I had some things I wanted to see, so I told him maybe tomorrow, as I quickly was out the door to explore the Old Town.

I explored the relics of Old Town Dubrovnik and the castle walls, home to the *Game of Thrones* film set. It was beautiful, and a challenging hike to a fortress on the top of the overlooking hill gave me a brilliant view of the castle just as the sun began to set. The next day, I had booked a boat ride to three islands, and Mama of the house graciously offered up her youngest son, Jakov, to drive me to the harbor to meet the boat. I could tell Jakov was slightly hung over from the night before with his poorly managed facial hair and tired eyes. He was indeed the party boy as he offered for me to join him at a rave downtown that night for Halloween. I was certain it would be a fun night, and it was nice to know I had options on the table from one of the brothers when I returned from my boat ride. My timing to places must be impeccable because this was the last boat tour of the three islands for the season. The lack of enthusiasm was apparent from the weary young boys running the boat that only had the energy to mutter, "Fish or Chicken" during the entire trip, leaving me to my own devices to explore each island with the lack of tour information.

The first island we were dropped off on I was given a time line of three hours to explore. I followed a small sign that lead me on quite a difficult climb over the belly of the island and down the other side to the sea. I was certain I was lost as I stumbled upon many old grave sites only recognizable by out-of-place flowers and small stones. When I arrived to the "beach," I wouldn't call it a beach by any means, but it had some giant boulders that made up the entry point, and it was calm and peaceful as I enjoyed the waves crashing around me. I evaluated my desire to take a swim with the likelihood of anyone else challenging that hike and my options for swim attire. Unfortunately, I chose white underwear, which was not the best to disguise as a bathing suit, but the sea was beckoning me with each crashing wave to jump in, so I did.

The water was great, even for late in the year. I enjoyed swimming to and from a mini island off the coast. As I decided to head back in, I was shocked to see a few of the tourists from the boat had decided to tackle the hike after all and were standing on the outcropping of the massive rocks, staring at me. No one wanted to jump in for a swim, but they found it fun to watch me as if I was an attraction on their tour. I swam out to a little island and perched myself on some rocks to plan my next move, hoping the tourists would grow bored and leave. My white underwear swimming attire was a bad choice as the sea had made them basically translucent, so I sat there perched on my rocks in the Adriatic like a mermaid, intent to wait out the unwanted guests in my hidden cove. I started to worry about my timing to get back to the boat, so I gave in and swam to the giant boulders that made up the beach, giving quite the show to the Japanese tourists who watched me emerge from the sea and shimmy into my jeans and blouse. I would tell myself I was like a siren of the sea, trading in my mermaid tail for legs and Levi's, but I'm sure the reality was I looked like a hot mess scrambling about the boulders barefoot in my undies like an American fool.

Back on the boat, I made friends with some folks from England as I used the next two islands as places to scavenge fresh fruit of oranges, pomegranate, limes, and rosemary to make sangria from the boring red wine and Sprite on the boat. It was a great day, and now it was time to plan for the night. When I returned home, there was sweet David, and I knew my option of a low-key night at a brewery was my best option. I got ready and painted my face like a clown to celebrate Halloween as JoJo, the family dog, kept me company. When I headed to the downstairs common room, I was startled to meet the oldest brother, Luka. He was using the common area to preserve and paint all the wooden decorations in the hostel and had the table covered in his creations. We got to talking, and I realized that he was the artist in the family. I felt right at home as I grabbed a paintbrush and helped him paint.

We looked like quite the assembly line as David and Jakov walked in, surprised to see me with their brother painting away. I could tell I had a choice to make. I had tentative plans with David or Jakov, but I was having a great time talking with Luka. David and Jakov sat idle by the table, hoping I would grow bored with their brother and choose to go out with them. Conversations with Luka got even more interesting as he frequently would have parts of his life that were influenced by the war. I would nod as if I knew what he spoke of, but in reality, my only knowledge of the conflict stemmed from watching *Behind Enemy Lines*. There were times when his family didn't have water for over eight months and times when the family was separated, but with Luka being the oldest, he was the only one of the brothers with fond memories of how hard times actually were. It made me admire this family even more, and I was intoxicated learning about them. The more I saw in this world, the less I realize I actually knew, and it humbled me.

With our primer coats done on all the wooden decor, I had a choice to make. I could go have a chill night at a local brewery with sweet, reserved David, who was patiently waiting in the common room, where he had started playing a video game...or put my party clothes on and head out with wild Jakov, who had pounded a couple of beers—I knew it would be a crazy night. But then there was option three, where I would add a bunch of colors to my painting boards and paint bohemian mandalas on the wooden guitar that was ready for the next coat. I had already explored the heights of the castle walls and fortresses of Old Town and swam in the depths of the Adriatic Sea, so whatever option I chose was a bonus to a wonderful visit. One brother was too sweet while the other too wild, but at home with Luka and a paintbrush was just right. I was Goldilocks and the three Croats, and I found my place for the night.

Wanderlust Diaries: The Fortune-Teller of Montenegro

When you have to walk across an actual moat to get to your hostel, you know the place was going to be pretty special. The town of Kotor was first mentioned in 136 BC, but in the Middle Ages was fortified into an Old Town that was surrounded by high walls with the giant limestone cliffs, overlooking the city and the Bay of Kotor. I hit another jackpot with my hostel with being given a single room that was made of rocks and mortar. The Old Town was like a cobblestone maze with small alleyways connecting the restaurants, gothic cathedrals, pubs, and souvenir shops. It was fun to get lost and know that my tiny little hostel was lurking somewhere in this fairy-tale place.

The other hostel guests were from around the globe, but unfortunately, I recognized the accent of the most obnoxious one of all. With her platinum blond hair with jet-black roots, she resembled more of a skunk than a woman and was decorated with long fake eyelashes and a thick caked-on makeup face. As she giggled at the boy on the couch that kind of resembled an Abercrombie male model, I could tell she was a California girl, and I was right. Sometimes it embarrasses me when there were Americans that made asses of themselves to other nationalities, but I sat down beside them and played along with an odd drinking game that complemented the National Geographic deep-sea fishing show playing on the TV. Every time the narrator said "Tuna," you had to drink. It was kinda clever and silly, but the loud giggles and overly flirtatious maneuvers from skunk woman grated on my nerves. Looks aside, she seemed more hollow and fake than the cheap genie lamps being sold on the sidewalk, and I hated that her remarks about current events reflected on my country. I wondered how long they had been sitting on that couch doing this when there was a no-shit castle to explore right outside the doorstep.

That night, as I nestled into my little cave room that I absolutely adored, I realized that the stone walls could not drown out the god-awful voice of skunk woman. Apparently, she was honing in on a Scotsman that had the room right beside mine. I could hear their voices clear as day as she rambled on about how she hated her sister because her sister's cat ate her prosciutto and how much she LOVED Miley Cyrus's new song. I could hear the Scotsman talk about his childhood and going to a boarding school while the audacious skunk woman consoled him. It didn't take too long before the headboard was banging against the wall, and that high-pitched California girl accent was screaming "Oh my gawd" all night. I tried to muffle out the noise by streaming a movie about old Yugoslavia to take my mind off the ridiculous noises on the other side of the wall.

The next morning, I woke early and set off for an epic road trip through the mountains. The road consisted of over seventy hairpin turns and went from asphalt to construction zone, to something that remotely resembled a rocky driveway that led me into the oblivion of Montenegro. The harrowing heights of the sheer cliff on one side mixed with the fear that welled up inside my belly when a truck was passing head on was enough to get the adrenaline pumping as I continued the adventure. I ended up at Lake Skadar that bordered Albania and came upon an adorable remnant of a town, Stari Most. Passing all the ghost towns along the way made me wonder what the towns were like in their heyday—before the war. There was something eerie and completely captivating about old ramshackle buildings. As they stood being overtaken by Mother Nature, I wished those stone walls could talk. *Were they bombed, or did the family just move to the big city, leaving the building to rot away?* I would never know, but my imagination ran wild with the possibilities. I made my way back to the coast and enjoyed the scenic views of Dalmatia on the winding road back to Kotor.

Back at my hostel, skunk woman was at it again, flirting with a few guys while a couple of others were huddled around a computer. I was just so confused with these travelers. I tried to make some small talk, but this group was a bunch of duds. We talked of things they have seen in the Balkans, but mostly, they had barely ventured from the hostel and didn't have much to offer for conversation; in fact, they were more of a fun sponge. I felt like the vein of knowledge in an intellectual wasteland, so I decided to have a little fun.

I made up a story about my travel plans, and I told them I was headed to Bohemia in the Czech Republic to see my family of gypsies that were caravanning across the country and that I came from a long line of fortune-tellers. This grabbed their attention, especially skunk woman as she leaned in to learn more. I told her my specialty was palm reading and that I had never been wrong. She quickly asked me to read her fortune, along with some of the guys sitting around the hookah pipe. I scanned the group of guys, listening for that undeniable Scottish accent that I had heard all night through my bedroom wall. As the boys and skunk woman found themselves in a frenzy to who would get their palm read first, I heard the unmistakable voice of a fair-skinned strawberry-blond boy. He was to be my first fortune. I took a puff off the hookah that was packed with cherry-flavored shisha and blew the smoke onto his hand. I spoke of how he was from Scotland but had went to boarding school in England while his parents were trading goods in Madagascar. He was completely shocked on how I knew such things as he exclaimed to the group that it was all true. Skunk woman was now in a complete hysterics, begging me to read her palm. She handed over her perfectly manicured hand as I examined it and furled my brow. I spoke of disagreements with a sister and of a cat. I went on to talk about her love life and even threw in her similarities to Miley Cyrus but then I acted completely shocked as I started to follow a line in her palm, tracing to her dainty wrist adorned with a Pandora bracelet loaded with charms. I foretold that she was having health problems, to which she got a confused look on her face. The group was perplexed as everyone leaned in for my diagnosis. I acted hesitant and clammed up, but she insisted I tell her what I saw.

Taking in a deep breath and with my piercing green witch eyes, I revealed that her palms were foretelling a case of wretched herpes and that she needed to go see a doctor and get some antibiotics, quick! I could barely hold back laughter. It was the sort of self-control that hurt so bad my nose began to sting. She got a panicked look in her face as the guys sat there, speechless and wide-eyed. She exclaimed that it was not true, but I just replied, "The palms don't lie...only people do." To add insult to injury, I grimaced as I released her hand and applied my antibacterial hand sanitizer as she animatedly swore it could not be true.

I know it was kind of an asshole thing to do, but sometimes people are just too annoying, and it was my way of getting revenge for lost sleep the night before. My charade might have caused the skunk woman to be the "unfortunate cookie," but maybe she would get out and see some of the world instead of just the common room of the hostel or the sheets of her next conquest. That night, there would be no animal noises from the next room. I couldn't help but laugh at my antics as I posed as the traveling fortune-teller from Montenegro, and they believed me!

Wanderlust Diaries: Blast from the Past

The remnants of the war were evident here. As I arrived in Mostar, Bosnia, I noticed the chunks of concrete missing from the buildings that had been peppered with mortar shells and the eerie resemblance of what was a house with a mass of rocks and grout holding up a few walls that withstood grenades and missiles. As I made my way on an exploration over the iconic Stari Most Bridge that divided east and west Mostar, I was completely unaware of the history lesson I would be getting the next couple of days. The bridge had a story, along with all the people of the former Yugoslavia. I did not understand the language, but that was when I was blessed to meet Miran, the owner of my hostel, a survivor of the war, a Bosnian soldier, and now someone I would call friend.

In 1992, I was nine years old, Bill Clinton was my president, and I remember that was a time in my life when I thought I had a rough childhood. I was taken from my mom by social services and lived with my grandmother in Texas during that time. This was a chapter when I thought I was dealt a rough hand at life. However, the memories I had of that time included playing with my cousins in the street in the suburbs of Dallas, good old Southern cooking with my grandma's famous pecan pie, and the nasty cigarette smell that permeated her Oldsmobile interior cloth lining when she drove me to school. I barely watched the news, but I do remember every once in a while hearing the president give speeches about the "Serbs" and war in Bosnia, but I had no idea what all that meant, and it was a world away from me in my childhood. Miran, on the other hand, was sixteen years old at that time. His memories should have been learning to drive, finishing high school, and maybe dating girls, but instead, his childhood was something unimaginable. As he told me the story from the top of a mountain overlooking his childhood home, tears streamed from his eyes as if it was only yesterday.

Miran remembered that day in 1992 when the world stood still for him—when the first blasts from the Serbian army rocked his city and he was forced to leave his home. He was lucky to flee across the river to stay with a relative, but many of his friends were not so lucky and were sent to concentration camps where they were beaten, starved, and mutilated. To get water, Miran had to take canisters to the only available spring, but snipers would pick off innocent civilians just for sport. Miran and his family found ways to protect themselves with metal shields on their back to avoid shrapnel from the thousands of bombs exploding over their city every day. Miran's father volunteered to the front lines of the Bosnian army, and sometimes he could come home to see his family where he would try to save some daily rations of bread to feed Miran and his siblings. Miran would clean his father's AK-47 and wonder how it was possible that his father in the front lines had only had nine bullets for ammo. The Bosnian army was not primarily made up of trained soldiers, but citizens wearing their blue jeans and ball caps that scavenged whatever ammo from their hunting expeditions they could find. They were fighting a war on two fronts with Serbian troops looking to ethnically cleanse the country and purge out the Muslims while Croatia looked to side with Serbia to create new borders and increase their footprint in the former Yugoslavic territory. Bosnia begged for help—to anyone that would help stop the genocide, mass murders, and rape camps. But with the USA acting as the global police, Clinton was slow to act, and no other country wanted to overstep Big Brother, so they all turned a blind eye to the atrocities and human rights violations happening right under Europe's nose.

Now who was I to say what role the USA had on foreign affairs of this nature, but the brutal fact was that the USA had always chosen to meddle in the affairs of other countries, and they looked to our government as the peacekeepers. My world travels confirmed this everywhere I went. What was sickening to me was that we were ready and willing to send our troops to Afghanistan when there was incentives like oil, but when innocent Bosniaks were being murdered by the thousands, women raped, safe zones ambushed—the cries from the people were ignored. This went on for four years before peace agreements were signed. Thousands of people were never found, and it could only be assumed they were one of the lost souls occupying the mass grave sites in the countryside.

Miran and I walked about the city delivering vegetables from the market to his grandmother. I hiked the mountains and remote villages while he stopped to pray to Allah many times. This did not bother me. The man I walked with, joked with, and learned from all day was not my enemy, but my friend...no matter who he called God. Our differences were few but our similarities many as we discussed our views on work ethic, politics, and family. It got me thinking about how warped the world could be sometimes. Why do we create war and kill people to prove a point that killing people is wrong? And why are the leaders that oppose oppression the first that seek to oppress? Religious wars had caused so much death and oppression, but why could I see the good in my Muslim friend in one day and see that our beliefs were all based on fragments; no one had all the pieces put together, but we did what we could to be good neighbors, spouses, friends, and generally just good people. *Why can't that be enough?*

Reflecting on the past, there were things in people's childhood that would never be forgotten; sometimes it was the smell of fresh-baked pecan pie in the oven or else cigarette smoke in that old beige Oldsmobile. But sometimes it was the sound of grenades exploding, sniper fire ricochets, or women screaming in the streets. Whatever hand of cards you were dealt in life, be thankful, be resilient, and be strong. There are many people in the world that would die for what you have. I was thankful for my time in Bosnia with Miran. His friendship was like the mortar shell indentation on the buildings of Mostar, meaningful and forever impressed in my heart.

Wanderlust Diaries: Spider Webs of Blood and Honey

The Balkans got its name from the Ottoman word "Bal," meaning blood and the word "Kan," meaning honey. I had experienced the sweet side with wonderful people and the beautiful land, but the blood that was shed had left the Balkan countries in a time of transition, and I wasn't convinced this ultimate chess game involving religions and borders was over.

Before my travels, I had no idea about the political turmoil and the tragedies that occurred. This was not generations ago—it was in the nineties. From hearing the firsthand stories, it had forced me to research so many things that were just white noise before. I now knew Tito was not just a brand of vodka, but he was the beloved leader of the old Yugoslavia and the thread that kept the territories together and religions living among each other in harmony. After Tito, things fell apart as nationalism took hold, and one by one, each territory wanted their freedom. New leaders created divides with religion, which led to the mass genocides. However, the spider web continued when the USA became involved, spearheading the Dayton Peace agreements. Though this may have stopped the war, the newly formed countries now had a form of government that wasn't working and was unbelievably corrupt. Unemployment was high, and wages were low, so the educated people chose other countries of the European Union that will pay more and left. Slowly, the Balkans were deteriorating, and it was only a matter of time before the land of blood remerged.

I was no history teacher, but the facts made me dig even deeper. The Kosovo conflict, where the US enforced the bombings of Serbian forces without NATO agreement still had consequences, despite the statue of Bill Clinton that still stands in Kosovo. He might be a hero to some in the Balkans, but those actions in the late nineties were said to have fueled some of the animosities with the Red Giant, Russia. It was the Kosovo conflict that made Boris Yeltsin lose face with his compatriots, and this was the starting point of the reign of Putin, who publicly denounced our American antics with solving problems with bombs. I couldn't help but look where we were present day and asked myself if history was repeating itself. The issues are different, but the bloodshed mixed with the powerful opposing allies is cause for concern. In the US, we are mainly taught our triumphs and victories and rarely are the times of US greed and negligence discussed, but that is how we learn from our mistakes. It is important to love our country but understand we are part of an intricate global system. Pulling on the wrong thread can unravel the world into more bloodshed—the spider webs of blood and honey.

Wanderlust Diaries: The Towelhead of the Red Sea

I had packed my PADI dive card just in case I had a chance to do some diving off the coast of Jordan in the Red Sea. It was considered some of the best diving in the world, and I was upset when my plane had been grounded in Istanbul for two days after leaving Bosnia, cutting into my planned time in Jordan. I was hell-bent on seeing Aqaba; the coastal town a stone's throws away from Israel and Saudi Arabia with the Egyptian coastline of the Sinai Peninsula in full view. As I strolled along the boardwalk, that familiar red-and-white diver's flag caught my eye. It wouldn't hurt to ask, I told myself, as I leisurely strolled into the dive store. On a chalkboard was written their planned dives for the day; it was a three-dive special with an old C-130 wreck, and two other shallow dives off the Egyptian/Jordanian coast. I inquired about the trip, and it was as if the stars aligned with the right cost and a trip leaving within the hour.

I thought about this briefly, knowing that I had recently suffered barotrauma in my left ear from the trekking the perilous altitudes of Peru and Bolivia four months prior, which tore my Eustachian tube and left me bleeding out my ear in Chilean Patagonia. I considered that the dives were relatively shallow and decided that this was a once-in-a-lifetime opportunity, so I signed up and reserved my spot on the boat. It was a beautiful day out, and as I slithered into my wet suit, it made me grateful for getting to be there. When I travel, it was like I got to be a new Melissa. The wet suit symbolized removing the robes that drug me down with day-to-day routines and slipping on a new skin, shimmying it over my messy dreadlocks, stretching it over my shoulders, and wriggling my fingers through the loose ends. I was in a boat on the Red Sea with wind blowing though my messy locks as we made waves throughout Jordanian, Israeli, Egyptian, and Saudi waters, and I felt alive.

As I took a giant step off the back of the boat with my bright-pink fins, I adjusted my buoyancy to sink with my dive team into the blue abyss. The waters were clear, and the fish schooled around, sporting their uniqueness and vivid colors. I saw many lionfish that darted about, and it made me slightly nervous when they came too close, knowing how poisonous they were. All of a sudden, a wave of red came across my goggles. I tossed around to see if someone in my dive squad was hurt, but they were casually scoping out an adjacent reef. The red became deeply saturated, and my vision was blurred, but I could make out the dive leader waving at me. *Was it me?* I circled my head around, searching for the culprit; I was now in a panic thinking I had been bit or had scraped my leg on coral. The red surrounded me like blood soup—it was my ear! The pressure had ruptured my ear tube, and it began to throb as I made my way to the surface with my dive tender. My ear poured blood all over my face and spilled to the bright white decking of the boat. I wasn't sure how worried to be. Sure, it was a lot of blood and hurt, but I didn't feel like it was going to be the end of me, by any means. The boat captain called on the radio for a medical emergency as a police boat in nearby waters came to our aid and opened up a medical kit. I insisted I was fine, but the exchange between my dive boat tenders and the patrol boat officers consisted of a bunch of Arabic jargon, and then they forced me into the police boat where a man started to examine my ear. My dive boat untied from the nested police boat, and off they went without me.

This made me more nervous than any of my injuries, especially when I looked to the mast of the boat to see a strange flag. The flag did not look like the red-black-and-green flag of Jordan. It was only red-and-black with an odd emblem in the middle. The man attending to me spoke broken English, but I started to panic as I realized I was on board a Saudi police boat. I had nothing—no passport, no ID—just a blood drenched wet suit and a white towel draped around my head with a giant red stain over my left ear. I thought back to the racist jokes I had heard in my past with Americans calling the people of the Middle East "Towelheads," but I couldn't help but laugh at the irony as I sat in the Saudi boat with my headdress. I was the minority here, and I had to play by their rules.

In the distance on the shore, the call to prayer sounded from a mosque on the hill. One of the men on the boat with a scruffy beard and leathered face moved to the bow and bowed his head. He chanted in familiar Arabic; even though I did not understand the language, this part I knew. The foreign tongue fiercely and anointedly praying to the heavens that *God is Great, God is great... There is no other God than God.* Knowing full well the praises were to Allah, it still gave me a feeling of peace. I prayed many times on that boat as well. I prayed for them not to fuck with me because I was a tourist. I prayed that they did not go to Saudi shore, and I prayed for my ear to stop bleeding. Finally, in what seemed like an eternity, my dive boat returned, and picked up its damaged cargo.

My dive team spoke of the beautiful things they saw with the colorful fish and carnage of the wrecked plane. The only wreck story I had to talk about was myself as I shared a couple of stories about the couple of routine police checks the patrol boat performed as I sat there in silence with just my thoughts and the sound of Arabic linguistics that I did not understand. My ear would heal over the next two days with an intense cleaning regimen explained to me by the local doctor. Backpacking was not always the photoshopped Instagram posts with hair blowing in the breeze or sitting on a golden beach while the sun kissed my skin—sometimes traveling was tough. It was tough on the mind and tough on the body as I experienced things out of my comfort zone. Sometimes you get lucky, but other times, you might find yourself in situations such as missed flights, natural disasters, ruptured ears, and damaged rental cars, but those are the stories that would always be remembered.

The thought of me sitting on that boat under the Saudi flag, completely vulnerable, was like a dramatic painting that plays over and over in my head as I recollect the details. My travels were a blank canvas where I got to paint in the story. There were no erasers or way to change what happened, but the opportunity to paint the best picture possible. I was the artist, and I chose what the day's creation would be. I chose the media, the subject matter, and the vivid hues to use, and that day, I painted red—a color that was symbolic of my angst, fear, blood, and the sea. My adventures in the Middle East ended up with me perched on a boat, scared shitless, as the Foreign Towelhead off the coast of Saudi Arabia, and despite it all, I was fine, and my ear would heal someday. If I had it to do all over again, I probably wouldn't change a thing.

Wanderlust Diaries: The Flood of Petra

I woke in my dark bedouin tent to the feeling of warmth from the hot sun coming over the rock formations. It was time to get out of my canvas shelter before I started to cook. I could smell the smoke on my clothes from the bonfire and shisha in the tent the night before. Outside, it was a magical wonderland—red rocks meeting the blue sky horizon as far as the eye could see. My friends that worked at the camp had to run some tourists to the Petra entrance, so I headed out on my own to hike one of my favorite places in the world. Petra was beautiful. I rarely repeat travel places, but there was something that made me feel at home there in my little world of bedouins.

I had coffee with my friend who ran a small tourist shop outside the gates as he insisted I park my car in front of his store. I had surprised him the day before by just dropping in. We had been in contact casually on Facebook, but I love a good surprise, and the look on his face was priceless when he realized I had returned. I had wrapped my hair in a scarf and wore giant Audrey Hepburn-like sunglasses that hid my face. As I strolled around his shop and he came to greet me, I took off my glasses as I asked him how many dinar for a simple black-and-white scarf. He immediately gave me a huge hug, and even though he was mad I didn't tell him, it is more fun to just show up and make him smile.

Through the gates of Petra, many of the local guides tried to conjure me to take a ride on their horse, camel, donkey, whatever they had to offer. I casually declined, and when the persistent ones refused to let up, I told them of my buddies that ran the bedouin camp. It was kind of like name-dropping, but when they knew I had friends here, they changed their tune and did not see dollar signs but a genuine interest in the Rasta blond girl that was friends with the notorious bedouin brothers of the camp. I just wanted to hike. The rich food from Bosnia had me wanting exercise, so I took every hike I could find and saved the best for last, the Monastery.

On the trails covered in dust and tables of souvenirs from vendors selling their wares, it started to rain. At first, it was a sprinkle, but then it started to come down in sheets. A local kept yelling at me, but I assumed it was one of the many men who see the White women walk by and offer to take them to their "cave," which I knew was code for something else, so I ignored him as I scampered through the mud puddles. The man was hot on my tail, and when I heard a familiar "Melissa!" I turned back to see Yosef, my handsome bedouin friend from the camp. I took shelter under a tent with Yosef and his Belgium tourists that were trying to stay dry and had some tea that was warmed by a makeshift fire. Yosef offered for me to come back with him, but the mountain was calling, and even though it was getting late in the day, I had nothing but time, so I went off on my own to challenge the main attraction hike over the mountain.

The hike was just as beautiful as I remembered, but I could see rain clouds nearby, and the thunder roared and echoed through the canyons, sending chills down my spine. I reached the top, and the glorious Monastery welcomed me back with its luminous red rock with detailed carvings on the facade. This magical place was legendary, and even though I had been hiking all day, it was worth every step to reach this awe-inspiring place. The thunder and lightning was gaining ground, so I started my descent. I felt like a billy goat, jumping from rock to rock, and skipping down the hundreds of ancient steps. As I came to the bottom, my cell phone had picked up reception, and I had numerous messages from all my friends in Petra. "Where are you? Are you safe? Call me now!" As I scrolled through the messages, I chalked it up to my overprotective bedouin brothers who still had never embraced my solo travels, but then...I saw the flood.

Police and ambulances were at the bottom of the hike. The bridge was washed out, and tourists were trapped on the rock formations as the flood rushed past them. They were screaming for help as the local guides risked their lives to try to help. I was hustled by the police to a road that was an offshoot to the park. Masses of tourists covered in mud stood in a giant congregation—some were confused, some angry, and some were very scared. I looked at the road before me and saw a winding road that seemed to extend to oblivion up the rocky cliffs. It was all uphill, and I could see specks of tourists tackling the accent to eventually reach Wadi Musa, the town on the outskirts of Petra. Some locals were raking in the cash as the offered rides to the top in the back of their beat-up Toyotas. They told me it was ten kilometers to the top and another ten kilometers to the city, and if I wanted a ride, it would be fifty bucks to the halfway point. As the swarms of tourists overloaded the pickups, I found the humor in it and just walked, watching the show. Young boys no more than five years old were bringing their donkeys out, and the children made quite a bit of pocket change as they shuttled tourists to the top and then ran barefoot back to the bottom to pick up their next fare.

I made it to the top and looked at my pedometer—fifty thousand steps for the day of all mountains, and the next pilgrimage to the village would add quite a bit more. It was utter chaos with hundreds of cars and tour buses in complete gridlock on the narrow streets. I took heed to avoid being trampled by the camels, donkeys, and smoking trucks that were working overtime shuttling the tourists that were evacuated up the giant hill. Then I saw the unmistakable little shit car of my friend, Hashem. He was my closest friend that called or messaged me almost every day since my trip two years prior. He was such a sweet boy then, but now he must had been about twenty-one years old, and his beater car had stickers about being "sexy" and "loving women"—it was such a hooptie ride, but seeing Hashem at that moment made me happy. I jumped in and gave him a huge hug and flashed a smile, but then I realized he was mad at me. He had been messaging me and was worried sick. He scolded me and would sometimes go off in an Arabic rant before coming back to English. He didn't like how I went about trekking on my own and told me stories about how he and his brothers had been rescuing tourists for hours, and all he could think about was praying I was safe. He was covered in mud and had lost his shoes, but it didn't stop him from peddling the clutch to get us to the hill, overlooking the city.

At the top, Hashem showed me videos of the town and what was happening right under my nose. If I had chosen to not take the monastery hike, I would have been caught right in the middle of the narrow gorge that was the entry to the ancient ruins. I counted my blessings for my divine luck but also for my friends that cared so much about my safety. I found my rental car outside the gates—a few logs smashed into it, and it had mud all over the side panels. I was thankful I took out full insurance on the rental as I navigated my way out of the village and through the winding roads back to camp.

After a shower to wash the mud off my legs, I snuggled up in the communal tent with my band of brothers on the colorful cushions that covered the floor. I felt at peace. Thousands of miles from the Pacific Northwest, this was the closest I could come to home while backpacking. I spent the night next to the fire with my friends enjoying hot tea and shisha while my bedouin brothers taught me a new card game. I looked at the smiling faces of my friends—their warmness filled the already cozy and smoky tent. Their eyes lined with coal shined as we laughed and enjoyed each other's company. It was moments like this that mean everything—moments when you realize how less is more, and you don't need much to be happy. Sometimes life's most shining days come in the middle of the night, in the blackness of the deserts of Jordan, with only the lights of campfires, shisha coals, and friendship.

Wanderlust Diaries: Uganda Tattoos and Witch Doctors

I pulled an all-nighter with a red eye from Amman, via Cairo to Entebbe, Uganda, arriving me to immigration at three in the morning. As I stood in line with the other passengers to get my visa, I became a little anxious when I saw everyone else holding paperwork alongside their passports. I had my yellow fever card, but what was this paperwork everyone was holding? I quickly sorted through my backpack to look through the copies of embassy regulations for the countries I intended to visit. I found the copies of the regulations for Uganda and read them silently to myself. "Visa permits are not available at Entebbe airport upon arrival. Visitors must apply for an E-visa at least two weeks prior to travel." *SHIT*! How did I miss this paramount detail? This was a fly-by-the-seat-of-my-pants kind of trip, but I always looked at the visa requirements, and I must have read it wrong before! Shaking like a leaf and already thinking of where I might be able to fly to instead, I approached the visa counter. "Can I help you?" the sweet African lady with braids and red lipstick asked me in her accent that seemed to be a second language to Lugandan. "I sure hope so," I replied as I explained my dilemma. To make a long story short, I got my visa, but in the wee hours of the night, I was thinking I was going to have to live in Entebbe airport for a little while until things were sorted out.

Speaking of the Entebbe airport, this was the place where the AirFrance plane was hijacked en route to Tel Aviv, where terrorists tried to negotiate the release of Palestinian prisoners in return for the Israeli passengers. The hostage negotiation was not a success as Special Forces raided the airport and released the Israelis. My visa situation at the airport was much less dramatic, and I grabbed a cab with ease and headed to a hostel that said they had twenty-four-hour reception. Down a dirt road with plentiful potholes, I arrived at a gated hostel with a security guard that had no plans for my arrival... or beds for that matter. I negotiated at the early hours of five in the morning that I would just sleep on the hammock until someone from reception arrived.

The next day, I was eager to explore. The economical way to get around in Uganda is a boda-boda, which was simply a shitty motorcycle taxi. I flagged one down to meander the town and see the local fare. The boda-boda was sketchy as it dodged the potholes and pedestrians, but it was exhilarating all the same. I realized on my explorations that I was undoubtedly the only White woman in the entire town, which was no surprise to me but made me feel privileged to get to see the other side of the world. Everyone walked to where they needed to go, with many carrying their handicrafts or supplies, such as fruits, baskets, or sugarcane on their head. Taking a bumpy turn a little too fast, my foot slipped off the foot peg of the motorcycle, and I instantly felt the undeniable pain of the heat from the exhaust pipe on my ankle. We pulled over to see a layer of my skin adhered to the exhaust and a nice burn, ironically in the shape of Uganda, on my ankle. It hurt pretty bad, and Leo, my boda-boda driver, insisted he take me to go get some medicine. I was reluctant, but fearing an infection in the wilds of Africa was looming in the back of my mind, so I agreed. I maintained good spirits as we joked about my "Uganda tattoo" while we navigated the dirt roads to the village center.

The shops in Uganda were unlike anything in the modern world, with just shacks made of sticks and mortar leaning against each other for support. There were no supermarkets, pharmacies, or convenience stores in the areas I was exploring. The local butcher was just a ramshackle structure with a bloody carcass hanging by a rope where you request a cut of the remains, so when we rolled up to the shack of the local doctor, I wasn't surprised when I saw jars of herbs and potions, and a dark man with a light gray beard came to greet me. I showed him my ankle that slightly resembled hamburger meat, and he quickly gathered some supplies off his dusty shelves. There was a sting from the astringent liquid he poured on my skin. The elderly man started to rub a whitish sorghum paste with other herbs in a mash that he mixed with a mortar and pestle. He then used dried papyrus sprigs and made a pseudo bandage that adhered to the gooey concoction that was spread on my ankle like bizarre cake icing. During the whole ordeal, I asked him questions to take my mind off the pain of my ankle.

I examined the potions in the dusty jars, and when I asked about a red flower that was stunningly beautiful sitting on the top shelf, he lifted his brow as he stopped to retrieve the jar of intriguing flowers. He said it was for love and motioned for me to hand him something from my purse. Of course, I assumed he wanted money, so I started to remove some shilling notes from by clutch. He animatedly shook his head no and pointed inside my purse. I wasn't sure what he was motioning to, but as I scavenged through my bag, he saw a bag of cough drops. I had purchased these in Guam, and after transiting eight different countries, they were tattered and aged with the wrappers glued to the candies. He grabbed the bag and shuffled the individual pieces on the table. He placed about a teaspoon of the unique red flowers in a bowl and added the wrapped cough drops while he chanted and touched my hand. The moment felt unreal and completely exotic as I sat in the shack with the witch doctor speaking in strange tongues while my boda-boda driver waited patiently in the corner. I left my Ugandan witch doctor with my bag of cough drops and instructions not to remove the papyrus dressing until the morning.

Back at the hostel, I opened a book I found in reception on Uganda and started to plan my adventures by candlelight in the main lodge. My goals for the next day were to avoid infection in my new Ugandan tattoo wound, find an interpreter/guide to lead me to the remote Bhatwa/Pygmy tribe in the Bwindi Impenetrable Forest, and to get some good photos while having a good time. In the morning, I awoke and slowly removed the dressing on my ankle. It was unbelievable—barely a trace it had ever been injured with just a small red outline tracing of the wound. I was bewildered, and looking at the old cough drops, I honestly wondered the power contained inside the slimy tattered wrappers. My first goal of healing my ankle was complete... Now to find an interpreter and head to the forest. Things were looking up already!

Wanderlust Diaries: Road Trip to the Bwindi Impenetrable Forest

So it was just me, Saleem, and a safari van. I was lucky to meet Saleem. He came highly recommended by all the locals I met when I explained what I wanted to get out of Uganda. I needed someone who could interpret the Bhatwa language of the indigenous tribes of the Pygmies that lived in the forest that bordered Uganda and the Democratic Republic of the Congo. Saleem was not only gifted in being my translator, but he had been a guide and also studied social economics, making him an excellent road trip partner. We talked about everything as he explained Uganda politics, history, and customs. One custom that I found bizarre was that many men had more than one wife, including Saleem. He explained his first wife was more of an arranged marriage made by his parents, but it was old school enough that he gave two cows for her. I exclaimed, "Only two cows!" as he giggled and said that he did throw in a goat as well. I asked what I was worth, and he said since I was highly educated and "worldly," I could easily get thirteen cows. I was indeed flattered.

Our safari van was a budget rental for thrifty travelers, and after two flats and a broken shock mount, we made it down the ridiculously rough unpaved roads to Queen Elizabeth National Park, where we pitched tents and enjoyed the evening. We saw almost every type of animal Africa had to offer, including elephants, leopards, lions, antelopes, warthogs, water buffalo, and too many others to count. Our tents were alongside a channel that connected two lakes and the sounds of hippos grunting and splashing in the water with hyenas cackling in the distance was like a midnight serenade. I slept under the African sky that was painted with thousands of sparkling diamond stars, enchanted by the absolute magic and wildness of my surroundings. Back on the road, it was never a dull moment with locals carrying anything imaginable on their head as they toted water canisters from the nearby well. Children ran barefoot alongside the van, waving at me, saying, "Ello!" The children's smiles were enough to warm your heart as I fell in love with them all.

Saleem and I would occasionally stop at a local pub while he hustled the regulars in pool on rickety tables, and I played with the local kids. I would fidget with the photo apps on my smartphone and take our pictures as puppies or with a rainbow spewing out of our mouths as they giggled with pure joy at my Snapchat filters. Kids just ran free here, which was something out of the norm for me and one of the things that sadly seemed to be a lost era in the United States. I remember playing outside and riding my bike to school, and now it seemed most kids were cooped up playing video games and parents shamed if they even let them walk alone to the bus stop. I didn't see any other White folks except for one tour group that was camping at the Bush Lodge I was staying at. It was fun to chat, but hearing their travel stories of itineraries and rigid time lines made me happy I had my own agenda. They had not even been able to meet any locals, so I wrangled a couple of them in my van and headed to the local bar where we enjoyed some Nile beer and got to know each other. The next day, they set out for their planned destination via an asphalt road while Saleem and I loaded up our packs into the van and headed into no man's land. I wanted to see Bwindi and the exotic people and mountain gorillas that inhabit it. There was something about the name that beckoned me. "Impenetrable Forest"—it was almost like a challenge.

Wanderlust Diaries: Gorillas and People and Moments in Between

The road to the Bwindi Impenetrable Forest was so much fun. Every twist in the unpaved mountain roads had another beautiful vista as the hordes of village children from the different communities ran alongside the van. As we skirted the Congo border, the kids would wave and say "UN" instead of the normal "hello." The Congo was having some pretty serious rebel issues that were sending heaps of international support, and I saw many white Jeeps with the stenciled "UN" on the side, so the children are accustomed to the only pale faces being aid workers from the United Nations.

I stayed in a small village outside the National Park gates to get my bearings. I learned that the Bhatwa tribe, or better known as the Pygmies, were forced out of the forest due to conservation reasons and were living on the outskirts of the park boundary. I spent a lot of time at the orphanage visiting the kids. There was over two hundred children in the small facility, and they slept three to a bed because there was no room. Most of the children were born to the wild Pygmies, and their parents surrendered them to the care of the orphanage in hopes they might have a better life than the nomadic ways of the forest. The kids would sing and dance with me and take turns teaching me their choreographed moves. The children melted my heart. The main reason I had come to Uganda was in search of an organization that was promoting anti-poaching, but I had been unsuccessful in finding the type if NGO I was willing to donate cider house money to. I had made a purple sweet potato cider that was a perfect candidate to donate profits and resonated with the vibe of Africa, but after spending so much quality time with these kids, I thought I found my mission, and I looked forward to contacting them about what the micro cider house can do for the macro cause.

But I still wanted to see the Bhatwa. Their way of life and customs were becoming just as much endangered as the neighboring mountain gorillas. Saleem and I made our way into a hillside and had arranged a visit with them from a local that knew their whereabouts. We walked deep into the forest to see small little huts arranged in a clearing. Their houses were no bigger than a hunter's deer blind, made of dried banana tree leaves, and an assortment of sticks. The Pygmies stood barely over four feet tall and welcomed the strange "Monzingo" into their world. The women showed me where they cooked, as Saleem translated for me. I learned that they are given a ration of maize and beans from the government, but it wasn't enough to survive, and they had to find other means. They use to set traps in the forest, but conservation efforts had tried to put a stop to this practice and encouraged them to assimilate with the general population. The Pygmies had no formal education or vocational skills, and their height was a dead giveaway to their origins, leaving assimilation difficult as they struggled for survival in the forest. I walked to get water with the women and ground up the sorghum grains into fine flour with a stone to make porage. The food was dreadful, and I found myself mostly chewing on a piece of charcoal to rid the ailments I felt churning in my belly from the bacteria I was not used to. The women made handicrafts, and I tried to make myself useful by pitching in. I asked many questions about their hunting and realized that the poaching was not as much for sport but a reality that it was the only skill they possessed and the way to merely survive. My goals of hoping to find an organization that stopped poaching by the Pygmies was further confirmed to be a deeper issue than I could help with. It would be like someone telling me not to like cheese and bacon when I was starving.

Life with the Pygmies was interesting, to say the least, and I was thankful to have been accepted into their tribe for my short stay. I decided to stay alongside the mountain in the small village. I had found a lodge that overlooked the entire valley and was nestled in the trees, so I bid my farewell to Saleem as he made plans to return the safari van to Kampala. He was such a blessing on this trip, and I truly hope stars would align and our paths in life would cross again. His smile and laughter were intoxicating, and he was a genuine soul that I was blessed to meet.

There was a small airstrip outside Bwindi, and the locals told me that the following day, an Englishman flew in supplies, and he would be able to take me back to Entebbe in his small plane. I preferred that option, as it gave me more time with the locals, with the children, and with the mountain gorillas, and avoided retracing steps I had already taken through Uganda. The next morning, I met at the park gates to be escorted with a couple of other trekkers to find the family of gorillas that inhabited that area. I hired a porter for fifteen dollars, and that was the best money ever spent as he helped me through the unyielding mountain and chopped the vines and branches with a machete to clear our path. I channeled my inner Diane Fossey as we looked for signs and listened quietly for their sounds in the forest. We found them, and it was a beautiful moment.

We watched two infant gorillas playing while their mother stood to watch. I snapped about a billion photos until I just stood there in reverence of the fascinating scene in front of me. Suddenly, a loud grunting and rustling of the brush startled me as I froze in my footsteps. The male silverback came thundering out of the bushes and brushed right past me as he sat mere inches from my feet, chasing the infants away as he started to eat his lunch of leaves. He had a broken finger that left his middle digit extended, as if he was shooting me the bird. I just sat there watching him and watching the babies play overhead in the treetop canopy. I could have stayed there forever, studying their mannerisms, admiring their strength, and enjoying their presence.

The next day, I patiently waited for George, the Englishman, to arrive at the village. Storms rolled in and cast flashes of lighting against the gloomy skies overhead. The thunder roared through the valleys as I took refuge from the pelting rain. The elder of the village looked to me and said, "Sky full, no plane." *What the hell did that mean*? I understood enough of his broken English to realize that the storm was going to change my plans of getting back to Entebbe. I played my cards wrong here and wished I had returned to the big city with Saleem.

Out of options, I looked for the closest international airport, which was in neighboring Rwanda. A bumpy boda-boda motorcycle ride left in me in the border town, which was really the only time I can say I felt unsafe my whole trip. Hagglers and touts surrounded me like a swarm of mosquitos, trying to sell me insurance and ask for bribes to get through immigration. It was frustrating, and I couldn't make sense of it all. I swatted the hustlers away like flies, but they would return to hinder me from analyzing what I needed to do. The border made no sense with just a maze of conex box offices with bars on the makeshift windows and signs that meant nothing to me in the native language. The lines of people would shrink and swell like a slinky as masses of folks waiting would suddenly switch lines and, then after a few minutes, try to return to their original queue. I went from exit of Uganda immigration, to a Rwanda immigration line, to customs, to the bank booth to pay for the visa, back to customs, and then returned to immigration to get my actual stamp in my passport. This place was desperately in need of a Six Sigma LEAN initiative because it was utter chaos.

At one point, I was completely fed up with the ludicrous behavior of grown adults cutting in line. They saw my white face and knew I probably was clueless of the process and took advantage by pretending I wasn't there. At one point, I realized the only way I was going to get my visa was to play hardball as I embraced my inner mountain gorilla and slung a man out of line as he tried to weasel his way into the inch of spare room in front of me. I was probably five minutes from biting his neck with my gorilla fangs, but I was sure that would have landed me in a Rwandan jail. It felt like a reverse Rosa Parks situation, and I wasn't going to stand to be in the back of the line any longer. At one point, I realized that much of the chaos was because if you didn't choose to use one of the local hagglers and offer a bribe, your paperwork was lost in a pile of hundreds of people. The immigration officials were merely puppets, and the routine bus drivers and young border boys ran the show here. When I became in tune with why my papers were being neglected, I found a young boy who had been running back and forth in and out of the immigration stall like he owned the place. A few bucks in his greedy little palm, and I was next in line and finally got my visa. I then was herded like cattle to the next bullshit stop for Ebola screening where I was more likely to contract the virus than be screened for as I made my way through the test line. At last, across the border, I just wanted to walk and get away from the insanity.

I headed up the road like a turtle with my bag on my back on foot. I missed the calm of my mountain gorillas… I missed the laughter of the orphans…and I missed Saleem; he would have never let that circus happen. About a mile down the road, I waited for the bus that would take me to Kigali. As it stopped, I laughed at the irony that the only available seat was next to the man that I threw out of the line in my gorilla rage. I recognized him by his torn Gucci shirt that he had underneath a business jacket. I remember thinking how silly he looked, and he sure as hell remembered me as I took my seat beside him. I distracted myself from his constant staring by plugging in my earbuds and ignoring him. I realized that I was the only White person I had seen in days. This trip indeed weeded out the whiny backpackers. Backpackers thin out when you must run on rice and bugs. Plans usually end where there were no easy trains and the billboards of beer advertisements disappeared, but that was where so many adventures abode—beyond the billboards. Bob Marley began to sing his profound melodies off my playlist and drowned out any white noise. Bob told me, "Everything was gonna be all right," so I chose to believe the words as I sat back in my chair and made my way to Kigali.

Wanderlust Diaries: Good and Evil

My time in Rwanda made me realize that I had traveled to almost all the sites of mass genocides—or at least the known ones: Germany, Cambodia, Namibia, Bosnia, and now Rwanda. Travelling to third-world countries gave me perspective; I absolutely loved navigating the different cultures, but unfortunately, this was where a lot of nasty things in the world happen as well. I thought back to what I was doing in 1994. I tried to remember hearing about Rwanda and the Tutsis and the Hutus. I couldn't recollect anything.

Out of all the human rights museums I had been to, this one might be one of the most informative as I learned about the horrific things that happened to the people of this country. This African nation didn't ask to be colonized, but the Germans forced it upon them as they shoved education and religion down their throat. It advanced them from their native ways, but it also created a separation of classes of people that didn't exist before. Then came the Belgians who helped them set up government and put certain class leaders in charge, widening the gap between the people and creating hatred among the citizens. After years of thoughtful planning, a coup d'état occurred that shot down the president's plane over the Kigali Airport. Within minutes of the crash landing, the awful plan was put in play to exterminate the Tutsis. People were brainwashed to kill the Tutsi and given Ten Commandments. Even though people of different classes had lived in harmony beside one another, the Hutus would break into their Tutsi neighbor's house to kill their family. Women were purposefully raped and mutilated by HIV-infected men, and young babies chopped up by machetes. I have seen a lot of terrible things that unfolded in history from my travels, but this one had me in tears. Over a million people were slaughtered, and over 90 percent of the children at that time saw someone in their family die in a horrific manner. It made me wonder the fundamental question in life, *Are people intrinsically wired for good or evil?*

The forbidden truth and taboo about it all is that evil does not always repel but frequently attracts, making good people not victims but accomplices. How on earth could someone kill a baby with a machete? I looked at the town differently after understanding this part of Rwanda. Everyone I passed in the street, I did a quick math calculation as to how old they probably were during the civil war, or more appropriately, genocide. I wondered if they had lost their parents or siblings or if they had been one who clubbed the innocent to death. I understood why they looked at me with hesitant eyes. Many Rwandans have lost the ability to trust anyone now after the onslaught that occurred just over twenty years ago.

I hopscotched the city by hopping on the back of boda-bodas and explored the women's craft markets and city center. I could tell the city was trying to make a reemergence. The locals talked of grand plans of Kigali to be like the Singapore of Africa, but there was a long way to go. Slums populated the main thoroughfares and were marked with giant spray-painted Xs to designate the intended demolition. The government seemed to be doing a lot to empower women, but I wondered if it extended beyond the public billboards and into the households. Being there made me so thankful to be from America, the land of the free, but as I watched the way normal life took place in everyday Rwanda, I pondered what free actually was anymore. Kids played with sticks and women bonded together walking to the markets to sell their handicrafts and fresh veggies they produced. When they had enough money, they bought what they needed, and that was enough. At home, I was slave to my job, technology, bills, and the hundreds of other obligations that gobbled up my time. Don't get me wrong, these were choices I made, but there must be a value placed that does not involve money when it comes to freedom, and that simplicity was very apparent in Africa and something special.

When you have the world at your fingertips, people only want more and more. They are so entangled with things that they are never truly free. Rwanda was desperately striving to move beyond the civil atrocities and become a destination. I hoped whatever advancements occurred in infrastructure and business, the Rwandans kept that simple "freedom." Even though the country strived for wealth, I wished the people who had been through so much realized that there are two ways of becoming rich—one is by acquiring much, and the other was by desiring little, and who was to say which one was better? Rwanda had learned the hard way on the dark side of industrialization, capitalism, and nationalism. I hoped they could hold true to something more powerful than all that. As I walked the Rwandan streets, all I could do was trust that the goodness in people and resilience was stronger than the evil and past misfortunes of the world.

Wanderlust Diaries: The Kite over London

It just felt too easy, which made me anxious, like I was missing something. I checked my bag for my passport, my phone, my wallet—everything was accounted for. As I loaded up on the train to Camden Town, I realized that I was indeed missing something in my travels. I was missing the psychological stomach flip I usually get with somewhere new. I had been to London a few times, and it almost seemed routine. I knew the trains to take, and I never found myself with an adrenaline rush of being lost.

In the Navy, I would roam the decks and passageways to try to lose my way. As much as I would try to disorient myself, I knew there would never be a time where I could not be saved. With traveling, it is the same but different. The urge to roam and get lost in different cultures and customs is intoxicating, but in the Navy, I always knew that on the bulkheads were bull's-eyes with hull frame designations to lead me to my bunk. In London, no matter how many thousands of miles from home I was, the familiar tube subway map with its organized structure and English language would get me to my hostel with ease. Though still foreign, I knew my US citizenship made me kin here, and I was already coming closer to home.

I tried to explore new things and sent myself on a scavenger hunt throughout the city to find the hidden Banksy street art that was painted on random alleyways, not obvious to the unkeen eye. This got me out of the normal tourist hubs, and I saw some districts that normally wouldn't have drawn me in. I loved the thrill of feeling like I had a mission to fulfill. I wondered if a psychoanalyst would argue that my wanderlust might have some deeper meaning than just the stamps in my passport. I was not sure why I enjoyed putting myself in such odd places that many would consider "harm's way," but I couldn't beat the thrill of it—it was like a drug. Why did Houdini have to evolve from simple ropes and chains to ornate boxes and chambers to wow his audience? It was the thrill of the escape. It is hard to explain, but the triumphant feeling of navigating through the world solo is a rush that not everyone understands. The dopamine hit when you make a friend across an ocean and the oxytocin injection to your brain when you bond with them and experience a new world together was something very special.

I met up with my friend, Lauren, whom I had met in a rowdy hostel in Buenos Aires. She was an Aussie living in London and had to settle down for a bit to save up some money until her next travel binge. Travelers understood the routine. You live it up and drink the nectar of the world as if there was no tomorrow, but then visas expire and bank accounts run low, so you return to reality for a bit to recharge and plan the next adventure. We lived like paupers but were rich as kings from the things we had seen and wouldn't trade any of it for a luxury hotel room with room service.

I could feel the reigns of reality slowly reeling me back in. Like Icarus, I had flown too close to the sun, and my wings were slightly burned from my escapades in Eastern Europe, the Middle East, and Africa. I was a wild kite flying with complete freedom, but as I roamed familiar England, I could feel the slack of my kite string tightening. I was slowly being drawn back in. Seeing happy dogs guided on leashes made me think of my fur babies back home, and I could already imagine their excitement when I saw them again. I knew my cider stash was pretty much gone, and my mind would wander about when I was going to whip up the next batch of kegs so my accounts didn't go dry. I would see couple affectionately kissing on the subway, and it made me think of my wonderful bearded man at home that was so understanding and patiently waiting for me to return.

I didn't even bother unpacking my bag in London. All my clothes were dirty, and even the "clean" ones were quite disgusting from washing them in rivers and letting them air-dry with grime everywhere in the villages of Uganda. I felt I was slowly letting go of my wings and returning to the atmosphere, but the drops of sand and rain from my exotic adventures were still in my messy dreadlocks and burned into my soul. I wondered why it felt at that current moment when all my friends had settled down with kids and I reflected on my own life, it seemed more likely that I would build a spaceship and fly to Mars. I remembered in my twenties having a ten-year plan, but looking at life now in my thirties, I wondered how literal that time limit was. What was time anyway? Motherhood seemed more like a looming deadline than an exciting chapter, which made me question my intentions. If all else failed, there were plenty of orphans that imprinted on my heart in Africa that would love a home, so what was the rush?

It felt like a game of musical chairs, and when the music stopped, I was to grab the nearest chair and take a seat, but I couldn't just sit down because the music was still playing, louder than ever. What if my list of places to roam grew longer instead if shorter and my thirst for new experiences and learning became unquenchable? Who was to say that was a bad thing? We all have our own roads in life, and maybe mine was just different. I didn't think there was a textbook "Happily Ever After," where the story ended, and what was truly important was if you were happy and doing what you loved. Maybe I preferred to make my own road by chopping down vines with machetes in the Bwindi Impenetrable Forest of Uganda or by hiking out of a canyon in Jordan after being evacuated from floods. You never know what life has to offer or what adventures are in store.

But for now, I headed home—to the familiar and to the ones I loved. There was a peace that came knowing my head would be on my fluffy pillow and my fur babies by my side. I couldn't ride the crest of a wave forever, and eventually, I needed to plan on crashing onto the shores of home. As I walked the streets of London, I felt like a full sponge. The thrill of seeing Big Ben and Westminster Abbey didn't give me the twinkle in my eye as it normally would. I realized that my living large the past couple of months had filled up my soul so full that I had no more room. My travel cup had runneth over, and I now was ready to reflect on what a great ride it was. Traveling can be brutal. As I looked at my beat-up body, I realized that each tsetse fly bite, bruise, torn rotator cuff, and ripped eustachian tube in my ear may have made life a little harder, but each had a purpose. Traveling forces you to lose the familiar and trust strangers and learn to be off-balance. You learn that nothing is yours, except the bag on you back, the air in your lungs, and the dreams in your head. I know my travel style is not for everyone, but don't live your life staying in one time zone—go explore and learn from people that think differently than you do and see things that make you question how you feel about the world. Cast off the bowlines and let the trade winds take you somewhere new. Make the opportunity to live life by a compass and not a watch. However, sometimes the best views in the world are not from the coastlines of Croatia or the Red Sea in Jordan but from your front porch looking in. So whatever you are doing in this chapter of life and no matter where you are doing it and who you are with, just make sure it makes you happy. I was thankful for all the kindred spirits and friends I made along the way and my anchors of loved ones that guided this crazy kite back home.

PROLOGUE

SINGAPORE, NEPAL, AND MYANMAR

I *had great hopes of traveling through Indochina, but the COVID-19 pandemic certainly played a role with this trip and changed my plans. When I left for my trip, the understanding of the virus was in its infancy, and the world waited with baited breath as more cases emerged and the death toll rose. One by one, each country put new quarantine measures in place with only a few maintaining open borders. I was enjoying the lack of tourism, but the scenes turned almost apocalyptic as I would out-run the pandemic but face being trapped in the next country. While the United States was forced to stay indoors, I managed to trek some of the most amazing parts of the world and connect with other travelers during a very difficult time.*

This wanderlust adventure proved my grit as a traveler with diffi-culties I would have never imagined possible. The month I chose to pur-sue this journey was the month that the world was turned upside down, and it was difficult to fully understand what was going on as the media was unreliable, and the news of the virus changed every minute. My family and friends were deeply worried about me, but I made it home like I always did, with a backpack and head full of travel memories that I would never be able to replace.

It was this final trip that gave me the ability to finish my book. When I finally made it home to Washington, I had a forced two-week quarantine from the shipyard, and the public facilities were on lock-down. It was the perfect time to put all the memories of my wanderlust diaries together. The book would now have life breathed into it as I spent over two weeks in mismatched pajamas hunkered over my laptop, taking breaks only to grab a quick bite or pour my "breakfast wine," as I liked to call it. My quarantine was my chance to make my adventures truly immortal. I had so many wonderful people I had met in my wanderlust adventures, and the places I had visited deserved more than my social media posts. It was time.

This trip was wild, raw, and unbridled—a perfect saga about my untamable wanderlust.

Wanderlust Diaries: Connections and Reflections in Futuristic Singapore

Singapore was merely planned to be my gateway city into Asia. Since my ticket to Beijing no longer was an option because of the hysteria with the coronavirus, I chose to just stop at Singapore for my layover and opt out of China. Immediately, I knew this place was going to be pretty amazing as I made my way through the meticulously organized art installations, robotic displays, and even a damn waterfall in the airport. I had just flown over twenty hours, so finding a hostel was the first thing to do on my list, but my initial impression of the country was high for my first stop.

It was easy—a search through Hostelworld on the airport's lighting fast Wi-Fi showed a cute hostel called the Bohemian, which seemed right up my alley. The coronavirus fearmongering had definitely played a role here. I was the only one on the bus. I was upgraded due to extra vacancies to a capsule dorm that even had its own TV in the bunk (for those of you who don't do the backpacking gig, this is unheard of; it's usually a squeaky bunk, and an upgrade is a free loaner towel). There were no Chinese tourists competing for pictures with their massive selfie sticks while spitting phlegm from their polluted lungs at me.

Singapore had been hit hard with the initial outbreak, but the city seemed to be recovering with sanitizer stations everywhere and guards checking body temperatures before access was granted to public places. I think my timing was impeccable despite the worries from my friends back home about my choice to go to Asia. The city was immaculate and a testament to urban planning. I felt safe, and with my mobile maps and camera, I was all set to explore. Like a hostel pro, I started day one with some coffee and the simple complimentary breakfast. I didn't eat much because I didn't want to waste belly room on cereal and toast when there was a smorgasbord of options outside the hostel threshold. My true intent was not for the budget food but to see if there were any like-minded travelers to accompany me for the day.

It was like shopping for new friends—the Danish boy on a pit stop that worked in the engine room of a tanker ship in the bay or maybe the German fella who doesn't have a plan at all but seemed kinda dull or the English bloke that kept playing on his phone but wanted to go to Sentosa with a strict agenda. *Hmmm.* Just as I was about to commit to a plan, in walked a sweet Australian brunette. I recognized her as my bunk mate, but being in a capsule dorm, I didn't really see my roomies much. I knew I woke her up the night before as my phone starting to ring from a panicked phone call from my papa in Texas that caught word I might be in China. She was charming and seemed to be on my wavelength with walking the different districts and exploring—bingo! We were off to explore Chinatown, Little India, and the Arab Quarter, which were the three distinct communities in Singapore with lots of different energy and history making them truly unique.

As she pulled her DSLR out of her bag, I realized I had a fellow shutterbug in my midst, which made for even a better day of snapping pics of the detailed murals and architecture without having to awkwardly ask a stranger to take my photo. We were like sisters, and our wanderings took us to the world-famous hotel, the Marina Bay Sands, whose iconic structure sets the backdrop for almost every Singapore postcard. We went to the top where we bought a steeply priced drink to take in the view, but all the booths and tables were taken, except for a reserved couch for a large party in a VIP section with the best view in the house and likely in all Singapore. It was a shame not to have an ass on that plush velvet sofa with the best sunset view imaginable, so after I struck up a friendly conversation, I learned that the real VIP was David, a local celebrating his birthday. Needless to say, I got an invite into his little rooftop VIP oasis, and we all sipped our cocktails as we watched the sun go to bed, casting the most vibrant hues over the futuristic skyscrapers. The city then took on a new light as the neon signs and street lamps glowed in the distance and the people emerged from the concrete jungle; now the heat of the day had subsided, the city came to life, and I absorbed every bit of its energy with my new friends.

The next day, I headed out to Sentosa Island, the adventure-seeker's capital of Singapore. I think it was a ploy to keep the foreigners separated from the locals with the adventure experiences, amusement parks, and anything you could imagine on a tourist's menu of things to do, but it was fun all the same. With the coronavirus scare, the island took on a completely different persona from what I imagined the usual boisterous activities would be. The animal encounters were quarantined off, and most of the amusement rides were closed until further notice. I only went for the beaches and hikes, so it didn't bother me, but seeing the gondolas at a standstill and closed signs everywhere seemed eerily apocalyptic. The silver lining for me was the trails and beaches were mine to explore without anyone on my heels or invading my space. The normal rules of reserving lounge chairs or waiting in lines was nonexistent.

There was only one lift operating that serviced a "luge" track that I couldn't pass up. As the lift made its way to the top of the hill, I turned in my seat to get a picture behind me of the stunning landscape, but I was a little dismayed when there was actually another person on the chair lift behind me. My first emotion was annoyance that I was going to have a person in my photo when I had been such a recluse all day and spoiled with scenic photos with no people, but once at the top, we were both eager to meet one another. Serendipitously, Chett was a Pennsylvania boy that moved to the Silicon Valley—a Yank! We raced our luge carts against one another and just kept making laps up the mountain to give it another go as we became friends over conversations on the chair lifts and taking turns with who squirted the next round of antibacterial hand sanitizer on our palms.

We ended up with a bucket of cider at the beach and a good sunburn to remember the day by. On our way back, we met a local girl who joined us for the night. Her name was Christina, and she had moved to Singapore a couple of years ago and hadn't made any real friends yet, so she jumped at the invite to peddle around downtown with the silly Americans that were slightly drunk but genuinely happy to get to know her. She taught English at the local university and was the perfect addition; with just a smile and a nod, our duo became three. The glowing skyscrapers towered over us, and we played around the downtown promenade and sampled the local cuisine from the hawkers' stands in the food pavilions.

On my way home that night, my phone, which was my compass, map, camera, notepad (pretty much everything) died. Looking up at all the towering skyscrapers that all had their logos of banks and fortune companies glowing in neon at the top of these modern marvels, I realized how much I was a slave to technology. The light show from the nearby gardens and melodies of opera music resonating off the buildings gave me clues to my whereabouts as I looked for familiar architecture to lead me home to Chinatown. I felt like a lost character from Avatar with all the robotics and lights. I had a feeling in my gut I couldn't turn off, beckoning me to find a plug and stop with the silly navigating by stars nonsense I was doing. I pondered on how many people were a slave to their devices that they lose their connection with people and real life. I thought about how people didn't read paper books or use maps anymore, on how technology drives everything we do, and people spend billions to figure out ways to simplify human lives—hell, people don't even have to do their own grocery shopping anymore. Just order your stuff on your phone, and voilà, someone brings it out to your car! Why do we put so much energy into figuring out how to do less? Isn't that moment of smelling the perfect pineapple or comparing the fat marbling on the steak options worth anything?

Conversations with Chett and his job with IT in the Silicon Valley surfaced to my consciousness as his endearing compliments of how much fun he had today compared to working on circuit boards swirled through my head. Sure, I loved some of the modern conveniences, but it was crazy just how much more advanced the world was since I was a kid. I couldn't imagine what the next decade would bring. The connectivity in our lives was disconnecting us from some of the best parts! The devices that we buy end up controlling us, and the natural resources to make all the little gadgets will run out one day. The world would find equilibrium, and honestly, it scared me a little wondering what that might be. With my dead phone zipped up in my purse, I noticed how the city looked different without my face scanning the map on my backlit screen. When the world was at your fingertips, I wondered how much I was actually missing out on as I navigated by sights, smells, and sounds of this beautiful city back to my hostel.

My walk really made me think of the current state of our world. A virus that might have started from bat soup was the fiber that linked so much of our daily lives—the feeling of safety, stock markets, TSP, schools, events, and politics. This one fiber in our intricate network of our world had caused complete hysteria about a looming pandemic, enough that multiple countries were quarantined and the shelves of supermarkets were bare. Whether it was purely media hype to distract the sheeple of the planet or something more serious, I would argue that our balance with technology, industry, and the future state of our human race was not in harmony.

As I made my way to my fancy capsule bed with a mounted TV in my little space in the world, I turned it off and reflected. I was so thankful for the connections I had made so far. I lay in my bunk, thinking about how every day we get to wake up and make choices, and those choices will have an impact on something. Every choice makes a difference, whether it is with a person, the environment, or our community. When we shamelessly let our light shine, we unconsciously give those around us permission to do the same and what a brighter world it becomes—no LEDs required! Who needs a TV in your bunk and a phone when I had the most important thing all along—a connection with other people and making memories together, and none of them needed a plug. While I knew I was not going to ditch my phone, I at least had a better perspective in understanding that the most important connections in life had nothing to do with broadband or wireless but with each other and our world around us, wherever you may be.

Wanderlust Diaries: The Mountain Is Calling—Now or Never

My flight from Singapore to Kathmandu was a rough one with turbulence tossing the jet around most of the trip, so arriving late in Kathmandu, I was eager to get off the plane and start adventures in a new country. I could not have chosen a complete "yin" to the "yang" of Singapore. Kathmandu was chaotic. I was reminded of the grit I needed to bear India with muscling my way through lines because there was no personal space and everyone cut in front of me. There was little order to the immigration process and no trains to get to town. My cabdriver could not find my hostel in the late night, and I was stuck, wandering the broken piles of concrete and rubbish through narrow alleys late at night to find my new place of refuge. Once I did, my dorm was probably one of the roughest I had ever been to. I wondered if the earthquake a few years prior was cause of this mayhem or if it was just the way of life. I liked roughing it, but my days in swanky Singapore set me up for a complete culture shock. My dorm had broken windows, no locks, a hard mattress, and cats that climbed in and out of my dorm room, using my bag as a scratching post. The nearby streetlamp glowed through my window into the bunk, and the sounds of stray dogs fighting and the honking of horns kept me awake. I lay in my bunk, cruising the internet with the Wi-Fi, the one thing that was in working order for the hostel. As I looked for things to do in Nepal, there was one thing that kept calling to me—the king daddy of them all, *Everest*.

I had NEVER intended to attempt this bucket-list trek, but after looking at a few photos of this beautiful mountain, the algorithms and the wizards of the internet populated every ad with Everest treks on each query I made. If my phone could talk, it would have been whispering in my ear as my Samsung screen lit up my tired face in my shabby bunk. I had thought it was too early in the season for Everest base camp and I was time constrained, but my late-night searches found a possible option. In the early mornings, there were helicopters that made their way from Kathmandu to Lukla to drop off gasoline and supplies and give local Sherpas a ride back home to their village. There were no prices listed on the internet, just a name of a company. I looked at my watch. It was four in the morning. I knew sleep wasn't in my cards as the friendly cat curled up next to me and the street noises continued the ballads of revving engines and cooing pigeons. As I distracted myself with cruising through social media, the mountain kept calling, and I knew it was now or never.

I washed my face, grabbed my bag that wasn't even unpacked, and found a taxi to take me back to the airport. The company listed on the internet had a small booth similar to what I would pop up for cider events, and I found it unbelievably casual to just show up and hitch a ride for cheap. The only real protocol I observed was the strict calculation of my weight and pack—if I was over the spare kilograms available in the helicopter, no ride for me. They told me this helicopter was not for tourists but for cargo, but I assured them I had no problem with that. After they weighed me for the second time, I was cleared to make my way to the helipad. I waited in the holding area as the boxes kept piling up for the cargo load, praying that each additional one did not bump me from the ride for too much weight. It was just me, a local Sherpa, and the pilot with loads of boxes and canisters of gasoline. I could see the bright red heli with a cool dragon graphic on the side. I couldn't have been more excited as they started the engine and the rotors began to hum.

The pilot told me it was time to go, and as we headed out to the loading zone, the chopper I thought was for me took off, leaving a smaller older black one behind it. It wasn't fancy, no graphics or anything special, and I could tell it was going to be cozy as I was directed to the front seat next to the pilot, where they started to load boxes onto my lap and in every bit of spare space available. Maybe it was my lack of sleep, but I did not care, load me up, I was in a chopper headed to the Himalayas. I was elated as the heli took off, and like a giddy schoolgirl, I snapped photos and took about a million videos. I have to be honest, there were times I was completely terrified and probably had a few moments that I feared for my life and have never been more scared. I like to live out of my comfort zone, but as the chopper jumped around, trying to grab hold of the thin air, my comfort zone was in a totally different orbit than life at that moment.

The pollution from Kathmandu created heavy smog over the city, but once out of that, the mountains would appear out of nowhere, and it was hard to tell what was a cloud and what was a mountain, and there would be dire consequences if the pilot didn't know what he was doing. Reality kicked in that I hadn't even shown my passport, and I didn't recall the company even writing down my name. As the chopper started to toss and turn in the thin air, I started thinking that the only way I would be identified if something happened was by the tag on my bag and articles in my purse. Crazy thoughts started going through my sleep-deprived head as I started to inspect the welds and rivets of the helicopter. I just stopped looking and paid attention to the foreign tongues speaking on my airway headset. I had no idea what they were saying, but I assumed if we were in any peril, the pilot would at least have a tone deflection and yell or something, so I tried to chill out and just enjoy beauty around me.

The pilot who had spoken zero words to me up until now finally warmed up by taking off his face mask and starting a conversation while pointing out the peaks. I learned his name was Samir, and he had been flying since 2005. He told me that 80 percent of his business was search and recovery of the mountain trekkers, and the rest was cargo runs and an occasional local hitching a ride. I learned that he usually retrieved at least three bodies from the mountain a year, but one year, he had to pick up twelve. The thought of corpses occupying that very helicopter was a little unsettling, knowing they met their demise chasing the dream I was about to pursue. As we soared through the different terrains, I admired the rivers with suspension bridges, villages, and high mountain deserts from my bird's eye view. Samir motioned to me as we arrived in Lukla, and with perfect timing, a tiny plane began its landing in front of us. I scrambled for my phone to catch a video of the spectacle of watching an actual landing in the world's most dangerous airport that dead-ended its narrow landing strip into a mountain face in the extreme altitudes of the Himalayas.

Once out of the chopper, Samir showed me where a crash had occurred, and a local policeman was killed instantly as a plane veered out of control off the strip, smashing him and a helicopter exactly where we were standing. Being such a small landing strip accessible only to choppers and tiny planes, the remains of the crashes over the years were neatly stacked in a pile off to the side like a ramshackle museum. I made arrangements with Samir to pick me up in a week at a landing zone a few kilometers past Everest base camp. He frequently brought supplies to a nearby village and had a planned drop off in that area, but it bookended me to making the trek in no more than seven days; otherwise, I would lose my ride back and have to spend another seven days hiking back down, which would not work for my time lines. We exchanged info, and I knew in seven days, I would be back on that chopper with a million stories and photos to show him...and not in a bag in the back cargo space.

I made my way to the itty-bitty mountainside village of Lukla and found a small lodge to stay for the night while I made my last-minute arrangements. I was able to organize my permits and minimalize my pack before settling in with the locals for dinner. Dinner turned into sharing giant bottles of Everest beer that we passed around as we sat on cushions scattered on the floor. Then guitars came out, and next thing you know, we were singing the night away in true Nepalese style. They even had a ukulele, and I joined in, belting out my favorite tunes with my new friends. Knowing just a few chords, I played along and sang all night, toasting to the start of an amazing journey. I knew I should go to bed, but the crisp clean mountain air had replaced the pollution of Kathmandu, and I felt I was doing exactly what I needed to be doing in that moment. There was another man that was going to starting his trek the next day, and I realized he was already short of breath in conversations from the altitude. I was singing with no ailments whatsoever, so I figured that at least I was in better shape than him, so why turn in early?

I had been brainwashed by the ads online that this rugged place would be treacherous, but after my new friends shared their pictures with me, I knew I could do it. I was in the best shape I had been in many years, and if I didn't do it now, it would always be something I regretted, and I don't live with regrets. As we sang the night away, eventually, I headed to bed. I took one last freezing cold shower and prepped my bag for the morning. The mountain was calling my name, and I knew that when daylight broke, I would answer her call. So it was off to the mountains I go...with my eyes and heart open to recharge my soul.

Wanderlust Diaries: Mt. Everest Monks, Mandalas, and One Yogi Bear

So this is really happening! I kept reassuring myself as I set off on the trail from Lukla. Trekking Mt. Everest was not something I should have done on a whim, but if the cards aligned so perfectly, I felt I would have karmic retribution for not making this happen. With the coronavirus scare, I was capitalizing on the lack of tourism by everything being available and locals willing to assist me with planning the proper route and even help me go through my pack to discard things I would never use but acquire the things that would make the trek more pleasant. Multiple outfits or specialized toiletries were a waste of space and weight. The locals of Lukla eased my fears with explaining the proper stops for my time lines and best teahouses to stay at. Even though I was alone, there was going to be enough other people on the trail. I felt confident I could manage.

Matt, the man I had met the day before, was leaving early in the morning, and we would be on the same schedule for the most part. Even though he was kind of an odd duck, it was nice to know there was another human I could lean on if needed. The first couple of days were relatively easy as we made our way through the perilous suspension bridges and would stop at the small Sherpa villages for a masala tea. As we rose in altitude, it became harder for us to hold a conversation, so to ease the awkwardness of the silence between us, I would trek ahead so we could spend whatever time we needed independently to catch our breath and let our heart rates slow down without feeling rushed by each other. I rather enjoyed trekking alone, tackling Mount Everest was a pilgrimage and a personal experience— hearing only my footsteps and sometimes embracing the quiet so intensely that I physically could hear the beating of my own heart was surreal.

Every now and again, a local Sherpa would gain on me, and hearing them on my heels would make me shift gears and walk faster. When they finally caught up, multiple times, I would hear them kindly tell me, "Namaste, Bistārai bistārai." I didn't find out until later that they were telling me to slow down. I guess I was like a stubborn trail horse—the one that hated for others to be in front of them and would nip the horse's ass in front if they didn't get their position in the head of the pack. I found myself pushing too hard when someone would walk behind me but learned to just enjoy the journey. The trek was a metaphor for life—sometimes you're ahead, sometimes you're behind. The trail is long, and it isn't a race; in the end, the only one you are competing with is yourself.

I would always stop in a scenic spot to get some photos and wait for Matt. I was concerned when his breathing became heavily labored and we weren't even halfway there. In our tea stops, I learned a lot about him that fascinated me but slightly annoyed me at the same time. He was a true yogi at heart, and any conversation would always lead back to this. Even when he was out of breath, he found the energy to share his knowledge on sound healing, reiki, yoga, and massage. He even carried around a rather large sachet of stones that all had special qualities he wanted in his pocket at all times. When we stopped for the night at teahouses, he would almost immediately light incense and stick them in little nooks around the room. I accidentally walked right into one and burned a small hole in my thermal underwear. I just wondered why the hell he brought all this stuff. I was waiting for him to pull out a crystal bowl at some point. I had minimized my pack to the bare essentials with only one outfit and minimal provisions. I did not look beautiful, but at least I was not carrying a yogi starter kit in my pack but to each their own. He had offered to help align my chakras by offering me a massage. He even had brought essential oils! The last thing in the world I wanted was oil on my freezing cold body. What I wanted was a parka and some peace and quiet. My chakras would be much better in tune if he could offer me that instead. Matt needed to acclimatize more than I did and planned to stay an extra day in Namche Bazaar, which seemed to become a trading post for the Tibetan yak caravans among the other trekkers. I had to continue making progress, and physically, I was doing okay. There were other trekkers that I had started to make friends with that were continuing on, so I said my farewells to my little yogi bear friend and continued my journey.

When I reached the beautiful Tengboche Monastery with its whitewashed walls, I thought it was a great stopping spot to recharge and warm up. I had arrived just in time for the evening prayer, and what I was about to witness was going to alter my mindset for the rest of the trek and possibly forever. Upon entering the monastery, I read some informational plaques that informed me how this place of peace had been destroyed once by an earthquake and again in the nineties by a fire, but it was again rebuilt out of stone to its previous glory. I wanted to make sure my presence was welcome to seek refuge from the bitter cold. As I looked around, I heard the sound of beautiful chants in a nearby corridor. I could tell it was younger boys by the higher octaves in the calming harmonies that entered my ears. As I followed the sounds, I was astonished to see a truly beautiful sight.

Five elderly monks were sitting in a circle, applying delicate layers and lines of sand to a giant sand mandala using tubes and simple tools. They used rocks from nearby areas that when crushed made different hues of sand that they had separated in little brass bowls. One monk adorned in his red robe covered in a fleece blanket seemed to be chaperoning the process, and when he saw my weary but curious face peeking from behind a pillar, he motioned for me to come closer. I maintained my distance not to intrude but knelt to observe this mesmerizing process. The monk motioned to a sign that said no photo for this area of the monastery, so I tucked my phone away and just watched them work in harmony together, applying the sand. For the first time in days, I felt completely at peace. I didn't have the frigid temperatures or altitude physically demanding my attention or Matt taking up my bandwidth with mindless chatter about yoga. It was only me in this beautiful place of refuge, watching these monks create a masterpiece. I had watched a documentary about this in the past, but never did I think I would ever be so privileged to witness it in person. The beautiful colors of yellow, blue, pink, green, and tan were intricately woven together by just focusing intensely on the task at hand; it was a lesson in itself.

I could hear my stomach growling, indicating it was time to eat. I stopped at one of the guesthouses for a warm tea and meal and plan for the next day's journey. Every guesthouse served the same thing, and it was funny how excited I could get over the simplest of meal. Most guesthouses served some sort of toast, egg, noodle dish, and my favorite, the momo. Momos were a Nepali staple that resembled a gyoza but had a different shape and flavor. At the lower altitudes, the momos had great curry flavor and spices, but the further up the trail I went, they became little blobs with random fillings, such as greens and yak cheese, but anything was better than my stash of granola. I had developed a routine of going through my pack while there was daylight and retrieving any necessary items and repacking it for the next day. In my experience, the most difficult part of the day trekking Everest wasn't the time on the trail but the nighttime and early morning. While I still had energy, I liked to make all necessary preps for the next day because the nights were almost unbearable with the cold temperatures. Due to the lack of tourism, any sort of hot shower or camp stove to warm yourself by was nonexistent. The most I could hope for would be that the teahouse I stopped at had the kitchen in the communal area, and I could sit close to the kettle to warm up. Occasionally, there was a woodburning stove that resembled a large rusty metal barrel where the innkeeper would keep a fire going, and you could hang up your socks or wet clothes to dry. Sleeping was actually one of the hardest things for me because of the frigid temperatures. At least there were extra blankets at the lodges from fewer trekkers, but it was still miserable. I would layer every article of clothing I brought—two layers of thermals, leggings, hiking trousers, sweatshirt, vest, fleece jacket, and my puffy-down jacket; I looked like Ralphie from *A Christmas Story*. Once I was all bundled up, I then wrapped myself in my fleece sleeping bag like a burrito and layered however many blankets I could pilfer on top of me and tuck myself in to not allow any air into my homemade blanket igloo. I would let my breath slowly warm up my cocoon, and when I felt like I was no longer going to die, I would allow only the smallest hole to be exposed to the outside air and stick my nose through it.

The next morning, I wanted one last look at that beautiful mandala before I set off on the trek. I made my way through the tiny monastery to where the monks had been working the day prior, but in its place was nothing but a large foundation board that had a chalk outline of the mandala design. There was not even any sand left to be tidied up, only the empty space that one day prior had held one of the most spectacular things I had ever seen. It was a lesson to admire the beautiful things of this world but know that it never really belongs to you. It was a lesson that sometimes the simplest things can be the most special. And lastly, it was a lesson that nothing lasts forever—time would take its toll on your body, and one day, we will return to the earth as ashes. Maybe we would be granted a full lifetime of beautiful experiences; but for some, a lifetime was only one day, and that day must be cherished and exalted for what it was—a gift.

Wanderlust Diaries: Everlasting Memories

The last day was brutal. The altitude was taking its toll on my body as it was all I could do to just walk ten steps and then take a break. I didn't know what was pounding harder, my heart or the massive headache I had from the thin air. I would allow myself what I called "imagination breaks" after my ten steps, where I let my mind wander for a while on random topics before I started trudging along again. There was one topic that my subconscious kept flocking to that became my treat I indulged in after each ten steps.

I thought about that beautiful sand mandala from the monastery a few stops back on the trail. I thought about how much effort went into making such a thing of beauty just to be wiped away. It made me think of so many parts of life and how maybe I could take a lesson from those bald little monks who let me take part in such a thing of beauty. I started to regret not hiring a porter, but at the time, I thought part of the experience was taking only what you need and testing your grit and gumption—well, I was at the end of my rope in that regard as my pack dug into my hip bones and the straps wreaked havoc on my shoulders. When I found myself focusing on the negative, I always put that mandala in the front of my brain. I thought about how pain was fleeting, and the journey was what mattered. The pain told me that I was lucky to have life in my body and that I should be thankful, not sullen, and those thoughts got me through the harder days.

Base Camp Everest was the final destination for most of the trekkers I had leapfrogged with the past six days, but it wasn't mine. I had one final summit and ice field to tackle to reach my rendezvous with Samir for my helicopter ride back to civilization, and my intended route made me head west toward the Kala Patthar peak, away from the masses of trekkers headed toward the summit. My itinerary I put together had some pros of not backtracking to Lukla and getting much closer to Everest with better views, but it also meant that I would likely be alone for one of the most difficult parts and almost all the guides and porters stayed in base camp unless their trekker was attempting the full summit. A few of us trekked a couple of hours past base camp together to a hidden oasis, Everest Hotel, which was only accessible by helicopter or trekking. It was a complete novelty in its location but offered panoramic views of the Himalayas and a peekaboo glimpse of Everest. It would be the last time I would see their sunburned faces from the solar reflections off the snow, and it was my final recharge before meeting Samir.

I made my way through the valley of giants that towered over me in the Rooftop of the World. There were seven mammoth mountains that all peaked over 5,000 meters, but the king of them all sat in the back, winning the claim to fame with its peak at 8,844 meters. There was something peculiar and ominous about Everest with its color darker than the rest and always watching me as I came closer and closer. I had made it. There was a single small shrine no bigger than fireplace with a few prayer flags adjacent to a small rock helipad in the vast nothingness of the Himalayas. There was a lone Sherpa woman sitting perched at the rendezvous flag with a grimace of pain from however long she had been trekking. I wondered why she was alone and what she was doing, but I was sure she wondered the same about me. I used my charade skills to comprehend that she was waiting for a helicopter ride too. I assumed one of Samir's locals that would catch a ride to Kathmandu for supplies. I felt comforted knowing I had accomplished such a feat, and now I only had to wait. I had one last thing to do, and as I looked around this magical panorama that will be forever burned into my soul, I knew it was the proper time and place for something I had been saving.

Even though I hadn't intended on hiking Everest, I did know that my travels would bring me somewhere beautiful, and when I saw it, I would know that the timing was right for what I was about to do. I took off my pack and dug out a Ziploc bag I had brought. It was a portion of my mother's cremated remains. For a quick backstory, I had bought a beautiful urn in Japan, but unfortunately, it was just a tad too small, and for years, I had part of my mom's ashes in a separate bag. I had decided that I was going to start putting those in beautiful places that made me think of her. As I looked at those mountains that words could not describe, I knew this was the place. For many years, I harbored regret in my heart about my relationship with my mother. I loved her more than anything, but there were parts of my upbringing that made me resent her, and as an adult, I kept her at a distance. I always thought there would be more time to make things right, but just like the sand mandala, time waits for no one, and one day, my life was forever changed when she left this world. As I looked at the pathetic little Ziploc, I tried to forget about the bitter cold as I removed my gloves. I thought of her face. I thought of her smile. I thought of how my family always thought she was the crazy one for the way she nomadically moved from place to place and the crazy stunts she pulled. I thought of her laugh and how she brightened whatever room she was in when she was happy but how it felt like the earth was shattering when she was mad. It was in these reflections that I realized that woman that I loved and envied but then sometimes hated and despised had never really left…but was inside me.

The only things we leave behind in this world are the impressions we make upon others, and what is left is only ashes. As I poured the remains into my frozen palm, I wasn't filled with sadness but an enlightened joy. As I looked toward the heavens with the majesty of Mount Everest looming over us, I let the wind take her away. There is nothing that lasts forever, only the impression we leave behind; if we master this for the good, we, too, become immortal.

This post is dedicated to my mother.

I pray the qualities that made her so unique, always live within me as I pass them onto those I encounter, and I pray that the demons of my past disappear into the wind like the ashes as they floated from my hand. I will endeavor to leave a positive impact on the world and that the life-changing experiences I have had on this mountain are never forgotten but woven into the way I see the world and humanity.

Wanderlust Diaries: "HOLI"-SHIT—the Festival and Tattoo

I expected Pokhara to be quaint, considering it was a lakeside village and base for Annapurna Mountain treks, but it was still a sprawling city with all the same city craziness. Once my soreness from Everest wore off and I wasn't walking like the Tin Man, I would try for another trek, but until then, I explored the town. As I was buying a street side samosa, making the usual pleasantries with the vendor, a lady stopped with enthusiasm after eavesdropping that I was American and engaged me in a conversation. She was somewhat an ex-pat Californian, who planned to stay the allowed five months a year in Nepal. She knew all the local spots including a small footpath through a Tibetan refugee camp to get to the infamous Peace Pagoda that sat perched atop a small mountain on the other side of the lake. Instead of the tourist boat that costs six hundred rupees, we took the long way around the lake and chitchatted as we got to know one another.

It was pure luck that she stumbled into me because I was invited out that night to meet her friends, which were basically international gypsies, migrating as sporadically as the wind blew. They all wore hemp and the stereotypical backpacker attire with baggy stitched shirts, adorned in vibrant colors and the sultan bottoms that somewhat resembled MC Hammer pants. My dreadlocks gave me a pass into the secret club, and I ditched any link to my "real" job and only told my travel stories that they found interesting and could relate to. I was just in time for one of the core reasons I wanted to come to Nepal—the Holi festival.

The infamous Holi festival, or the Festival of Colors, was mainly celebrated in India and Nepal. It focused on Hindi beliefs and was the celebration of the triumph of good over evil and welcoming the spring and good harvests. It was the festive day to rid oneself of past errors, end conflicts with foes, and a day to forgive and forget. The legends that drove this dogma ran deep with the stories of Vishnu and the endeavor for true love, but nowadays, it seemed a lot like a reason for locals and tourists to get crazy drunk, dance, and smear colors all over stranger's faces as they walked past. Germophobes take heed because there was nothing stopping the mob of people if they determined you needed more color—it was hands smearing streaks on my cheeks as they all exclaimed "Happy Holi!" I took part in the shenanigans, but I was extra cautious as I saw some of the madness that could turn a good day sour. I kept my phone hidden away to keep it safe from the rainbow powders that hovered over the crowds. As night came upon us, only the rowdy stayed up as the locals barbecued by the lake. I partook in some delicious skewers of pork and chicken and even adorned a sweet street dog with some vibrant Holi colors as he relaxed at my feet, hoping for a piece of my dinner.

The next morning, I did not have much to do but explore the town, which seemed to be catering to tourists in a sort of undesirable way. It is a difficult balance for third-world countries; promoting tourism can be a self-defeating cycle, and it left me frustrated. I wanted to see these beautiful countries to understand their culture and the way of life for the people. I didn't come here for the street stands of trinkets and restaurants, offering pizza and cheeseburgers. I worried that the fact that tourism was so important to the economy, the country would lose something much more important—their heritage. I wished my white face was more than a dollar sign, and I wished tourists did not come with such a stigma of what should be available. *If I want food, I'll eat what you eat. If I want music, I'll listen to what you play. If I need clothes, I'll buy something you made.* I didn't need all that other junk, and it clouded the beauty of what was truly special. However, with nothing else to occupy my time but roaming the streets, I did engage in some friendly conversation with a tattoo artist in an adjacent street stall while I was enjoying some momos at a street stand by my hostel.

It wasn't one of the fancier tattoo parlors on the main street but off the beaten path, which appealed to me. I thought of how cool it might be to get a design I had been muddling over for years but never found the time back in the States. The design even fit in perfect with my mindset since arriving in Nepal. I loved the symbolism of a unalome and had one designed that was stored in the images in my phone. The unalome is a symbol that represents the path one takes to enlightenment and is about your individual journey in life. Everyone's path is different, and it is full of life lessons as your time on earth ebbs and flows from the choices you make. The unalome is a specialized line drawing that twists and turns but finally straightens out, which symbolizes one reaching an enlightened moment. I wanted a mandala lotus flower to be a part of the tattoo design because of the symbolism of overcoming adversity and learning from mistakes. The tattoo artist hastily said he could do this, and for three thousand rupees, I could have the tattoo of my dreams once I downed my last momo. That was crazy cheap and so hassle-free that in the spirit of Holi, I said yes, but before I go on, I will now say in hindsight that my lesson in the day was that the unalome is curvy for a reason, and at that moment, my internal unalome made a sharp turn south as I watched my tattoo artist struggle to assemble the tattoo gun.

Once he started, I realized this was a HUGE mistake. At first, I thought maybe it would get better, but as he started to free hand my dream tattoo, just a simple circle looked like something a kindergarten student would have mastered better than he did. I told him to stop as I pointed at the horrendous excuse to the start of a mandala. With another oopsie, he then told me he was up all night for Holi and the photos of the tattoo work he had showed me wasn't his work but another guy who could come and fix it once he was done taking a monster shit in the bathroom. With the language barrier, I learned that charading a lotus flower and unalome wasn't the best idea, but at least I got out while I could before any more damage was done.

I couldn't be mad. Life was full of choices, and I chose to go in that seedy little studio and mime out a tattoo design. It would now be a daily reminder of the choices in life I made, but the next choice I would make once the abomination healed would be to march into my tattoo parlor back home and let my guy work his magic, but maybe I would let him keep a little part of the monstrosity as a reminder of my "Holi-Shit" moment when I let a hungover amateur artist tattoo my arm in Nepal. Holi would always be remembered as the day I was plastered in colors—some washed off and some were permanent, and I would have to celebrate that all the same. Happy HOLI!

Wanderlust Diaries: Trekking the Annapurna Mountains

Spending time in Pokhara, I caught glimpses of the majestic peaks of the Annapurnas that kept watchful eye over the city. The heavy haze that lingered over the town made me realize that I had one more trek to do for my Nepal bucket list to get up close and personal to these beauties. My legs were still weary from the Everest hike, but I figured the best way to fight fatigue in my body was to make it stronger, so back to the mountains I went.

The mountain roads zigzagged through the countryside, and I desperately wanted to ask the driver to pull over for a photo, but it seemed we were on a mission, so I sat back and enjoyed the bumpy ride. The weather in the Annapurnas was much milder than Everest, and as I began the trek, I realized the importance of layers. I would start the early mornings all bundled up like a Sherpa, but then as the sun came out and reflected off the snow peaks, I ended up rolling my long johns into shorts, looking utterly ridiculous with my pink wool socks and hiking boots, but the mountains passed no judgment. By the time evening came around, I was back in my full layers, searching for hot tea and a fire.

A huge surprise I had upon starting the trek was all the cute little villages I would pass through. I had packed a tent, but this just wasn't how it worked there. Each village consisted of a few little "guesthouses" all painted in vibrant blue, orange, and white; they all served the same menu options of food and offered a place to sleep. Since tourism was at an all-time low due to the coronavirus scare, innkeepers would offer free lodging if I would at least buy their food. Considering a room with a mattress and blankets was only three hundred rupees (about $2.50), I felt no need to haggle or take them up on their offer but gladly paid my room and board and was thankful for whatever they would prepare me to eat. The locals had no idea their worth; $2.50 for refuge seemed almost criminal, considering the hospitality and kindness I was shown. I couldn't fathom how on the cliffs of these mountainsides the locals could build such lovely guesthouses. It was nothing fancy, especially to American standards, but when I started the trek, expecting to camp and freeze my ass off and ended up sitting next to communal woodburning stove while the mom made me masala tea, my expectations were overwhelmed by how pleasant the trekking was.

Even though these mountains were not as notorious as Mt. Everest, they were still mammoths with thirteen of the peaks towering over seven thousand meters, and the most prominent peak over eight thousand, being one of the tallest in the world. Since I had no real agenda, I always enjoyed stopping for tea with locals that had little children running around. Once the parents figured out I was friendly and not bothered by their curiosity, I frequently engaged in a quick game of tag or even found myself in a water balloon war with a few little boys who thought I was funny.

I met some other trekkers that became my friends along the way, and we stayed up playing games with some Kama Sutra cards I picked up as a souvenir. With us all being from different countries, the only game I could easily explain the rules was Old Maid. Imagine a Frenchman, a Singapore girl, an English couple, a Nepali man, and a boisterous American dreadhead sitting around a table, playing a child's game with fifty-two different sexual positions to laugh and giggle about. No matter what our native tongue, laughter was the universal language that chilly evening. It was nights like these that made the trek even more unforgettable as we compared our cards. It didn't matter who won. We just enjoyed each other's company and played the cards we were dealt.

The morning of day three was the pinnacle day for my Annapurna trek, the summit to Poon Hill at sunrise. Don't be fooled by the name, Poon Hill sat at 3,210 meters (10,532 feet), and with the icy footpaths, it took its toll on many unprepared trekkers, including myself. I didn't expect to need the insane gear I needed in Everest like spikes for my boots or an ice axe, and what I brought was pretty minimal. On the summit, I found myself slipping all over the place from the treacherous ice patches that took me down a few times. Once at the top, it was a witness to God's beauty as I admired a vision of soft colors that became more vibrant as the sun peered over the mountain range. The snow peaks glistened with pinkish hues from the reflections in the heavens above. It was as if I had summited to see a masterpiece, full of serenity, calm, and beauty. My old faithful friend, Mr. Altitude Sickness, was starting to creep in as I felt a light-headedness giving me warning it was time to descend. When I hit the ice patch, I watched trekkers slip and fall as they cautiously tried to gingerly step their way through it. I was not even going to play that game as I sat on my butt and glissaded my way down as the other trekkers laughed. I will take a sore ass rather than a broken leg any day. I took in one last breath of fresh mountain air and loaded up my pack as I set off for the steep trek back full of flagstone steps that were hell on the knees but a necessary evil to admire the beauty from the top.

Back at Pokhara, I realized that I had no more clean clothes—it was only dirty and dirtier. I took advantage of some downtime to do laundry and catch up on e-mails. With my colorful underwear drying on the hostel laundry line like a Nepali prayer flag, I opened up my e-mail that I hadn't checked in days. What I was about to see wasn't going to add to a day of leisure. My flight out of Nepal was canceled due to the virus scare and impact to the airline industry. With nothing except a few travel bans holding me back, I sat at a little café, drinking some masala tea. There was nothing shackling me to an itinerary anymore. Where shall I go next? The world was my oyster, and I was looking for pearls.

Wanderlust Diaries: "FITFO" Kathman-DO-or-DIE!

My guys at work have a phrase—it's called "FITFO," or better explained, "Figure it the f—— out!" Upon realizing my flight out of country was canceled because of the dirty C word (don't make me say it), I weighed my options. Looking at the map, it seemed I was kinda screwed. Every country surrounding Nepal had closed borders because of the damn virus scare. I had almost booked a flight to Vietnam to see my friend, but before I could complete the transaction, I double-checked and found out they were closed for business too. With India, Thailand, Philippines, Vietnam, Cambodia, Japan, Korea, Mongolia, China (obviously), and most other countries not allowing travelers, I had to treat my wanderlust like a very strategic chess game.

The first order of business was to get to Kathmandu. To make any sort of plan to the next country, I had to "FITFO" this and get to Kathmandu by the next morning to make a strategic flight out of Nepal that would not leave me stranded. Nepal was closing its borders in the next couple of days, and I needed to get out—and fast. All budget airline flights out of the tiny Pokhara Airport were booked solid, and as I walked past the buses that were overloaded with tourists, trying to get out of country to meet quarantine deadlines, I found myself having little interest in dealing with the ridiculousness of loading in a sardine can for hours. As I walked down the main street of Lakeside in Pokhara, the motorbike rentals caught my eye and gave me an idea. *What if I rented a bike and made my OWN way to Kathmandu?* Now that option had potential. The time line worked, economical, super adventurous with a little spice of danger—the perfect recipe for the way I like to travel. Now I just needed a bike.

I asked a few shopkeepers if they would loan me a bike for a one way to Kathmandu, but most of them were hesitant because they needed their bikes in Pokhara. However, I didn't give up and kept asking, and I found a taker. There was one shopkeeper that ran a small hole in the wall store that sold Nepali sim cards and telephone data plans. He had a small sign to inquire about scooter rental, so I did. He was fine with me taking the bike to Bharatpur to his brother's house, which would get me halfway to Kathmandu, where I could more easily hop a bus or budget plane into the big city. The scooter rental would only be seven hundred rupees a day (less than six dollars), and for that price, we made a deal. To be honest, it was a little sketchy, but this was what I wanted to do, and my path to start heading south. Not having an international driver's license, he told me, "Okay, no problem," as he handed me a tattered stash of paperwork. He told me if I got pulled over by the police to simply state "Prassuram is my friend. He let me borrow bike to go to hospital." Looking at my bandaged arm from my horrendous tattoo, I played the script over in my head and figured I could pull it off. He told me it was possible that I might get pulled over just because I was White, but if so, just give the cop five hundred rupees, and they would let me go (for anyone's interest, this only happened once, and I only bribed sixty rupees—what a bargain!). I knew this probably wasn't the wisest thing to do, but I couldn't shake the idea of me, a bike and the open road through Nepal.

I was already somewhat familiar with the roads to the Annapurna circuit treks, and I figured the backroads could get me where I needed to go. My friend Judy was walking with me as I haggled for a bike, and when she saw the glow of excitement in my eyes once I found a way to make it work, she hurried to find a bike she could rent too. She wanted to join me for part of the ride. My last night in Pokhara was filled with so much love. The gypsy friends I made became so close you would have thought we were friends for twenty years. It was so inclusive with this group—it didn't matter your race, age, handicaps, only the essence of your heart was what allowed entrance into this tribe. We spent the last night at an open-mic night, listening to a few sing while we all shared parts of ourselves with one another. Natalia, the Russian girl, took beautiful photos that she shared with everyone. Simi, an Indian man, shared with me some poems he wrote once he saw I liked to write too when we became friends on social media. Some others sang and played guitar as I sat on my floor cushion and just basked in all the love in this place.

The next morning, Judy and I were off early on our bikes to avoid the city traffic, but that didn't stop her from ramming an unsuspecting biker the first five minutes of being on the road. We just rolled on as the poor disgruntled rider gave Judy a glare. I dubbed her the nickname of the *California Enema* after that stunt. As we started the mountain roads that were mostly dirt and gravel with giant potholes, I realized having Judy along might have been more of a liability than a buddy rule safety measure as she crashed again, and her bike slid out from under her. Like a good soldier, she got back up every time as we continued on some of the wildest and most undeveloped roads I had ever seen.

After a stop for momos, I said bye to Judy as I continued on to Bharatpur solo. I started to embrace the chaos of riding in Nepal. I learned to just let go of any expectations of rules of the road. Nepalis drive on the other side of the road from the United States, but it really didn't matter. If there was a path, you took it. When other drivers were nearby, when in doubt, you just beeped it out as I followed suit with the other riders by honking my horn on blind turns and when I was going to overtake a car. Once arriving in Bharatpur, I found the brother's house and dropped off the scooter and continued on. I found a cheap twenty-minute flight from Bharatpur to Kathmandu that was going to get me to the capital city, so now it was to the airport I went.

The airports of Nepal were so outdated and small. I sat on the roof, watching the tiny planes take off and the Nepalese military train on the fields in the distance. I boarded my tiny twin prop plane for the capital city that was packed full with Nepalese, Indians, an English family, and a handful of Americans. It was supposed to be less than twenty minutes, basically a takeoff and a landing, but what I was about to experience was the scariest moment of my life—it was actually hard to write about. As soon as we took off, something went wrong. The mountain weather must have taken a turn for the worst, and possibly the tiny plane was overloaded, but the plane shook and tossed and turned in the sky. I had felt awful turbulence before, but this was worse than anything I had ever flown in. The pilot struggled to ascend in altitude as the plane thrashed in the atmosphere. It felt like our tiny plane was being flushed down a toilet. The plane would try to gain altitude but struggled as the pilot tried upward angles that absolutely terrified me as the aircraft would drop like a rock before gaining control again.

Most passengers were panicked, honestly, including myself. The lady behind me was screaming and praying at the top of her lungs and was only silenced when she puked in her barf bag. The stench of her curry lunch filled the cabin. A mother and daughter in the adjacent seats clutched each other in an embrace as they wept. I wondered if possibly this might be just a rough ride and contemplated, asking the Nepali man sitting next to me if this was normal, but any minute I spent talking was a moment I wasn't praying for safe landing of our plane. As I looked at him, he was studying the emergency procedures anyway, so that answered my question about how "normal" this was as I grabbed my procedure to review. The info was useless as I thought of how flotation devices were pointless if we crashed into a mountain face in the Himalayas.

As more passengers began their prayers, I thought about how faith was a house with many rooms—many gods were called upon that day as prayers in all tongues filled the curry-stenched cabin. At one point, I looked at my watch, and we were almost an hour into a planned twenty-minute flight. I knew something was wrong as I looked at my offline map with a GPS tracker, and we were now somewhere over Northern India, trapped inside the mountain weather. I just white-knuckled to my seat and prayed. I thought of everyone who was important to me and fervently requested I would see them again. Finally, in what seemed like an eternity, I could see Kathmandu in the distance. At last, I felt it was possible that this Yeti Airlines flight would make it to its destination and not be a small press article of a downed flight with twelve Nepali, five Indian, two English, and four Americans crash landing in the Himalayas—an article where I was merely a statistic that would be lost in the mass hysteria of the media frenzy of the coronavirus.

When we landed, a weight was lifted as everyone cheered. We all emptied out of the tuna can onto the tarmac. The sun on my face never felt so good as my stomach expelled its contents of masala tea onto the asphalt. For the rest of the day, I was quite shaken up, and the thought of getting on a plane again was looming over me, but I knew I had to do it. I couldn't rent a motorbike across the Pacific, so I needed to just accept it was a fluke and carry on.

Kathmandu was pandemonium with scooters and taxis whizzing around on the damaged streets lined with vendors who were not bothered by the chaos. Kathmandu was wild—with the pollution and trash, it was hard to see that behind the rubbish, there was a gem. I walked to a couple of temples that were inhabited by monkeys that jumped from the statues and rooftops. As I took photos and admired the architecture, I took a moment to reflect as I looked at the deities that were exalted in the temples. As I gave a prayer wheel a spin, I was thankful. I did not care which God answered our prayers that day, whether it be Jesus, Allah, Buddha, Shiva, Ganesha, or whoever, I owed them a debt of gratitude, but I would NEVER, and I mean NEVER EVER, fly Yeti Airlines over the Himalayas again.

So looking at the map, it was my move. What was next on the chessboard of travel for me? The next morning, I boarded my flight. I ordered two mini wine bottles immediately. With an odd look from the flight attendant, she handed me my hooch, probably just writing me off as an obtuse American. If I was going to leave this world, especially from a damn plane, I was at least going to do it in style—with head full of memories, a heart full of love, and maybe, just a little drunk.

Wanderlust Diaries: Gilded, Golden, and Unforgettable

Yangon, where do I start? It was a land that broke the paradigms of traditional travel and welcomed my foreign white face with open arms. I think locals actually asked for more photos with me than I did of them. The only thing that could compare to the kindness shining from the locals was the brilliance of the golden gilded pagodas. With foreign travelers being recently allowed into Myanmar, the dark side of tourism had not taken hold, and for that, I was grateful.

The roadside markets weren't selling cheap trinkets and souvenirs but power drills and combo wrenches. With the exports to China being stopped, Myanmar had a surplus of watermelons. As I tried to walk down the road, I would almost trip over them as the locals would try to basically give them away. I would graciously decline the offer of a giant two-cent watermelon for them to think I was haggling or playing hardball and then offer two watermelons and a giant laundry basket to carry them in. The men wore sarongs while the women decorated their face in a tree paste called thanaka with smears of cream color on their brown skin that looked like times when I might have drunkenly applied the wrong color foundation to my face. Upon arriving at my hostel, the first day, I ended up hanging out with a bunch of twentysomething-year-olds. God bless them. The naivety of their actions and words they spoke made me giggle to myself so many times as they thought thirty-year-olds were ancient and they had everything figured out.

We made our way to an abandoned amusement park with locked gates and no entry signs, but I knew there was a secret way in. Just as the group was about to give up, I asked a local construction worker who was giving us a funny look as he saw us prowling the gates. He pointed toward a building that had a broken window, and voilà, we were in as we snaked through the window and into this apocalyptic land. After an afternoon of walking through the rusty hunks of metal now covered in vines, me and an English girl stayed in town to go check out the pagodas while the twenty-year-olds went back to the hostel to take a nap (LOL, the thirtysomethings didn't need naps!). The vibe of the country matched the rhythm I longed for. It had the culture and architecture like India without the intense hustle and the dynamic landscapes and delicious food like Thailand, but none of the tourist hassle and fake friendliness. The locals did not see dollar signs but for the most part wanted only selfies or to practice English with me.

An evening at the Shwedagon Pagoda was absolutely mesmerizing as I admired the golden hues that only became more dazzling as the sun went down and it shined like a twenty-four-karat marvel. At night, the buzz of the city was Chinatown, where you could grab meat skewers of almost any type of animal or insect imaginable, and they grilled it up while you could wash it down with a local beer. I befriended a couple of guys from the Peace Corps that were in a holding pattern, waiting to see if the United States was going to force them back home because of the virus scare. One fellow that was a lot of fun was Dayton, a North Carolina boy with blond hair and glasses. He spoke Burmese, which was a blessing for allowing me to figure out the ropes of the culture and methods to interact with the locals without learning the hard way through charades and making an ass out of myself for the first day. As he helped me figure out the whole BBQ and beer situation, we all sat in the streets, having a fantastic night.

As the night pressed on, the twenty-year-olds all wanted to go to a club on the outskirts of town. Dayton and one of his Burmese friends that met him in Yangon agreed to take them, but after a full day in the hot sun and a few beers in my belly, I passed up the offer and headed back to my hostel. It was such a wonderful first day in Myanmar. I could not imagine what could top it. I caught minimal sleep, and as I woke up before dawn, I lay in my bunk, admiring the beauty in my photos I had captured. With my phone in my grasp, I was very surprised when all of a sudden, I started getting multiple WhatsApp messages from Cho, the Burmese friend of Dayton. We had exchanged numbers in case I ever needed a ride somewhere. Dayton's job for the Peace Corps was an English teacher, and he freelanced English lessons in his small village outside Yangon, where he met Cho and had been teaching him English. I answered him back as he told me he was outside with Dayton, and something was wrong.

I headed downstairs and opened up the locked security gate to see Cho, and in a pathetic heap was Dayton, all hunkered over on the sidewalk. I ran over to him to make sure he was alive, but through a series of pantomimes and a few English words Cho knew, I came to understand that Dayton must have taken some sort of illegal drug that turned him basically comatose. Cho did not know what else to do since the twenty-year-olds left him and my hostel was locked up.

Cho and I carried him up two flights of narrow stairs and laid him out on his bunk. He was starting to become lucid, or at least enough to thank me and Cho. It was now the early morning, and waking up to this, Cho and I decided to grab a coffee.

When he asked me what my plans for the day was, I told him I was interested in catching a bus to the Kyaiktiyo Pagoda. It was a long drive but a very sacred site that supposedly held the hairs of Buddha. As I was sure I was pronouncing it incorrectly, I showed him a screenshot of the site on my phone with the directions I had found to the bus. "Golden Rock!" Cho exclaimed as he insisted he take me. Cho had a car, and we just had a very bonding moment from dealing with the twenty-year-old shenanigans. He was my age with a family, and I thought of how perfect this encounter was as I happily accepted his offer. I still was really rough on the Burmese culture, and the smallest action could be incredibly offensive, so having my new local friend was perfect.

As we headed out of town on the four-hour journey, I asked what music he liked as he handed me a CD case. As I opened it up, I was shocked to see nothing by Southern rock and classic country CDs with the name "Dayton" written in black Sharpie on the face of the discs. Apparently, a trick Dayton used with Cho and other locals was to play American tunes and have them learn them and sing along, where he then would teach them the meaning of the words. I loved the technique as I hoped Dayton was well and thankful for this chance meeting of his friend. We spent the first hour of the trip singing while I explained the song slowly afterward. Cho had a hearty English lesson thanks to me, Conway Twitty, George Strait, and Dwight Yoakam, and the CDs of our blitzed friend sleeping it off in the hostel. Dayton might not have had the best judgment, but at least he had good taste in music.

After a couple of hours, Cho was tired, so he took a nap in the back while I took a turn behind the wheel. Outside Yangon, it was country roads with nothing but watermelon and jackfruit stands as far as the eye could see. We made it to the town of Kipun, which was the launching spot to the trek to the spiritual mecca of the Buddhists, but nowadays, the walking was substituted with loading into the back of these giant diesel trucks that hauled loads of people up the mountainside. It was insanity as Cho helped me scramble into the truck, and we crammed people into every square inch of the back while vendors tried to sell random snacks to the trapped passengers. I was in love with the pandemonium as the sun kissed my face and wind caught my dreadlocks on the bumpy ride up the mountain. I was the only pale face, not one person spoke English unless you counted Cho's limited vocabulary. With the virus scare, there were only a few Thai tourists, but other than that, it was just me and the truckloads of worshippers.

Cho insisted on buying me a silly straw hat to protect my fair skin. It was hard to explain to Cho that I wanted the sun as all the locals applied tree paste to their cheeks and covered their heads with straw hats. The infamous Golden Rock had revealed itself, sitting perched precariously atop another giant boulder and painted in gold. The only English in the complex was a sign for foreigners to sign in where I received the new tradition of the temperature-checking gun held to my forehead to make sure I was not a contagion for their sacred site. I was issued a badge to be worn at all times to signify I was a foreigner, as if my white face and platinum dreads was not a dead giveaway. But there was one other English sign: "Ladies Are Not Allowed to Enter." To touch this sacred rock, apparently, only men get that privilege as I was only allowed to capture photos from adjacent viewpoints.

I got a dose of understanding the expectations of the different sexes as I kept realizing that some of the smallest gestures were considered uncouth. Cho kept wanting to take my photo, but my normal way of posing I guess wasn't ladylike as he made sure I placed my hands on my knees in order to not look provocative. Nevertheless, the locals made me feel like Cinderella at Disneyland. Every time I would finally get a good spot for a photo op, I had a delicate tap on my shoulder as someone wanted a selfie with me. I couldn't ever get a good photo of that beautiful pagoda because I had a line forming to have photos taken with me. Finally, Cho helped me out of that mess as he escorted me around.

Cho and I had a truly picture-perfect day—a little chaos mixed in with culture and new experiences. The language barrier caused difficulties, but I laughed at some of the misunderstandings we had during the day. As we spoke, he kept talking about his sister in his thick Burmese accent, "Mi Seesta come have shan noodles..." "Mi Seesta want come to pagoda now..." I kept thinking we were waiting for his sister and kept missing her until finally I had to stop him to ask where his sister was. Confused, he replied, "You Mi Seesta." Oh! Mi Seesta is me! (Melissa in a Burmese heavy accent.) We laughed about the confusion as I joked that I guess he was my brother now. We filled almost every possible hour in the day by heading to an ancient city of Bago to check out the sites. There does become a point to where you are Pagoda'd out. I had seen enough for a day, and we headed back to Yangon.

Still at the hostel were the twentysomethings hanging around the communal table. They still hadn't mustered the energy to do anything for the day, and I had covered enough to fill three days in one outing and made a new family member/friend as well. I offered them to join me the next day for a train ride that circled around Yangon where you can watch the locals hop on and off the train while selling local foods. It was a spectacle to see as the vendors would make their way up and down the rickety train, selling eggs, strawberries, oranges, watermelon, and even soup! It was a real experience to watch for only two hundred kyat (fourteen cents) and worth every penny, but the youngins stayed back to prep for night two out on the town.

Your twenties is a magical time, full of new experiences, but is also the time when we shape our character and build the foundation of the person we become. Your thirties is determined by how strong a foundation you built. You will be either paying for mistakes of your twenties or learning that the road to becoming the best person you can be is a never-ending path but full of happiness if you learn along the way to love yourself. So, young ones, take heed...build your foundation well. You can change many things about yourself—your hair, your eyes, your weight, addictions—but you can't change your character.

Wanderlust Diaries: Pandemics and Pagodas

With the coronavirus scare, I had skirted being stranded multiple times, but the wave of luck I was riding was bringing me to places with perfect timing. I finished my treks in Nepal a week before they stopped permits and froze foreign travel. I managed to wiggle into the countries I wanted before borders closed. Some travelers spook a little easier than I do because after a day of near perfection with my new friend Cho in Yangon, I came back to my hostel to find my friends from the previous day gone, leaving me only a message on WhatsApp that they were scared and decided to fly home. The Europeans were all packing up, and I wondered what on earth could have happened in one day to flip the switch in these traveler's minds to give up and head home.

I took a quick scroll through the news to see President Trump was still limiting European nationals from entering the United States, and the normal social media banter ranging from the "end of the world…bunker down" to "you people have lost your minds." I didn't even care where I was on the spectrum anymore. I was in Myanmar, and I going to enjoy every minute of that time and look at the positives. I now almost had the hostels to myself unless there was another traveler just as crazy as me. It helped me filter out the titty-babies quicker. Airline travel was now almost cheaper than crowded local buses, and my flight for twenty dollars from Yangon to Bagan was COMPLETELY empty—no need to wear a mask if I was the only one! It was as if I was traveling on Air Force One with coffee and pretty little flight attendants checking on me all the time. I knew I couldn't ride the pandemic wave of luck forever, but for the mean time, it was surfs up!

The only thing on this whole trip that was very important to me was a bucket-list experience of riding in a hot air balloon over the ancient city of Bagan. Seeing photos in travel articles had made me antsy for this experience for over eight years as I held a small photo of this magical place in my desk to give me motivation to make it there one day, and now I had arrived. Myanmar was like that quaint coffee shop or café that you secretly loved, but you didn't want to tell anyone about for fear of hipsters finding out and taking over the place, ruining the vibe—well, that was Myanmar. While Thailand, Vietnam, Bali, and even Nepal were wonderful places with great food, architecture, and beaches, Myanmar had all those things too, just not in the touristic way. I had gotten to experience life of the Burmese with smiles instead of locals wanting their palm greased. There really were not any rules that made me color inside the lines with my travel style. It was raw and inviting, and I loved it.

I had prayed so many times for the balloons to still be running as this coronavirus scare made its way across the globe. Still riding the wave of luck, I opened my e-mail from the Balloon Company. They wanted to confirm my departure for the sunrise hot-air balloon over Bagan the next day. After all the turmoil and travel plans that had changed, I made it. I escaped the hostel that was nothing but mind-less jibber jabber talking about the virus. Everyone had their own sob story about travel plans that changed and plotting their next move. I realized no one really wanted advice, only to commiserate together. I practiced my social distancing by telling anyone that wanted to hang with me that the virus topic was off-limits. If they wanted to talk about that, they could go call a travel agent or go bitch with the others. I was in Bagan, and no one was going to ruin my day with tears of woe.

As I arrived early the next morning to the balloon-launching site, I was in complete heaven. I couldn't have been further away from the strife of social media as tears welled in my eyes. I was so proud of myself for making it here. To be honest, it was kind of a rough ride navigating through canceled planes, trains, buses, and borders crossings, but none of that mattered anymore. The only other people in my balloon were Germans speaking their own language, which was fine by me. They could have been talking about the virus, food, sex, I wouldn't know. I was happy to be excluded, so I wasn't distracted by anything else except this moment—the moment I had been waiting for.

I hopped in the basket and took my place. As the burners were turned on, slowly, the bright yellow balloon with an eagle printed on the fabric billowed and tightened and lifted the basket off the ground. As we rose to the heights above the ruins, my spirits lifted as well. The bright red sun began to peak out over the hazy horizon. The hundreds of temples dotted the landscape with an eerie mist that brought the picturesque view together. I had to put on my signature heart-shaped sunglasses, not because of the sunlight but because I had started to cry. The world can be shit sometimes if you let all the garbage of the media creep into your head. The only thing that spreads faster than the virus is fear, and it has wiped out the planet. I had been watching it unfold throughout my travels as hostels become wastelands in a day from panicked travelers that decided to open their phones to the media instead of their eyes to the world and forego their plans and head home instead. Everyone has their own reasons for their actions and can choose whatever outlet to validate those choices, but the past few weeks, I was proud of mine— they led me here. In this moment, I knew what I had been through to get to the middle of nowhere Burma and the headspace I fought to maintain to achieve this goal. When your passion and purpose are greater than your fears, you will find a way, and I did. I chose to live my dreams instead of my fears, and when countless doors shut in my face with canceled flights and rejections, I kung fu kicked the damn doors down and said, "Fuck you, I'm here! What now?"

As the balloon started to plot its course for landing, reality set in that I, too, must do the same. All my plane flights were canceled. I needed to figure out what shore this wave of luck was going to crash me into. The journey wasn't over, but my eyes were now set on how to get home across the Pacific. The Asian countries were dropping like flies with who maintained open borders. I had started a map on my phone and started crossing them off as the pandemic spread. I now had only one option to get home after Indonesia announced its farewell to traveler visas. I needed Indonesia, but I still could do this. So it was off to the next place. I had been blessed to celebrate every sunrise and sunset in Bagan, and it was a metaphor to the craziness of the world right now—this too shall pass. We will continue our journey around the sun, and no matter what press article ran that day, you could always depend on a faithful sunrise and sunset. One day, things will become normal again. It was pointless to book flights in advance anymore, so I packed my bag. Where to now?

Wanderlust Diaries: Long Way Home...Maybe

I was two days in to a five-day trek across the belly of Myanmar when another trekker going the opposite direction informed me that the USA put a level four travel ban into effect. That meant come home immediately, or face the possibility of not being able to return to the

United States. *Well, shit.* There wasn't much I could do now. My large bag was already at my destination in Nyaungshwe, waiting on me to hoof it 120 kilometers.

Since my travel plans (or lack thereof) were completely amiss, I had decided to take advantage of being "stuck" in Myanmar by truly getting into the guts of the country. My plan A of Malaysia followed by my plan B of Indonesia falling through with the countries on lockdown made me develop a plan C of hiking my way through the countryside on foot. One of the most beautiful things about Myanmar was the people, and to truly experience it, I needed to get away from places taxis could go and deep into the villages. There were no bus stations, guesthouses, or any amenities a tourist would want, and at this point, I was one of the few travelers left. All guided tours had shut down, but a trekking company was kind enough to send my heavy pack to the final destination and hook me up with a family member to show me the way on days three through five, where I would meet her at a rendezvous point.

I spent the first two days escaping all forms of reality and living in my personal heaven. I had researched an elephant camp buried deep in the forest that was a two-day trek away through a beautiful mountain jungle. Once I arrived, the camp was shut down to visitors, but they let me join the staff for the day, completing the chores to care for the elephants. These beautiful beasts eat over 150 kilograms of food a day, and the mahouts grew weary of the same old routine. When I eagerly offered to feed them, the mahouts just relaxed, smoking their Burmese cigars and drinking whiskey at ten in the morning while I spent hours feeding all the hungry elephants. I couldn't pronounce their names, so I just gave them nicknames with my favorites being "Little Old Lady," who was sixty-nine years old and showed her age with her deep indentations in her temples from where time was withering her away but not her spirit. There was "Sister," a precocious female that was my age and quite demanding but so loveable. There was "Hungry Boy," the only male that was twelve years old and ate double the fare of the girls, but he was so sweet and angelic. I even was privileged enough to join the mahout for some bath time at the river under a waterfall. I scrubbed his little trunk and forehead with softened bark and smothered him in kisses as he happily sat in the water, soaking it all in. "Betty Page" was a memorable girl, who was in the prime of her life and had the most perfect markings and color speckles on her ears. From her years of hard work in the lumber industry, she had a big star tattoo on her butt to signify she was now government property. She would strike a picture perfect pose as the mahout would give her a signal, and she would prop up her massive leg on a post for footpad inspections. I could have lived here with these beauties. I felt connected to their soul as I gazed into their eyes that glistened with wisdom from around the creases of deep wrinkles and long eyelashes. But it was time to go. My travels weren't merely just to "see" but to do—to listen, feel, taste, and experience ALL that was Myanmar. I knew it was time to move on.

It was the beginning of day three when I met Thuli, the local who would show me the rest of the way to Inle Lake. It was also at this point that I found out about the travel warning that I could do nothing about. In tow with Thuli was four other travelers. Apparently, with all guided treks being shut down, this left an opportunity for Thuli. It was like a corona soup with a mixture of an Iranian girl, Jasmine, who had met the Swiss boy, Matteo, during travels in Tehran. Now that they were a couple, he vowed to stay with her despite she was now basically trapped and not allowed entry into any neighboring countries because of her nationality. He didn't mind too much because most countries were blocking Europeans as well, so they were just going to overstay their visa in Myanmar until they could figure something else out. Then there was a South Korean and a Japanese girl that joined the tribe. The Japanese girl couldn't speak any English, but I tried to dig up a few phrases in my repertoire from my time in Japan, and she would make a goofy smile and giggle in her high-pitched voice and clap her hands like an anime character. Apparently, Myanmar was the last frontier, and from blockades of all surrounding countries, it was now the melting pot of who was left and couldn't find a way home. The only other nationality we needed to make this a complete medley would be a Chinese traveler to add to the irony of my travel companions.

We made our way over almost every terrain imaginable, from high mountains to dry desert, passing through villages inhabited by the local tribes. Thuli had arranged for us to stay in the home of a local the first night, and it was one of the most memorable experiences I have ever had. Imagine living in the middle of nowhere with all your neighbors being your only contact. Everyone woke at dawn and worked the fields of potato, ginger, cauliflower, and other staple crops. They used simplistic farm implements and their buffalo to help till the soil. The older children would either help on the farm or at home with the chores while the young ones played in the dirt streets or on a bamboo seesaw. The working day ended when the sun went down, and everyone retired to their bamboo huts and made dinner on their simple camp stoves. The inside of the two-room homes were charred black from the smoke of the cooking fires, and the meals were always the same—noodles, egg, and tomatoes…maybe some papaya if the lady of the house could jiggle one loose from the tree.

After the first night, Jasmine developed a cough. Thuli was alarmed because of her being from Iran as she asked me many probing questions about her. As her cough continued, Thuli took me aside and pinpointed a few locations on my offline maps. She said she had a daughter and did not want the virus and had to leave… and just like that, she disappeared over the hillsides, leaving me with the corona soup troop. I was torn in what to do because I, too, did not want to be around a coughing Iranian, but we all were headed in the same direction, and I couldn't just bail out. Since I was on a five-day trek instead of a three-day like the rest, my backpack was bigger, and I had brought a first aid kit and medications just in case. The rest of them had just assumed this would be like the offered tour in the guidebooks, bringing only minimal items in their tiny bags. I paid the price as the kilometers progressed, and my backpack that was not engineered for this type of trekking dug deep into my sun-burned shoulders. There became moments where it was a borderline *Lord of the Flies* situation when Jasmine could not keep up, but I had to make tracks. I did not have the luxury of just doodling along and overstaying a visa, knowing that I had to go back home ASAP was in the back of my mind as I kept on trekking, despite the heat and discomfort.

It was psychological warfare with myself—my head said press on, but my shoulders and pinky toes kept crying out, "Stop! Give us a break!" My head would then take command and tell my other body parts to "Piss off! We keep on moving!" It's an odd thing to have an argument with yourself, but oddly enough, you always win one way or another, I suppose. Jasmine just wasn't meant for trekking. She didn't like to go uphill or downhill. She didn't like the sun or to carry a bag. We weren't obliged to each other, and when she wanted to loaf around and I kindly told her the route, but that I had to go; she insisted I give her my first aid kit and medicine. I laughed at her way of thinking; I had paid for it, brought it, carried it. I had been leading the way despite not being the tour guide, but that wasn't enough—she wanted more. I was a nomad at the point and bridled to no one as I told her to "Keep up, shape up, or ship out." The other two militantly kept on my heels as we made our way through buffalo paths through the valleys.

I had a *Thelma and Louise* moment when, on the last day, I could almost see the lake, but as we crossed over a ridge, there in front of us was what felt like the Grand Canyon of Myanmar. I had no idea how to cross it, but it had to be done. We finally found a narrow footpath, but my hackles were up at one point, wondering if I had come this far to be stopped my Mother Nature, but of course, she had made a way for us. With Thuli gone, locals were warned by media outlets that foreigners likely had "the virus," so staying with a local family wasn't an option anymore, but luckily, monasteries dotted the countryside and offered a place of refuge. It wasn't anything fancy, but the monks would string a line, separating out part of the main parlor with linens and gave us small mats to sleep on. I would awake to the sounds of chants from the monks as they started their pilgrimage for food donations with their small metal bowls. As the sun came out, light would twinkle in from the holes in the tin roof over my head, appearing as little stars as the early morning light crept in and brightened the monastery. Staying with the monks meant we had to either scavenge food from villages or from the trail because the monks stopped eating at noon, and it would not be appropriate to make food in front of them, or at least I did not think it was polite considering the hospitality they had offered.

Finally, Inle Lake was in the distance; it was not a mirage—it was real. The agave and cactus scenes turned to palms and banana trees with thatch bamboo houses on stilts built up upon the narrow waterways. Rice paddies dominated the landscape as I watched the farmers diligently harvesting and replanting in the ponds. We hopped on a small wooden canoe that took us across the lake to the town of Nyaungshwe. The wind and spray on my face felt like a reward as I gazed upon the mountains in the distance I had crossed to get there. My boots were filthy, my clothes were torn, but upon checking into my wonderful hostel, I saw my faithful green pack. I indulged in a shower and watched the dirt circle down the drain. There goes so many wild memories of Myanmar that are burned in my soul. As I dried off, I felt refreshed and ready for this next round of figuring out my next move.

It was a chess game, and I had lost a piece every time I opened my e-mail, so with heavy anxiety, I connected to Wi-Fi. I lost BIG this round... Singapore was gone now too. On this chessboard of life, it was corona on one side with a fully stacked army, and then on the other side, alone, there stood only one piece, the queen...me. But this bitch was flexible, and I was sure I could find another trick up my sleeve. As I ordered a mojito from the rooftop bar, I scratched my head. *It's my move.*

Wanderlust Diaries: Home

Don't ask me about Thailand—it was kind of a "whatever happens in Thailand, stays in Thailand" kind of thing, but not for any fun reasons. I had no tales of ping-pong shows or Khaosan Road debauchery, but more like horror stories of quarantine rooms with health and immigration officers questioning me about my health certificate. My flight home was canceled because Japan changed the rules, and I no longer could freely leave Haneda Airport to go to Narita in Tokyo, so I had to concoct another plan to get me to Seattle. I was in no man's land, not allowed entry into Bangkok, but nowhere to go.

This is when I discovered airport lounges; for forty bucks, this was my home as got my money's worth of cheap wine and snacks while I figured out a plan on their Wi-Fi. To be honest, these last few days were pretty rough, but that was part of the journey. When I was away from the comforts of home and in peril, that was when I could find out how strong I truly was. I was blessed with so many wonderful days on this trip, and even though the last segment had been tough, I chose not to fester on the negative. Sometimes life gives you lemons and you make lemonade, and sometimes it gives you a prickly cactus, but you don't have to sit on it! I chose to use my time waiting on a flight to open up and think about what a wild ride it had been.

Clutching my passport, I looked at all the stamps I had collected, including the one from Thailand that got etched out by the immigration official, followed by a briefing stating "I never entered the Kingdom of Thailand!" Some of the craziest stories were held between these stamps in this tiny little book. As I realized I had squeezed every bit of juice I could out of these countries before I was forced to come home, I knew I had to ask myself, "Was it all worth it?" and "If I had it to do over again, would I?" The answer was simple—*abso-fucking-lutely yes*.

There was a whole world outside my doorstep, and I would be a fool to miss it. I suppose it would have been an easier method of travel to have had a well-documented plan and travel from point A to point B, but that was part of the fun—the unsureness of where I would wake up the next morning, the conversations in foreign tongues that I could not fully comprehend. Everything was new and exciting, and I felt like a child learning from the locals on how to eat, talk, dress, and even cross the street—that was a feeling that couldn't be found in a comfort zone or routine. I knew I was going home to a mandatory quarantine, but this life of crazy chaos was what I needed to feed my soul. A life without the perpetual stomach flip of travel was like a rainbow without colors, a tree without leaves, or a city without people. My life in a puzzle would likely never fit inside the borders anymore, but I had brought new pieces to the table to include.

This trip reminded me of how some of the most special things are simple, such as a friendly smile, sharing a homemade meal, or even just a walk off the beaten path. The simple things are special. I thought of the basics like water, air, and fire—they all have something that makes them wonderful, just as the places I explored. Singapore was water, the cleansing oasis that rushed in new with the old, and the ebbs and flows never ceased to bring in fresh ideas with the changing tides. Nepal was air. The pollution of Kathmandu was replaced with the crisp mountain air in my lungs. The altitude of the mountains as I trekked to the Rooftop of the World made me thankful for the breath in my body as I let the wind take the ashes of my mother away into the heavens. Myanmar was fire. I had never celebrated the rising and falling of the sun as I did in the heat of Myanmar. I celebrated the sun from a motorbike, the jungle, and even from a hot-air balloon. The red ball of fire was the only predictable thing as the world went to chaos, but reminded me that one day, things would return to normal.

I had found my way home and would soon board a plane bound for Japan that would then take me across the pond to Washington. From my month of globe-trotting, I wasn't sure how I would deal with being caged up with the stay-at-home orders from the government, but the more I thought about it, the more I longed for my life back in my log cabin with the fur babies and people I loved. I could already taste a juicy cheeseburger and fancy cheeses I requested in my quarantine care package. The journey was coming to an end, and I could feel the bookends closing to my adventure. But that was the thing with travel—the voyage never really ends but was a story that played over and over in the quietest chambers of my mind.

Never let the opinions of others fuel your choices. You will run out of gas with that way of thinking. If I did that, I would have a pretty boring life. The cost of not following your dream, your heart, or your gut is spending the rest of your life wishing that you had, and that was an expense I will never be willing to incur. To travel is to live, and a way to look at life through a different lens. If your life isn't exactly what you want or something you aren't proud of, I hope you have the courage and gumption to change it. No matter your circumstance—how poor, your race, your age, or where you come from—it is never too late to be who you are meant to be and to follow your purpose in life.

If you are reading this, I hope you have enjoyed my tales along the way and are inspired to make your own adventure story. It's the many stories we all do every day that make up the novel of your life, so do what you can to make it a best seller, even if it is only for yourself. Thank you for reading my story. I want to thank the many kindred spirits I met across the globe that gave vibrance to my writing but also to my friends back home that gave me the motivation to write and share my stories. I enjoyed putting life to the fun people and experiences I have encountered, and I truly feel that when you travel, you open yourself up to so much that the world has to offer. This book took many years to create, and I hope it is more than mere words on paper. My goal in writing this was not for myself but to create something immortal. I hope the words speak to you and encourage you to pursue your dreams. Life is short, and I hope you make the best of it.

ABOUT THE AUTHOR

*M*elissa Kittrell has traveled the world, and after a wild ride back home from Asia as the COVID-19 pandemic spread across the globe, she was ready to tell her story. She was born in Texas and raised in Oklahoma, but has called many places home as she honorably served in the US Navy as a Nuclear Machinist's Mate. She now lives in Washington State, where she runs a small farm raising goats, pigs, and many other types of fur babies. She has her master's degree in organizational leadership and undergraduate degree in workforce education and development, along with her extensive training for the military as a nuclear operator. Melissa is currently employed by the US Navy and is a project manager for submarines in the Pacific Fleet. She is also the owner of Bushel and Barrel Ciderhouse, a company she founded to showcase her craft cider and a vessel to donate a percentage of profits back to the community and global causes. She loves animals, cooking, spending time with friends, and travel, of course! *My Wanderlust Diaries* is her contribution to kindred spirits that live life by a compass and not a rule book and desire life to be anything BUT *ordinary.*